ONE OF US
HAS TO GO

Katja Schulz

For contact:

email address:

author.katjaschulz@gmail.com

Based on a True Story

ALL NAMES OF characters based on real people have been changed or withheld, as well as the names of workplaces. The use of 'Gadburg', 'Dabendorf' and 'Fessdorf' is fictitious. A few events have been amended from their original timelines for the purpose of improving the narration, e.g. Sonja's father making a drawing regarding family attention occurred later in reality than in this story.

Certain characters' genders have been changed to support anonymity.

Written for healing

I Have A Plan

July 2014

My mobile phone buzzes in front of me on the bare windowsill.

One message.

Lock me in at 11, as usual, Sonja writes.

Same message she sent yesterday at this time. Same as the day before. And the day before that... She reminds me every night. As if I didn't know.

I hesitate. I don't like 'the usual' any more.

I pick up my phone.

I can't keep locking you in! I reply.

Thirty seconds later.

Yes, you can. And you haven't stopped in almost 9 years, she writes.

True, but I'm fed up with it now. You're using me, and I've got to move on. With Roger, I send back.

Thirty seconds later.

No message.

Forty seconds later.

Still no message.

Instead, several rapid knocks on my door. I sigh, rolling my eyes.

The door of my room flies open. The rickety handle bangs against the wall, making the hole in it deeper.

"I didn't say come in!" I tell Sonja.

She plants herself in front of me, legs slightly parted. Her long blonde hair dishevelled. She doesn't care about looks. If I talked about ageing, and the fact that we could soon get our first grey hairs, she wouldn't be interested.

Now she's frowning at me, her face scarlet.

"You know what? You've got no choice but to lock me in," she blurts out.

"Of course I have a choice!"

She isn't the tiniest bit taller than me. Physically not stronger either. Same size, really. If our slender arms and fists flew at each other now in a fight, they'd smash into splinters like matches. And yet, her five-foot-five height, and the way she's posing right now, would normally intimidate me. *Normally.*

"No, you don't! See this?" She's holding the screen of her phone toward me, showing a picture of me next to a guy on a bench in the park where I often take my au-pair children.

"Yes, and?" I say.

"You two seem very close, right?"

"So what?"

"You're hugging. Embracing. Roger surely won't like this."

I was watching my au-pair children play the other day, and then that man started talking to me. He suddenly got emotional about his divorce.

"What are you telling me, Sonja? Are you trying to blackmail me? To get me to stay here, keep locking you in every night, and not move in with him?"

Sonja grins. Her blue eyes are very cold tonight, in

contrast to the first time I saw her when we were young. Back then, I didn't mind that she came close to being a mirror image of me. Now I hate it. Now I know *why* we look similar.

"It was only a comforting hug. That's okay when someone is upset," I say.

"Yeah, but Roger doesn't know that. He'd see this picture, nothing else. It would take me only a couple of clicks to send it to him." She narrows her eyes. The death stare.

"You tricked me, Sonja?"

She shrugs her shoulders, turns around, walks out of my room and slams the door. I twitch.

Bitch.

What. A. Damn. Bitch!

Okay, this is it. It's got to happen. Tonight. And this time, I have to succeed. She. Has. To. Go. If I don't succeed today, I probably never will.

*   *   *

SONJA LIVES IN the room next to mine. Now and again, I hear her. It all started a long time ago – two girls who got along extremely well. Almost twenty-eight years. It feels like a lifetime. That's why it's so difficult; that's why she thinks she can do with me whatever she wants.

We've all heard about these kinds of relationships when two people have been together for ages; when all appears fine. But we also know that we can be deceived sometimes, right? That, deep down, one would like to leave but can't. So please understand why I've spent all this time with her.

Our rooms are positioned at a ninety-degree angle to each other. When I open my door, Sonja's is to my right in the corner of this third floor. To my left is another room with its door facing the same way as mine. A man lives in there. I call him Mr Stumble-Late. He often comes home long after midnight, drunk. And so I wake up. I have no idea who he really is. We don't talk, but nod when we accidentally meet in the corridor.

I can't say I *live* in my room. I exist. Ever since we moved here, I haven't bothered trying to make my place look cosy. I've done it too many times, I'm tired of it. The only personal thing I've put up is a picture of Roger. It's leaning against the little radio on my bedside table. Well, *the* bedside table – it isn't mine, but part of this furnished room. The radio belongs to me, too, but I don't regard it as something personal. This room is pretty empty, and I don't like it. Who would? It's rather sterile, and the smell of the new plastic floor doesn't want to fade. If I talked to myself, I mean out loud, there would be an echo.

I thought I knew Sonja. Inside out. But I seem to have been wrong. It's horrible thinking you know somebody well when you discover that you don't. Again, we've all heard about it, right? It's like when hubby comes home and suddenly breaks the news that he's leaving you for another woman. Or when you've done everything for your queen but surprise, surprise, she says she has fallen in love with her new boss. Or, imagine your parents turning their backs on you? Is that the worst?

How can all these things be? You wonder how you did not see them coming.

I didn't. Not really. I'd never have believed Sonja was capable of blackmailing me. But she just did it. Bitch. She's going to destroy my precious romance if I leave her. She tells me she can't be without me and that I must stay. But

I'm exhausted. Life's passing me by. God, you know! Please, God, if you exist, you know that I have reached the end of my tether. You know I'm done, and you do understand, don't you? I have no other choice this time.

* * *

IT'S NOT QUITE eight o'clock. The outside world is flooded in gold by the sun hanging low in the sky. Completely the opposite of what the neon tube on the ceiling does to my room.

Today is the 22nd July 2014. I'm standing here by my window; the slats of the blinds are open. I can easily peek through the gaps. A few of those golden sunrays tickle my bare arms. I like that. I want to be out there but must guard Sonja instead.

I can see into the yard behind this building and over to the neighbouring one. People in business clothes regularly stand there during office hours, smoking. I don't like smoking, but I like those people. I know them all and have a close relationship with each of them. They are my friends. My only friends, to be honest. And that person out there right now, the guy I'm talking to, that's WHWM-Dad. Sometimes he's with WHWM-Brother, but honestly, I love it most when it's just him and me. 'WHWM' stands for 'wish he was my'.

WHWM-Dad is such a good listener. He does late shifts almost every evening, which is one of the reasons I chose him. He's always there for me. I mean, most evenings I talk to WHWM-Dad a lot. Sometimes in French; I'm fluent now. I've told him all about my plan, and that I've tried before but failed. He's listened to everything, although he most likely doesn't even know I exist. He never looks up here to my window. But I still tell him that my plan will be implemented *tonight*.

Unless I'm deceived by *his* appearance, WHWM-Dad is warm and loving. Like a strong, friendly bear from a kids' story. He would protect his princess-daughter with his big paws. Whenever he comes out through the door with his colleagues, he holds it open for everybody and smiles. So charmingly. His small belly would be perfect for me to nestle myself in when we'd have a WHWM-daddy-daughter hug. Sure, I might be a bit too grown up to talk like this. But I once used to be a child, and he'd have hugged me back then. And I'd still go and sling my arms around his neck these days, resting my head on his shoulder.

I know he won't be a former high-school teacher. He may only have a job doing simple tasks like piecing things together. But I don't care. I'd even treasure it that he wouldn't threaten me with logical, annoying and heartless principles and make me lose argument after argument. I wouldn't shed tears over WHWM-Dad.

The slats of my blinds are dusty. They need cleaning. Softly, I move my finger over one at chest height. Sonja wouldn't stick her finger into that kind of dirt. Not without protecting it. She would use something like a tissue. Maybe even put rubber gloves on. Brushing dust off the slats with a naked finger is forbidden. But it's not the dust that is the problem. No, the dust is not the dirty thing. It's the slats of the blinds themselves. *Made in Germany* is written on one of them. That's why they are dirty. She still hasn't come to terms with her own roots.

I've wiped about a third of the slats. I used my fingers. The dust has fallen on the floor. I sneezed a couple of times

— as I said, the blinds need cleaning.

It's past 8pm now, but far too early for Sonja to get ready for bed. She doesn't like it and keeps putting it off. When she eventually starts, the routine will last a very long time. She currently takes two and a half hours, but there have been times when she took four.

Well, I'll carry on for a while, standing here by my window, moving my fingers over some more of the dusty slats. WHWM-Dad has gone back inside, but I hope he'll come out again for another chat with me.

Please, let the hours pass quickly until 3am – that's when Sonja should be tucked up in bed, asleep.

I turn back to the text messages on my mobile phone.

Okay, will lock you in at 11 then, as usual, I lie, then put the phone back on the windowsill.

BEFORE I KNEW SONJA

Mid 1980s

I STILL HADN'T had my first bite of that beautiful, white piece of cream cake that was standing on a plate right in front of me. I'd have preferred some more of Mum's savoury bratwurst and sauerkraut. Well, actually, I *had* had a first bite: I had eaten the one and only dry, whole hazelnut from the top.

My brother, who sat at the other side of the table, was spooning up the whipped cream off his plate.

"Can I have another piece?" he asked Mum.

"A second one? That's a bit unhealthy, don't you think?" she said.

"Give me four vitamin pills instead of two tonight, then," my brother suggested.

"He won't die from another piece!" Dad shot back at Mum.

Mum hesitated, then cut another, smaller piece off that big, beautifully decorated, creamy thing and let it slide down the cake slice onto my brother's plate.

The living room fell into an awkward silence, broken only

by the ticking of the old clock on the wall. That ticking made it all the more awkward. Like a bomb was about to go off.

Mum got up. I watched as she walked over to the hi-fi. Keeping my eyes fastened on her felt safest – Dad was sitting right opposite me. Mum's pants appeared a little tight; they were brand new, and Mum wasn't the skinniest anyway. She had tried a few diets, mainly to please Dad, but had to accept that Dad could eat as much cake as he fancied without putting on an ounce of fat. I suddenly realised I hadn't seen Mum in a skirt. My teacher at school was often dressed in one. Mum, never.

She pressed the button for the radio to come on. Nena's *99 Luftballons* was playing.

"We haven't had music while eating for some time," she said.

"It's been a long time since I heard that song," I said, trying to support Mum's distraction. "Has the singer been sick?"

My brother snorted. Dad looked amused, too.

"No – you don't really believe that Nena is at the radio station right now, singing this song live, do you?" My brother was ready to laugh.

I tried hard to give him a firm look but failed. I felt hot, and surely my face was turning red very quickly. Yes, damn it, he was right – I was that naive at nine years old. He couldn't contain himself any longer and burst out laughing.

"Why don't you eat your cake, Finja?" Mum asked.

"Don't know. I just can't. The feeling of the whipped cream in my mouth is so weird," I said.

"What? No, it's not. Maybe it's you that's weird." My brother seemed amazed at my aversion, since he had a second piece already while my first was still untouched except for that missing hazelnut.

"Do you want some of this?" Mum pointed at the other cake on the table, which was whipped-cream-free, and somewhat dry, with only light icing and sprinkles.

My brother was closest to it, so he reached for the knife and cut the first piece.

"Here, have this one with these pink sprinkles on," he said.

"Thanks, but can I have the next piece, Mum? With yellow sprinkles?"

"You're really weird," my brother said. "In my class *every* girl's favourite colour is pink!"

Mum took control. She put the pink-sprinkled piece by the side of the cake and gave me a yellow one, resulting in Dad rolling his eyes at her.

*   *   *

I WORRIED I wasn't like most children. At school, when the other girls had Nutella sandwiches, mine were salami with mustard. Whenever Mum didn't put enough mustard on the salami slices, I reminded her later at home.

Was I weird?

Some time ago, Mum had told me that when she was pregnant with me, she had wished for a girl, because she already had a boy. She said she prayed to God and told him she would accept and love a girl even if she wasn't perfect. I was a girl. But while I was a little different, I didn't really believe I was weird.

I was in Year Four. I liked going to school, learning, and playing during the breaks in the schoolyard. I loved maths and art. But my love for German was not unconditional. Our teacher enjoyed having her pupils learn poems by heart. The only way I could learn German poetry was the way Grandma (Mum's mother) taught me, line by line, with facial expressions and hand gestures. When it was my turn to stand in front of the class and recite the poem, I had to do it exactly as Grandma did. Our teacher became obsessed with this and always saved me until last as her treat. How I hated her for that.

I did enjoy the writing part of German, though.

I disliked music class, because I didn't like the teacher or her cotton-wool tufts of hair that wiggled on her head whenever she conducted the class as we sang. I wasn't born to make music. Mum and Grandma never understood that. Grandma had given me her father's old piano to play on, and a private teacher came every week. I couldn't manage pieces longer than two pages, and I was only able to read one of the two staves. I knew the treble for the right hand but not the bass for the left. I learned the sound of each song after Mr Fink had played it to me a few times. I tried copying him when he sat next to me. Sometimes he corrected the notes I hit, but most of the time he fell asleep in his chair, full of the cake and coffee Mum fed him each Monday afternoon.

It took plenty of Monday afternoons until I finally learned a new song, because each Monday morning I used my eraser on the little homework book where Mr Fink noted the songs I had to practise. Dozy old Mr Fink always used a pencil to write down my homework.

Dad didn't care about me playing piano, and I'm sure he was relieved that Mum was willing to drive me all the way to town to attend my weekly ballet lessons. But he was happy to take me to the neighbouring village for tennis.

Dad wasn't always easy to approach; literally or figuratively. Mum used to say he was a bit like the weather.

There was a little plastic house screwed to the wall of our house outside on the terrace. Two small weather dolls lived inside that house, and they came out of it on either side; one through the left door, one through the right door. They never came out at the same time. One doll was blue, the other one was pink. Mum had told me that the weather would be nice when the pink doll was out; and bad when the blue one showed up. I didn't know what a barometer was, but could of course tell the difference between blue and pink.

Did Dad appear in two different colours? Was that what Mum had meant? He didn't look blue or pink to me, but I still felt it was always best to find out how he 'was' before approaching him. If I stepped into his office at home, it was like a challenge: I wanted to make Dad 'pink'. But of course he was often working, so I had to be quiet. He was a teacher and would be sitting at his desk, head bent over a notebook of a high-school pupil, a big stack of more notebooks next to him. He usually gave one mark worse by default whenever a pupil hadn't folded each page down the middle to form a vertical line, leaving exactly half the page blank for Dad to write his red comments on. If he didn't react when I'd come into his office, I'd move along a shelf. I'd pull out a book, and then push it back into its place. Or I'd read the words on a recent gift (a papier-mâché megaphone) he'd received from his graduating pupils: *So that we understand you also at the back of the class.* Dad's philosophy was to speak softer and softer, the more inattentive and noisier his pupils became.

If he still didn't react to me in his office, I'd leave again and come back later when he would read a newspaper. Then I'd stand next to him at the desk and put my arm around his back, hoping and waiting for the pink doll to come out. Sometimes he'd then put his arm around me, too.

Mum was always the same weather. She was also a teacher and did her marking and lesson planning at the other desk in that office. She had even let me sit on her lap when I was very little, and hand her the pens and pencils she used in turns. To be fair to Dad, Mum's work was a lot less demanding since she 'only' taught up to Year Six.

Once, Dad drove me to a local tennis tournament where I met another girl about nine years old. Dad stood by the side of the court, watching me as we started playing. I had his full attention; he even cheered me on. God, but was I proud.

The other girl got many more points than me. I couldn't return her first serves since she hit them from above her head. I was only able to do a low serve like a forehand. She whacked ball after ball around and past me.

I heard Dad from the sideline: "What about your forehand? You've got a strong one. Use it!"

I tried following his advice, but it didn't work. I lost in the first round of that tournament in straight sets: love-six, love-six (0-6, 0-6). Only then did Dad tell me I had played against the champion of the *Bundesland*, the champion of the county – the best female player of my age group.

"I didn't want to tell you who she was when I saw it on the board," he said. "I didn't want to discourage you before you started."

I appreciated the gesture, but I still felt disappointment. I wanted to impress Dad.

April 1986

I KNEW SOMETHING bad had happened. I didn't understand

how bad it was, but Mum wouldn't stop pacing up and down in the living room in front of the TV. I saw the images: fire, an explosion and big smoking chimneys – the nuclear catastrophe in Chernobyl.

We were living in a sleepy village, Fessdorf, in northern Germany, far away from Chernobyl. However, Mum explained there was a wind coming from the east. And rain. Suddenly Fessdorf seemed under a strange threat as Mum wouldn't let my brother and me leave the house for three days. All the other children of the village did go out, though, and attended school. One of my brother's friends brought our homework. He probably expected us to be tucked up in bed with fevers. I wasn't embarrassed that he found us fit as fiddles. I thought his mum should have kept him off school, too. But no other mum did. Just mine.

I could tell Mum wasn't happy to see the boy turning up, though not because she didn't like him.

"Stop, stop, you're bringing all the radiation from outside into the house. It'll contaminate the carpet!"

I considered holding my hands over my ears. Mum's hysterical screaming was just so loud. It was the first time in my life that I'd heard the word 'contaminate'.

"Take your shoes off!" she commanded.

The boy did so and stepped onto the carpet in his socks.

This wasn't the only precaution Mum took. She persuaded Dad to go to the biggest supermarket in the area to stock up on food. My parents' pantry was jammed with long-life milk, and even milk powder so we could mix our own for several years to come.

"Mum, is a war going to break out?" I asked.

Grandma had told me plenty of stories from World War II. Mum explained the dangers of the radiation, the fallout, and that we could become very ill if we weren't careful. I didn't understand what radiation was. Especially because it was invisible. How could it exist when I couldn't even see it?

I was curious about this mysterious radiation. I stared out of the window, forbidden to leave the house and unable to see the danger. Although I couldn't see anything, I was scared of it. After three days inside, and once the rain had gone, Mum let my brother and me go outside for an hour to play some table tennis. My brother set up the table.

"Are you coming?" he called. "Where are you, Finja?"

I was still in the house, hesitant about going out 'into the radiation'. I summoned the courage to join him in front of the garage, right next to the road. He gave me a bat and we started hitting the ball. Whenever it was my turn to pick it up from the road, I checked: I needed to see the radiation; maybe it would come around the corner. I imagined it flowing about a metre high, and looking like hot air when it shimmers above asphalt. But I saw nothing.

"Come on. Play! What are you looking at?" my brother said.

I quickly glanced down the other side of the road. Still, I saw nothing.

Roger

July 2014

I've dusted all the slats of my blinds. They're clean now. It's 8.15pm and WHWM-Dad appears again in the neighbouring yard with a bag in his hand. He doesn't stop for another cigarette. No chat. Too bad. Have a great evening, then, WHWM-Dad. Now I'm on my own.

Bzzz, bzzz. My mobile phone still sits in front of me on the windowsill.

One message.

Hey, Princess, are you coming over? Roger writes.

I smile. Roger's texts always have a sense of love about them. Always. We've been together for over four months. My father was wrong when he told me I wouldn't get a man unless I changed the way I am. I'm *not* an alien.

Roger is English. He loves football as much as I do. Should England ever beat Germany again, we'll need to reconsider our relationship. Ha ha – just kidding.

Hey! I reply. *I'd love to, but can't tonight.*

Seconds later: *Oh, are you babysitting?*

No, I've some things to do at mine.

Shall I come and help you?

Oh my God. No! He shall not.

I could set off in 10 mins, he texts again.

Panic!

Roger doesn't know about my plan. He knows Sonja, though, and why she wants me to lock her in every night at 11pm. But he's not aware that I must get rid of her. Tonight.

What if I tell him? Would he do something? Of course he wouldn't call the police. I mean, I'm doing this for him. Well, I'm doing it for *us*. Would he see it as proof of my love?

I've told him how hard it is for me to split from Sonja after all this time. He says he understands, but I would prefer it if he persuaded me to get rid of her. Years ago, my then-boyfriend claimed that Sonja was a problem in our relationship. He broke up with me because of her. I don't want to repeat that mistake. She has to go.

No, it's okay, you don't need to come, I reply. *But thanks!*

What are you so busy with then, my princess?

Arrrrrgh, stop asking, *please*! I don't know what to text back.

It's okay, don't worry. You don't have to tell me, Roger texts again.

I feel a sting in my heart. He's always so understanding; never puts me under pressure. He knows when I feel rough.

I'd hoped to see you tonight, but it's totally fine if I don't. Really! he writes.

I know it's fine. I know he's not angry if I don't tell him why.

A sudden inspiration – thank goodness for that. *Can I call it a surprise?*

Of course you can. See you tomorrow then?

Yes!

Looking forward to it. Sleep well tonight. Thinking of you. I love you!

I feel my heart make a little jump. Those three words are so very strong. I rarely heard them before I met Roger. I understand them, and yet I don't. It's hard to shake the feeling that I'm unlovable. Maybe he doesn't really mean them. I'm unable to say the three words myself, so I reply to him with two emoticons instead: a smiley face and a heart.

WHAT. A. SURPRISE.

1987

IT WAS EARLY March, during my last year at primary school. Less cold, but lots of snow was still around, heavy and wet. I never liked the snow to go away. I went out in the garden, taking my doll, Sally, with me. She needed some fresh air. I searched for my old children's wheelbarrow. It was way too small for me and pretty rusty, but it still worked. I took it to the neighbouring garden, which belonged to the house my step-grandmother lived in. Step-Grandmother was 'Grandma' when we were together, as that was what she wanted to be called. Otherwise, she was Bertha; latest since the day before the last Mother's Day when I'd come back from the fields and asked her to hide my present for Mum at hers. She'd mocked me for the horrible wild flowers I had plucked: "You seriously want to give *these* to your mum?"

Bertha's mind was as multifaceted and warm as the decoration in her house: two smooth ceramic birds and one artificial flower sat in her living-room window. The rest of the wide windowsill was reserved for an easy pass of her feather duster. I'm sure the only reason she had a real tree at Christmas was that the instructions for assembling a plastic one would have been too difficult for her to follow.

Also, she was most likely the only person in Fessdorf driving an automatic – and still she'd managed to crash into the window front of the village's only supermarket while attempting to leave her parking spot.

Now, her garden was full of snow, just like ours. And yet I had the impression that the snow melted first and faster in our garden. I shovelled wheelbarrow after wheelbarrow full of snow from her garden, then transported the lovely white goods and dumped them in ours. I explained every single step to Sally. After an hour, I was tired and put shovel and wheelbarrow back in their places. I took Sally and returned to the house.

My brother and Dad were laughing when I came in. I made sure I disappeared quickly into my bedroom.

My bedroom looked like a proper girl's room. Because Sally lived in there. Whereas I always wore jumpers and trousers, some of which had been passed down to me from my brother, Sally always wore blouses with puffed sleeves, floral skirts or dresses with ruffles. Besides her adorable clothing, she had everything a girl needed: a hair-brush and hair clips, shoes, her own small table, her little seat to be fed in, a cooker, and a super-cute little washing machine. And, of course, she had a princess bed.

I stared out the window of my room at my snow-work. It was pleasing; the view was lovely. Sally was pleased, too.

They laughed at me. So what?!

"They just don't understand how nice I have made our garden. And how nice snow is," I muttered to myself.

They think I'm weird, don't they? I suddenly felt as if something as heavy as the snow I had shovelled was weighing on my mood. Had I just proved it? Was I really a bit weird? Or very? My brother and Dad didn't understand what I was doing; what I was feeling. They probably never understood me.

I felt disconnected. Disconnected from them. I blew up an Imaginary Comfort Bubble to slip inside – my special psychological refuge. It was nice and warm in there. I curled up, rested my back against its wall, and from within the bubble's confines my snow-work looked even better.

* * *

AFTER A WHILE, I re-emerged. I turned away from the window and went to my desk. I had homework to do. Homework that had to be finished for the next day, which was a Saturday. I had to go to school every second Saturday for a couple of lessons; mostly something light, like art or textiles. I really liked art, but textiles was different. Whether or not I did well depended on what we had to do. If it was embroidering, I did okay. But when we had to knit or crochet, I wasn't very good. The scarf I had knitted started much narrower than it finished. Crocheting, I didn't get at all. I could only do the very first line, which I kept going on with, never making any shapes. For this Saturday, I had to take a finished pair of oven cloths back to school. *Two* oven cloths, and I hadn't even started on one. There was no way that I could get them done. Well, almost no way: there was always Grandma. She was visiting with us and came to my rescue.

I left my bedroom and found her downstairs in the basement doing some ironing, helping with Mum's housework.

"Grandma?"

"Yes, my dear?"

"Look at this." I held out two balls of wool – a purple one and a red one. "I have to crochet a pair of oven cloths for school, made with two different colours. For tomorrow! Grandma, can you help me, please?"

"Of course, my poppet."

She took the two balls of wool out of my hands, then carried on with her ironing. I went back upstairs to my bedroom, trusting that my beloved grandmother would come up with the best result for me.

One hour later, she knocked at my door and came in with two completed, very tightly and neatly crocheted oven cloths. They were purple with a red trim, and even had a loop to hang them up with.

"Wow, Grandma, how did you do that so quickly?"

She smiled and handed them to me. "I hope you like them."

Indeed I did. I wrapped my arms around Grandma's wide, cuddly waist and nestled my head against her chest like a cat. Her hand ran through my hair.

* * *

THE NEXT MORNING, when I arrived at school, something was different. Something was… I didn't know, but I was suddenly confused.

I stood in front of my desk inside my classroom. It was next-to-last of a line of desks. The very last one had been empty since the beginning of the school year. Now, there was somebody there! A new child was sitting in the empty chair, at that empty desk. A new pupil had joined my class. What. A. Surprise.

My eyes searched this newcomer as if they were covered

in a woolly oven-cloth web that had been crocheted by Grandma. I was tracing the yarn from beginning to end, top to bottom. Why on earth was somebody joining our class in the middle of the school year? On a Saturday at the beginning of March? And why were they sat next to me? *Just* me? Why not next to Annika, or Sophie? They too had empty chairs next to them!

Nobody had said anything about anybody new coming. I didn't know if this new pupil had been announced to our teacher but, all of a sudden, I had a neighbour to my right whereas I used to only have one to my left – my friend Susanne. She'd sat there since the start of the year.

The new classmate was a girl. I sat in my chair, glanced at her. Then my eyes moved away. And dared to return. And away again. I wasn't sure whether I liked this new situation; this new girl. Would the fact that I was her only neighbour – her only *direct* contact – bring obligations? Was I supposed to accompany her in our class? Or was she there so *I* had another person to socialise with? As if Susanne wasn't enough.

I reached into my little bag. It wasn't my proper school bag, because I only had textiles today. I got my homework out and put it in front of me on the desk. Susanne, who had also arrived, eyed my purple-and-red oven cloths, while she got her own pair out. Hers were green and yellow. I preferred mine – well, Grandma's.

The new girl didn't put any oven cloths on her desk. She had none. But she was staring at mine! Had Susanne known about her? I tried studying the new girl, turning my head as little as necessary. She seemed quiet, almost shy. Was she in an Imaginary Comfort Bubble? Right now?

"What are you doing here?" I finally asked.

"I've moved here with my parents," she said.

"Does that mean you'll be here every day now?"

She nodded. "Can I see your oven cloths?" she asked.

I hesitated but slid them onto her desk. She took them, and I watched closely. Her hands stroked them. *Caressed* them. And I wasn't sure if I liked that.

Susanne turned to her. "You wanna feel mine?" she asked.

The girl shook her head. She stroked my oven cloths a couple more times and then put them back on my desk.

"What's your name?" I asked.

"Sonja."

What? *Sonja?!* I felt my reservations about her justified: she had a name ending in 'ja', like mine – *too much* like mine! Okay, admittedly, I wasn't keen on my name. It was hard for me to say it out loud. And it was worse with my last name. The latter was also Dad's, and whenever he said it, picking up the phone, it sounded so dry, so dark. Just as he sometimes shot back at Mum. But now this new girl had a name ending the same way as mine – even with 'n' before the 'ja'. There was no other girl in our class whose name finished like that, and I suddenly felt that this put Sonja close to me. Too close, maybe.

On reflection, however, I quickly remembered there being a Nadja, a Tanja, and even a Ronja in my brother's class. I cooled down.

Well, okay then: "Ah ha. And I'm Finja."

Our teacher came into the classroom, closed the door, and walked to her desk. She must have been in the room some minutes before. There were boxes with cloth, balls of wool, crochet hooks and knitting needles on her desk in preparation for the lesson.

"Good morning, everybody!" Mrs Motte trilled.

I suddenly felt a little sick. I stuck my arm up and raised a finger. Without waiting until Mrs Motte asked me to speak up, I did so.

"Can I please go to the toilet? I'm feeling sick!"

"Oh dear!"

"So please, can I?"

She nodded once, and I stood up and ran from the classroom. It was the first time I had ever left during a lesson. Before then, I'd always managed to time my need for a pee, or any other emergency, between lessons.

I rushed downstairs and crossed the big hall. I went past the stage, reached the toilets and went inside. Instead of going into a cubicle, I stood at a sink, staring at the mirror. My face was pale. I wiped my hands over it and looked into the mirror again. For a couple of minutes, I didn't do anything other than stare at myself.

I didn't really need to but I sat on the toilet anyway. Then I went back to the same sink to wash my hands and thought about the new girl, Sonja, up in the classroom. *I don't know if I'm going to like her!* My stomach still didn't feel right. I waited for something to happen, retched a little but that was it.

The tap was still running. I washed my mouth and face, turned the water off, took some paper towels to dry my hands and face, and checked myself one more time in the mirror. The colour of my skin was more normal, so I left the bathroom and walked back upstairs to my classroom.

*   *   *

I CLOSED THE door silently and returned to my desk. Mrs Motte had started calling up one pupil after another to show their oven cloths and get their marks. The new girl was watching carefully.

It was Susanne's turn to take her homework to Mrs Motte. I would be called next. When Susanne came away from Mrs Motte's desk, I stood up and walked in front of the class. My heart started to beat faster the moment I handed Mrs Motte Grandma's oven cloths. They were so neat and tight that I wasn't sure whether they weren't *too* neat and tight for the work of a child! Staring at Mrs Motte's face, a lightning thought occurred to me: did she know what Grandma's oven cloths looked like? Had my brother been good at making them too?

Mrs Motte inspected both sides of my cloths. I was shaky by then. But I needn't have worried.

"Well done," she said, handing them back to me.

My whole body relaxed. I smiled as I got a one, which was the top mark. *Well done, Grandma.*

When all of the pupils, except Sonja since she was new, had received their marks, we carried on with more textiles stuff that Mrs Motte had prepared for us. During the next one and a half hours, I stayed unusually quiet. Mrs Motte normally let us chat while crocheting. Of course, kids will always take advantage of that. I didn't. Not that Saturday. I didn't talk to Susanne, but let her chat to her other neighbour.

Sonja didn't speak a single word to me, as if she didn't know what to say. First, I was rather glad she stayed silent. Then I didn't mind. And then my curiosity awoke: *If she's going to be here now every day, I need to know where exactly in Fessdorf she lives.* But I just chewed my lips all through the lesson and glanced every few minutes at her hands and what they were crafting.

CONTROLLING THE KEYS

July 2014

MY LEGS FEEL tired from standing, from waiting for the evening to go by and the night to arrive. Actually, they hurt. I've only been here by my window for a few minutes but need to get my chair and sit down. I'm not good at standing any more. I'm too old. Yes, old at thirty-seven.

Aches and pains make my life hard, and they're down to Sonja's lifestyle. I blame her for all the times I suffered from migraine, when it completely tore me apart; when I vomited numerous times. Each time I begged her to leave me alone or hand me a gun to shoot myself. But, of course, she never had one.

She's managed to shrink my life to a small, oppressive box that she wants to continue to control. I blame her for my sorrow and devastation. And if I hadn't managed to just about keep my head up, I'd bang it against the wall until I felt nothing any more.

My physical problems started a couple of years ago when body parts began to feel temporarily numb. I get pins and needles in different places – on my back, lower arms, fingertips and shins. My left leg causes problems: I get pains up to hip height and need treatment. My throat is sore regularly, and I often have a cold or get ulcers in my mouth – a crap immune system. I'm oversensitive to noise. Going out means I must block my ears so I can stand the noise of the traffic. And so on and so on.

The medication I currently take is *only* made in Germany. So I haven't been able to avoid it, even though we're in France. Sonja would freak out if she looked into the little cupboard above my sink. She'd try to make me not take this particular medication, ignoring the fact that she'd be gravely endangering my health. She's done it before.

Roger thinks I can recover from my physical problems. I'm not so sure about that. But anyway, I'd better get the job done tonight, so Sonja can't continue wearing me out. Roll on 3am! But it's only 8.30pm and darkness hasn't even started falling over Paris. I've got to wait so long until Sonja will finally be in bed.

Sonja does the same things every evening. She controls, checks, makes sure, looks, and double-checks again and again. One of her light switches sits right next to my head whenever I'm in bed. When she has a problem with it, I have one too. Only if I put in my earplugs and play loud music can I not hear her never-ending switch-on-switch-off. But then there is my hypersensitivity to noise... so I can't play music *too* loud.

Sonja also washes herself a bloody lot. Washing her hands takes nine minutes on its own.

I expect she will knock on my door just before eleven o'clock. She'll hand me her key. It's always been so annoying to be involved in her routine. But now, this time, I can't wait!

She has two keys. One has been 'locked up' in a

gold-coloured envelope since we've lived here. She wrote the date across the sealing line when she closed it, just like a wax seal. She thinks that will let her know if the envelope has been opened and resealed, because the numbers won't look neat any more. She sealed this golden envelope some years ago.

Sonja has nothing to write with in her room. This way, she's unable to write anything else on the golden envelope with the key inside, and so she knows for sure the envelope hasn't been opened. She threw away the pen she used to write the 'wax seal' on the day she bought it.

Why does she do this? She wants to make sure she doesn't leave her room during the night, after I've locked her in. While she's asleep, she doesn't have control. She wants evidence each morning that she hasn't left.

Her second key is the one she uses to go out and come back home – the one she hands me in the evening. First she sends me a text to remind me. Later, shortly before eleven o'clock, she comes over, gives me the key, and asks me to lock her in. In the morning, when she feels fully awake and in control, she sends me another text, asking me to unlock her door again. In an emergency, she could get out of her room with that other key that is put away in the gold-coloured envelope. But she never has any emergencies. The golden envelope is kept safely 'out of reach'. It's stored on its own on a shelf inside her wardrobe; on the second one down, left-hand side.

As I lock her up every night, I'm in control when she's asleep. What else could I wish for now that I'm planning to kill her? It's a gift, isn't it? She'll say, "Please lock my door. Make sure you turn the key twice, okay?" Oh yes, I will turn it twice.

THE RULE

1987

IT WAS MONDAY morning – two days after that Saturday when Sonja joined my class and sat next to me. Mum woke me. I went to the toilet, got dressed, and sat at the kitchen table. In front of me stood a bowl of cornflakes. I poured in the 'fresh' milk Mum had made, mixing dusty, guaranteed-radiation-free milk powder with water.

I picked at my breakfast and thought about Sonja. I expected to see her again within the next hour. What would it be like? The pink and blue weather dolls from our terrace flashed up briefly.

Mum didn't know about Sonja yet. I hadn't said anything. Dad didn't know either. Nobody at home knew.

I left for school earlier than I had on Saturday, because Mum didn't let me go by bike this time. It was too frosty. I was dressed warmly, and walked. My brother took a bus to the high school in Dabendorf – the neighbouring village.

Just as I reached my school at the other end of Fessdorf and walked up the stairs to the main entrance, Susanne arrived. She came every day by bus, since she had to come from a different village. We went into our classroom, and Sonja was already there.

"Hello," I said.

"Hello."

I now had to put my school bag to my left instead of my right. Sonja's bag looked somewhat familiar. I eyed it more closely: red with a yellow trim, same as mine! It was nothing unusual when pupils had the same bags; some school items were particularly popular. However, I was surprised to see her with 'my' school bag, because no one else in our class had it. Unlike with the ending of our names, I just shrugged this off. I suddenly didn't mind she might be close to me. Funny, that.

I settled into my seat. The first lesson was about to start. German. I felt Sonja hadn't settled. She kept glancing to her left and right as if she was checking something. Repeatedly. Over her shoulders, then down her upper arms and onto the floor. I couldn't tell why she was acting like that. She had enough room. There was nothing, really. She only had one neighbour – me – and then there was just space to her right.

Mrs Motte came into class. Sonja stopped checking and looked up. We had to do some writing. I got my fountain pen out of my pencil case; a red one with a silver cap. I liked writing with that pen. I saw Sonja taking her fountain pen out of her pencil case. She had a blue one. Susanne also had a red pen, but hers was a slightly different shape than mine. We all started writing in our exercise books and followed Mrs Motte's instructions.

I peeked at Sonja's writing, and at Susanne's, then back at Sonja's. And at her, her head bent over her exercise book. She had straight blonde hair, tied in a ponytail. It was a similar colour to my hair. Susanne's was slightly darker and she didn't have so much of it; her ponytail was almost too thin whenever she had one.

It was the first time that I really looked at Sonja, since she had become my new neighbour. Did she know I was studying her?

She didn't look back at me. Or say anything. But I'm sure she noticed out of the corner of her eye that I was observing her and her first proper action in our class. She hadn't done very much in textiles two days earlier.

My eyes were fixed on Sonja's blue fountain pen, how the tip skated over the paper in her exercise book, forming letter after letter. It reminded me of Mum's calligraphy book. I loved Sonja's writing, and thought I should try and do better with mine.

She didn't seem distracted by my staring but stayed totally focused. Her composure, her calm appearance, or maybe her 'pink' look… something like that suddenly prompted a smile from me.

* * *

THE SECOND LESSON of that Monday was art. Even though it wasn't that springlike outside, it wasn't too long before Easter, so we painted pictures for that. My paintbox stood on my desk. So did Susanne's. Both were messy, like the mixing trays of wannabe artists. We had used them many times. Sonja opened hers. She lifted the lid and put it down on the desk. Her colours were all virgin and clean, not messy at all. I put my painting pad in front of me and opened it. It still had my painting from our last art lesson in there: a brown rabbit with lots of bright green around it, and Easter eggs. It wasn't finished. Susanne and I had worked together during the previous art lesson. I had almost a copy of her picture on my sheet. Sonja's sheets were all blank.

Susanne and I dunked our brushes into glasses of water. Sonja watched.

"Violet!" Susanne said.

"Violet what?" I asked.

"I'll paint my Easter eggs violet."

"Ah, cool, me too."

We wetted our blue and red colour pots.

"Oh dear, my red and blue now look the same," I said.

The two pots in my paintbox were next to each other. I transferred the colour mix onto my painting, inside the outlines of the Easter eggs. Sonja now started to paint as well. She took a big brush, made it wet, and went with it into the bright green of her box. With several strokes, she painted her blank sheet completely green and then blew it dry. Then she mixed blue and red and painted three violet Easter eggs onto her paper. Susanne and I watched.

"Well, my Easter eggs are too blue. I'm going to make them more like purple," Susanne suddenly said.

She pushed her brush into her red, brushed around with some water and added only a little bit of blue. Then she transferred the mix onto her paper, changing the colour of her Easter eggs. I decided to do the same with mine. So did Sonja. We carried on mixing and mixing, changing the look of our Easter eggs until Susanne's and my pots of red and blue were brushed out to their bottoms. The Easter eggs were too damp now. Mrs Motte waved from her desk; she had a hairdryer next to her. I went forward and handed her my painting. Once it was dry enough, Sonja stood up from her chair and went to Mrs Motte. Then Susanne.

Some minutes later, Susanne sat back down at her desk, and Sonja did her checking again. She stared down the lines of her shoulders, arms and sides as carefully as if she were playing the hand-eye coordination game in which one mustn't touch the metal loop against the wire to avoid a shocking noise.

The three of us decorated our purple-violet Easter eggs with bright spots. Then, my art was finished. I was pleased with it. I viewed Susanne's work and then Sonja's. They also seemed well done.

Just then, as I was looking at Sonja's painting, her body twitched. Lots of purple water on her desk. My glass still stood in front of me, but Susanne had accidentally knocked hers over. The water was pouring towards my desk and further onto Sonja's. I jumped up from my chair to avoid getting wet. Sonja got up as well, but when she had twitched she'd pushed her painting pad against her paintbox. It was now on the floor.

"Oh no," I said.

I bent down to look under the table and saw water dripping from the edge, hitting Sonja's paintbox. Purple drops landed exactly inside the pot of red, filling it up slowly.

Sonja appeared like she had witnessed a serious accident. She flopped back into her chair, putting her lower arms on the dry edge of the table and resting her right cheek on them. The purple water formed a pool over the rest of the table, surrounding her head. It made me think of blood – whenever Mum and Dad watched Detective Chief Inspector Derrick on TV, the victims so often lay in purple at a desk or on the floor…

I sat back in my chair. Carefully, I put my right hand on Sonja's shoulder.

"Hey, don't worry. Your painting has no water on it. It's fine. The water has only gone underneath your painting pad. Your paintbox isn't broken either," I said.

My own pad had also got wet, but Mrs Motte already arrived armed with an old kitchen towel to dry up the mess. She lifted our painting pads and wiped them underneath. She picked up Sonja's paintbox from the floor, dried it, and placed it back on Sonja's desk. Susanne used paper towels to soak up the water on her desk.

"Wow, you've done well. They're beautiful." Mrs Motte viewed our works.

I liked her comment. Sonja didn't seem to care, though. She wasn't resting with her arms on her desk any more, but stayed frozen. I was puzzled. Why was she so unhappy? Everything appeared fine! Yet her face was still so sad. So unmoved. So paralysed. So dead.

When the art lesson was over, we had a break of twenty minutes. Long enough to go into the schoolyard and play. I stared at Sonja who still seemed so upset in the chair next to me. In the next moment, I realised she and I were all alone in the classroom. Every other child had already run from it. Mrs Motte had gone, too. *Huh, Susanne hasn't asked me to come out and play!* I hesitated, but then asked Sonja, "Shall we go together into the yard?" And she nodded.

* * *

NORMALLY, I WOULD have played with Susanne and some other children. We used to play simple outdoor games like hopscotch, or do some skipping, either individually or with several other girls. I saw them playing in the usual area, but now I was walking with the new girl somewhere else in the schoolyard. I didn't know that I was never going to play with any of the others again.

I couldn't stop wondering what troubled Sonja.

"What's wrong?" I asked.

"The water on the table from earlier," she said.

"I thought so. But nothing happened. Not really. I mean, Mrs Motte cleaned everything up. Nothing has been spoiled."

"Yes it has." She sighed.

"But our pictures stayed dry. Nobody got wet. No clothes dirty, nothing. Didn't you see that?"

"But for me, something did get dirty."

"What?"

"My paintbox."

"Eh? Because it fell on the floor?"

"No, not because of that."

"Why, then?" I was confused.

"The water has made it dirty," she said.

"The water?"

"Yes."

"Ah. Because it wasn't clean? But it's not so bad, really. It's been dried off, you know. It's gone now."

"No, not because it wasn't clean."

"I still don't get it. Why, then?"

"Because it was *Susanne's* water. And it dropped all around the pot of my red colour and probably splashed on some others."

I remained confused. Completely. The problem wasn't that it was dirty water but that it was Susanne's?

"Why is Susanne's water a problem?" I asked.

"I'm not sure. It just is."

"I don't understand."

"I can't touch Susanne or anything of hers."

"Why not?" I was really intrigued now.

"Because that's The Rule. Anything she has touched is

dirty. And if it touches my belongings, they become dirty, too," Sonja said.

"Dirty?"

"Yes."

"Don't you like Susanne?"

I glanced across the schoolyard to see if I could catch sight of Susanne. She was skipping with some girls, seemingly having fun. Nobody appeared to be missing me. Not even Susanne, as she was able to just play with other girls.

"She's okay. Seems nice. But her water was dirty, even before she'd put her brushes into it. And it makes me dirty," Sonja said.

"What? How can clean water be dirty?"

"Because it was hers."

How did that work? No matter whether the water was dirty or clean, it made Sonja dirty. And what had she said earlier? "That's The Rule." *What rule?*

The school bell rang. Before Sonja and I made our way back into the building, I needed to know one more thing:

"What if the water had been mine? Would your paintbox still be dirty now?"

"No," she said.

We walked up the stairs to our classroom, and I saw Susanne already further up. Surely, she wasn't aware that her water was a problem, and that there appeared to be a rule saying that she and her belongings must not touch Sonja.

* * *

ONCE IN THE classroom, we sat down at our desks. It was time for maths, and I loved it. I was settled in my chair. Sonja did her checking again. Down her arms, sides and onto the floor.

"Your paintbox is still on your desk," I pointed out. "Don't you want to put it on the shelf where all the others are? And your painting pad?"

The latter stood on its side on the floor, leaning against the leg of Sonja's desk. Mrs Motte had put it there to dry after taking out Sonja's Easter egg painting.

"No, I'll leave them as they are," Sonja said.

She didn't move her paintbox the tiniest fraction, despite having less space on her desk. She placed her maths and exercise books, as well as her pencil case, around it.

Mrs Kling came in. I liked her. She was young and dynamic, and I found her way of teaching very good. I also liked Mrs Motte, but I never struggled with Mrs Kling's assignments, unlike with Mrs Motte's crocheting. The arithmetic from Mrs Kling was always easy. I liked numbers and wished I could have crocheted them instead.

The maths lesson was finished within a blink of an eye. After science, another twenty-minute-break and religion, school was out. I was hungry and wanted to get home as soon as possible. I packed my books and pencil case into my school bag and put my jacket on. Sonja and Susanne were doing the same. However, Sonja didn't quite put all her things from her desk into her school bag. Her paintbox was still on the table, her painting pad still leaning against the leg.

"Bye. See you tomorrow," Susanne said.

"Yes, see you tomorrow. Bye," I said.

Then I turned to Sonja. "What are you doing with your pad and paintbox?"

"I'll carry them."

"Home? You'll get cold hands!"

"That's okay."

"Why don't you leave your things here in the classroom, like everyone else? Put them on the shelf. You don't need to carry them home."

"But I want to. I have to!"

I gave up. I said bye to Sonja and left the classroom.

* * *

BEFORE HEADING HOME, I went into the toilets. Not because I felt sick again, but because I needed a pee. Then I left the school. Sonja was walking on the pavement, some distance ahead of me, holding her paintbox and pad in her bare hands. I was convinced they were already freezing. Where exactly did she live? This question was now burning inside me. I ran to catch up with her.

"Hey, where do you live?"

"Next to the railway track. That way." She pointed, holding her paintbox in the same hand.

There was a single railway track crossing Fessdorf. It connected several villages away from Gadburg – a bigger city nearby. The route wasn't very busy.

"Really? That's where I'm going, too. I normally take my bike, but my mum said it was too slippery today," I said.

"My bike is broken. My father needs to fix it," she said.

"On which side of the railway is your house?"

"On this side. It's a new one."

"Oh," I said. "There's only one new house. It has a wooden front."

"Yes, that's where I live," she said.

I knew exactly which house she meant. I had seen it being built and come past it almost daily. It had been built very quickly.

"That's really funny! I live just around the corner," I said.

"Really?" And then I saw her smiling for the first time.

"Do you want me to help and carry your paintbox? Or maybe the pad? Then you can warm one hand in your pocket before you swap, and I'll do the same," I said.

"No, thanks. I don't want to contaminate you. You can't see the dirt but it's there. It's invisible."

I experienced déjà vu. Her remarks sounded like when Mum had spoken of that radiation about a year before. She hadn't wanted the carpet to get contaminated when my brother's friend came round to bring homework. She told me about clouds and the dirty rain coming down on us, bringing something dangerous although I couldn't see it. Now this was the second time in my life that I heard the word 'contaminate'.

"You said the water wouldn't have been a problem if it had been mine. Why is Susanne's a problem?" I said.

"Because she's dirty."

I didn't really like that statement. "No, she's not!"

"She isn't dirty like dirt on the ground. She's... um... I don't know. Maybe not truly dirty, but it's simply what The Rule says."

That rule again. What bloody rule?

"The Rule. The Rule tells me I'm not allowed to touch her," Sonja said.

"Weird, this rule," I said. "And where does it come from? Whose rule is it?"

"Nobody's, really."

"Nobody?"

"No. I don't know where it's from," she said. "It's just there!"

"I've never heard about a rule like that. Is it written anywhere?"

"No. Not this one."

I was about to ask Sonja how many other rules there were, and where they were written, when we went past a litter bin. She dumped both her paintbox and her pad!

"Huh?" My jaw dropped.

"I had to do it. Otherwise they'd cause me too much trouble. Now I only have to wash my hands at home, and everything will be fine," she said.

"Is it what The Rule says?"

She nodded.

I was curious. "How are you going to explain this to your mum, then? I mean, that you need a new paintbox and pad *already*?"

"I don't know yet. I'll have to come up with something."

I figured her parents didn't know about The Rule.

The railway track was in sight. We reached the point where our paths separated. Sonja needed to cross the road after about another fifty yards and walk down a little grass path to get to her home. I needed to turn left and walk halfway down that road to get to mine. That was how close we lived.

* * *

AFTER LUNCH, I did my maths homework. I enjoyed doing it. Then I thought of Sonja. I didn't know much at all about her. It felt so weird now that I had a classmate who lived around the corner. Not just a classmate – a friend, maybe?

I left my bedroom and searched for Mum. *I need to tell her.* Normally, I told her everything as soon as I had a chance. But this time I hadn't even mentioned that I had felt sick during the art lesson last Saturday.

I asked to go over to Sonja's house, but Mum reminded me it was Monday. Mr Fink would come in half an hour – my dozy old piano teacher. I rushed back into my bedroom, got my eraser out of my pencil case and removed all the names of the pieces I still couldn't play, before he would be sitting next to me, eating cake, slurping coffee and dropping off.

I was always okay when he fell asleep, but this Monday I was particularly glad he did. Focusing on playing the piano was impossible, because Sonja was in my head. I made sure I hit a few notes every now and again. *Mum shouldn't come in and ask if something is wrong!* I watched Mr Fink's heavy eyelids and the long, white wart that stuck out from one like the toothpick from Dad's Swiss army knife. If only I could have sneaked out through the window. I so much wanted to spend my time with Sonja, to get to know her!

*   *   *

I HAD TO wait until the next morning at school. I was excited when I saw her. She didn't seem upset or bothered about her 'dirty' paintbox and painting pad any more. I was pleased she didn't. I thought her mum would buy the replacements new.

We had music. We didn't play instruments, but had to sing. Instead of going to the music room, we went to the stage in the school hall to sit on its steps. Mrs Baumschmidt wanted us to do canon singing in a choir. Unlike most of our teachers, Mrs Baumschmidt was ill a lot. I thought she was ill more often than not. Weak and skinny, she stood in front of us, waving her arms around to conduct our singing. The fluffy cotton-wool tufts were keeping good time. Sonja was to my left. Susanne wasn't next to me this time. She sat in the front row, whereas Sonja and I were sitting in the middle row above. I was between Sonja and Frank, and to Sonja's left was Lucie.

After about twenty minutes, Mrs Baumschmidt decided to give us, and herself, a break. We were allowed to move and run around. Most of the boys even went outside into the yard. Most girls stayed inside, walking around in the hall. Some went to the toilet. Some had a drink and sat down on the benches by the side of the big windows. I didn't need to go to the toilet, and I wasn't thirsty either. I remained sitting on the steps of the stage. But Sonja had stood up. She descended the steps and walked across the hall. I didn't follow her, but watched where she was going. She made her way through the hall and towards the stairs leading up to the first floor where our classroom was. No other child had gone there. Maybe Sonja was thirsty and had left her drink in the classroom. I leant against the step behind me to relax my back and wait until Mrs Baumschmidt and my classmates, including Sonja, returned.

However, it seemed that I was waiting for her a long time. *What is she doing?* I started worrying, and decided to get up from the stage and see. Perhaps she needed help.

The door to our classroom was closed. Was Sonja not inside? I pressed the handle down and pulled the door open. Yes, she was. But she wasn't having a drink. She wasn't even rummaging in her school bag or at her desk. Instead, she was right by the wall next to the blackboard, behind the teacher's desk, scraping her left arm. I had recently seen a children's programme with a bear in it, doing a similar thing against a tree.

"Sonja, what are you doing?"

"I'll be back soon, don't worry."

"But what are you doing there?"

She kept on scraping her left arm along the bricks of the wall. I went closer. Beads of sweat trickled down her brow.

"Cleaning my sleeve," she said.

"Uh, cleaning your sleeve?"

"Yes, I'm brushing off the bits from Lucie. This wall works well; it's rough." She rubbed her arm up and down against the wall and walked forward at the same time.

"Is it dirty again? Like yesterday?"

"Yes."

"Dirt from Lucie this time?"

"I'm not allowed to touch Lucie either."

"The Rule says?"

"Yes, The Rule."

"Bizarre stuff, your rule. Really bizarre," I said. "It must hurt. I mean, your arm against the hard wall?"

"It does. But I don't care. I've gone all along that wall." She pointed across the classroom towards the wall by the door.

"Really?"

"Yes, it's better the more I do it. I mean, to get rid of all the bits. Then I'll be safe."

"Safe?"

"Yeah, safe!"

"Well, are you safe now? We need to go back to the choir; the break must be over."

She stopped scraping her sleeve. She was breathing faster than normal. "Okay." She nodded.

We left the classroom and went back down into the hall. I took my place again on the steps of the stage between Sonja and Frank. Lucie returned and Sonja moved closer to me. The fluffy cotton-wool tufts returned and resumed action.

*　*　*

SOME HOURS LATER, when school was out, I walked all the way home next to Sonja again. It was mild enough to ride my bike, but I had deliberately left it at home.

"Why does The Rule say Lucie is dirty?" I asked.

"It's not just Lucie; it's *all* the girls. I can't touch any of them. Only you!"

Suddenly I felt Sonja's arm on my back; her head close to mine.

"Do you want to come round to my house? We could play together," she said.

My heart was engulfed with warmth. Wow – Sonja didn't touch any other girl in our class, because they were dirty. But her arm was currently wrapped around my back, and she even asked me to come to her house! When I had become friends with Susanne, it had taken weeks before she invited me.

Sonja's question wasn't difficult to answer: My brother showed no real interest in me; I was tolerated but not a popular playmate. Dad didn't get involved much with my life, except for a bit of tennis; I didn't think I was special to him; no engulfing there. True, Mum and Grandma were there for me; Mum's orange vitamin pills by the edge of my supper plate each night were proof of her love, and so were her strokes on my back I received every school morning when she woke me. Given that Susanne was able to play hopscotch with just the other girls, I only had my Imaginary Comfort Bubble as a true friend. So I really wanted Sonja now.

"Yeah."

THE BROWN FAMILY
MEETING FOLDER

IT WAS WEDNESDAY afternoon. On my way to Sonja's home,
I skipped down the grass path, then ran the final few metres
to get to the door. I rang the bell, and Sonja opened the
door almost immediately.

"Hi, Finja!" she said.

"Hi!"

"Come in." She grabbed my hand and pulled me inside
the house.

Unlike in my home, not all the rooms of Sonja's were
on the same floor. She showed me around. I saw the living
room and kitchen downstairs. Everything appeared pretty
new. Her bedroom was on the first floor, so we walked up
some stairs.

"Is your mum not here?" I said.

"No. She's out doing some shopping."

"And your dad?"

"My father is in the garden, on the other side from where
you came."

I didn't mind that he was in the garden. Meeting Sonja's
mum would be easier anyway, I thought. I never had many
grown up guys around me; my teachers were all female. And
Mum always sounded rather jolly whenever she said, "Dad

is staying away longer today. He's got a meeting!"

Sonja opened the door to her bedroom. We went inside. Then I counted: nine bottles stood in the middle of the room. Different shapes, all made of glass. Green ones and white ones, all empty. I thought it was odd to play with glass bottles, since I saw no dolls or other girly stuff.

"Well, my father put them there," Sonja said. "Shall we sit on my bed? Or on the sofa?"

"I don't mind."

She decided we would sit on her bed.

I couldn't take my eyes off the bottles. "And why has your dad put them there?"

"Because I didn't take them down to the storage room in the cellar where we collect them."

"To return to the supermarket?"

"Yes."

"Why hasn't *he* taken them down?" I asked.

"Because that's my job for this week. But I haven't done it, so he put them here."

"Your job?"

"Yes, it's actually one of *two*," she said. "Each week I have two to do in the house."

"And what's your second?"

"Taking the rubbish from the kitchen out to the dustbin."

We were both quiet for a moment. I didn't know if Sonja expected me to say something, or if she could guess my next question.

"And if you don't take it out, your dad puts it here as well?"

"Yes." She sighed.

I was pleased there was no rubbish in her bedroom while I was there.

"So you'd better make sure you take it out," I said.

Sonja said nothing.

"Why didn't you take the bottles down if it's your job?" I asked.

"Because I don't know how to touch them once they've been in the holder my father puts them in. I find that thing dirty."

There was that word 'dirty' again.

"What do you mean?"

"My father puts them here when the holder is full and I haven't taken them down."

"And your mum?"

"She knows I don't like the holder, so she doesn't put them in there."

"Ah, that's nice of your mum. Why doesn't your dad do the same?"

"Because he doesn't care." She tilted her head slightly down, chin towards her chest, and sighed again. I realised she spoke about him as 'my father', never 'my dad'.

"That's not so nice," I said.

"Well, on Sunday, I'll change my jobs anyway."

"Huh?"

"Yeah. Every Sunday, we hold a family meeting; after lunch. We sit around the table with the family meeting folder; discuss things; orders and rules. At the end, my father gives me my pocket money."

I was speechless. I'd never heard of a family meeting folder.

"Let me see if I can get it," Sonja said.

She left. I was sitting alone on her bed and stared at the empty bottles. Wasn't it mean of her father to have put them there?

Sonja came back and brought a brown folder with her.

"My father's in the garden. Should be okay that I've taken it," she said.

She sat back on the bed next to me and opened the folder. She started off with the last page. It was from the most recent family meeting, the previous Sunday. I saw some written notes, and she explained they were a report of what they had discussed during the meeting. Further down, I saw her jobs for the week noted. The last things on the page were the signatures of Sonja and both her parents.

"Can I hold it myself?" I asked.

She hesitated, then handed it to me.

"Can I look at some of the other pages?"

She nodded. Something told me to treat this folder with reverence, as if I was turning pages of the Bible.

During supper, if a family member wants to eat the last piece of any type of cheese or sausage, they have to ask the others first if they also want it. If yes, it will be discussed who will have it.

Everybody shall only take as much food out of a pot (or from other supplies on the table) as they can eat. The person who puts too much food on their plate and doesn't finish it will pay some money for it to Mum, who determines the value.

Every family member has to clean up their place at the table after eating. Dishes must be put on top of the dishwasher, and no remains of food should be left on any place mat. The place mat also needs to be wiped with a wet cloth if necessary. Consequence in case of failure: another family member can put crumbs and food remains into the bed of the person who didn't clean up properly after themselves.

I read about running around the house without shoes and socks (also, in winter, even in snow) as a possible punishment for failing at something.

Another rule said:

Nobody is allowed to go for a poo in the toilet in the bathroom. Anybody who needs to do a poo has to do it in the guest toilet and open the window wide after finishing. Consequence in case of failure: the next time the family member needs a poo, they will have to do it on the kitchen floor and then clean it up after themselves.

I had to stop reading. Sonja had been quiet all the time I turned the folder's pages. But she seemed to have followed what I read.

"Have you ever done this? I mean, a poo in your kitchen?" I said.

"No, I make sure it doesn't happen to me."

I was still holding the folder on my lap. It was hard to believe what was written there. Many of the things seemed bizarre, and not nice. But the last thing was just crazy. Were they serious? Well, they all had signed to agree to it.

Some pages were from a long time ago, like over five years. Dates were noted at the top of each of them. Sonja's parents had launched that family meeting when she was very young. On really old pages, her signatures were drawn rather than written. And she must have been very little on the day she drew her name like this:

What a weird family they were. Now I wasn't only okay with her father being in the garden; I was glad!

Admittedly, I also had to help at home. Like setting the table for supper, clearing it up again, or emptying the dishwasher. But Dad putting glass bottles in my bedroom as a punishment? Threatening to poo on the kitchen floor? I'd have hated him for that!

I closed the brown folder and gave it back to Sonja.

"Are you okay with everything in there?" I asked.

"Not really. But my parents like it. My father really does. He wants it to be done."

She left the room again and returned the folder to the living room. Then we played Ludo, sitting on her bed.

* * *

AT FIVE TO six, I had to leave. Mum had said I had to be home by six. Sonja took me downstairs to the door and held it open for me to slip through. But suddenly, her father came out from the kitchen, holding a rubbish bag in his hand. He stared at me, and I stared at him, like a who-blinks-first challenge. He was tall. His back straight; so was his head, as he looked down on me. I couldn't make out the colour of his eyes – they were narrowed. I'd never seen a face as serious as his. My heart beat so fast that I lost the challenge, my eyes drawn to that rubbish bag. Was it for Sonja's bedroom? Or was it maybe… oh my God! The brown family meeting folder popped up in my mind. I stared back into Sonja's father's face, imagining him squatting on a tiled floor, wiping his bum. Had he really?

"Hello," he said to me.

I don't know why, but I wondered if he wanted me to

be formal with him. A curtsy, maybe?

"Err… err…" I stuttered. "I've got to go."

"See you tomorrow?" Sonja said.

"Err, um, yes… sure."

I went through the door and got the hell out of there. I ran home, and couldn't wait to see Mum.

A MIND GAME

THE NEXT MORNING, at seven thirty, Sonja was standing on the pavement when I came out of my house.

"Oh, what are you doing here?" I asked.

"I thought we should walk together." She'd waited for me.

I left my bike at home, because hers was still broken. She took my hand, and didn't let it go until we reached our school. This made me almost dizzy – I hadn't had a friend, or playmate, who would hold my hand for so long. I didn't mind the dizziness; actually it felt nice.

All day, Sonja tried to make sure she didn't touch any of the other girls in our class, as The Rule said. Not easy – kids are lively! Remarkably, she never avoided any of the boys. The Rule wasn't for them.

After school, she and I walked home together. Holding hands. Before we parted, she asked me if I'd come over again in the afternoon. I thought of that folder and its rules.

"Will your father be there?"

"Not sure. In the garden, probably."

"Hmm." I was undecided.

"Oh, *please*," she said, her eyes big and round.

I hesitated, but then said, "All right."

She slung her arms around me, and pressed a cheek against mine. It was strange: I hadn't even known her a full week, but she'd given me so much affection already – more than Susanne had in all those months; more than Dad in all those years.

When I had done my homework and was free to play, I briefly wished it was Monday. I thought putting up with Mr Fink would be easier than being faced with rubbish bags or Sonja's father, but then still walked alongside the railway on the grassy path and arrived at Sonja's.

Strangely, the door was ajar. I wasn't sure what to do. Go inside, or ring the bell and wait? Before I had made a decision, I heard some noise from inside the house, as if somebody was crying. Huh – was Sonja upset in her bedroom? Had there been a lot of rubbish in the middle of it when she got home today? Maybe she was crying, because she didn't know how to solve the problem.

Without ringing the bell, I went into the house. I followed the sound upstairs, leaving the door open behind me. I didn't see either of her parents, and guessed her father was in the garden, her mum shopping again.

I had reached the top of the stairs when the noise made me stop. Was that really Sonja? I hadn't seen her crying, but I could actually hear her when she spoke. *She* wasn't crying.

I slowly approached the door of her bedroom which was also ajar. The corridor was dark, whereas daylight made it very bright in the bedroom. I could easily see inside. I saw Sonja and a woman, both sitting on the carpet facing each other. No bottles. No rubbish. The woman rested her face in her hands and was sobbing terribly. Sonja had her hands on the woman's lower arms, close to the elbows, stroking them.

"Mum, please. Please, tell me. What's up? Mum!" Sonja shook her mother slightly. "Mum, please don't cry. Please talk to me. What's wrong? Mum?"

Sonja's mum wiped her face and looked up. She didn't

seem able to speak; took several deep breaths. My heart was beating so fast — I had intruded in their house and was now watching Sonja and her devastated mum! What if they saw me?

"He doesn't talk to me," Sonja's mum said. "Dad treats me as if I was made of air."

"Again?" Sonja said.

She went on her knees, slightly taller than before, and wrapped her arms around her mum's neck. In response, her mum folded Sonja into her arms.

Suddenly, I twitched. A door had been closed and the whole corridor was flooded with light. Someone was coming into the house. I was stuck and I needed a place to hide. Desperately. It didn't feel like a good idea to be caught. I was lucky, spotting a vacuum cleaner and a cardboard box in a gap between a cupboard and the wall. There was just enough space for a small person. I squeezed in, squatted and used the box and vacuum cleaner as a cover. My heart bashed as loud as the steps I heard coming up the stairs. I peeked from behind the vacuum cleaner, holding its tube upright. It was Sonja's father.

"Shh, don't say anything to him," I heard Sonja's mum say in the bedroom.

"Okay. Don't worry, Mum," Sonja whispered.

But Sonja's father didn't go to the bedroom. Nor did he come any closer to me. He stayed at the top of the stairs and grabbed hold of the banister, not moving. It was as if he'd forgotten why he came up, and he turned around a moment later and walked back down. I could clearly see his face before it disappeared but he hadn't spotted me. My hands unclenched, nearly dropping the tube of the vacuum cleaner. Downstairs, he switched off the light again. I heard the same door opening and then closing. Seconds later, a car started and Sonja's father seemed to drive away.

Now I had to decide whether to show up in front of Sonja and her mum, or try to escape from the house without being seen. I felt it was wrong to appear à la jack-in-the-box from behind the vacuum cleaner.

The door to Sonja's bedroom was being closed from the inside. It was now pretty dark in the corridor. Only a little bit of light from downstairs made it grey rather than black. I waited until my eyes adjusted and then carefully freed myself from between the wall and the cupboard, putting the vacuum cleaner back in place as if nothing had been touched. I tiptoed down the stairs and slowly opened the front door. Sonja's father was nowhere to be seen. I closed the door with as little noise as possible. Then I wanted to go home – Sonja's place was scary! I walked down the grass path but couldn't forget about her big, round eyes. She'd *begged* me to come to hers. I stood still, carried on walking. Then I stopped again, turned, walked back to Sonja's and rang the bell.

It wasn't long before Sonja opened the door.

"Hi, Sonja!"

"Hi! Come in," she urged, and we walked upstairs. "Um, my mum is in my room."

"Ah, okay."

In the bedroom, Sonja's mum was now sitting on the sofa, a hanky in her hand. Her face was red, moist, and a little swollen.

"Hey," she said, and smiled at me.

I was glad she had at least stopped crying. I stayed quiet. She invited me to sit next to her on the sofa, seemingly making an effort to pull herself together. It was weird, because I had no clue how to cheer up an adult. I just stared at her eyes, hoping to see no more tears.

"It's okay, don't worry," she said, patting my shoulder. "I'll go downstairs so you can play. I've got things to do anyway."

She stood abruptly. Sonja rushed to give her a hug. She gave Sonja a kiss on her head and then left the room.

And then it was just the two of us on the sofa. She seemed to be searching for an explanation.

"My father doesn't talk to her. He ignores her. It's started today and my mum knows it's going to be like that for days. Maybe weeks. He'll treat her as if she was made of air."

"Why does he do that?"

"He's angry with her. And if it's really, really bad, he won't speak to her until she kneels before him, holding her hands like this." Sonja clasped her hands as if in prayer.

"Huh!" I felt my hand move up to my mouth, covering it.

"My mum was actually crying before you came."

I nodded.

"It's really bad when he's like that. I can't do anything about it. I hate it when my mum cries," Sonja said.

"And why is he so nasty to her?"

"Because she took down the empty glass bottles that were here."

"Really? That's why?"

"Yes. She did me the favour because there were too many. Now he's angry, because it was *my* job."

I wanted to know if Sonja's father was also angry with her and therefore didn't speak to her either. The answer was that he did speak to her, despite her not having done her job. Ignoring and not speaking was only meant to punish her mother.

"He's even very nice to me when he's angry with her," Sonja said.

I was confused.

"I kinda like it when he's like that. But it's too bad, really, because he's angry with my mum. And I'm nice to him, too. If not—I'd feel bad."

I knew that feeling. I also had bad feelings towards my father. "Oh, I know what you mean. It happens on my birthdays, and at Christmas, when I get presents. And when I go to my parents afterwards and say thank you for them."

"Really?" Sonja said.

"Yes. I open all my presents and my dad watches on with my mum, my grandma and my brother. He crosses his arms in front of him like this." I crossed my arms. "When I go to hug him and say thank you, he says, 'Thank your mother for it.' Maybe he's sulky. Or angry. I don't know. I just feel weird. He seems unhappy every time."

I believed Sonja knew exactly what I was talking about. We'd shared something I didn't share with anybody else. Not with my brother, although Dad behaved the same way on his birthdays. But I wasn't sure he even noticed. And Susanne had always been happy; totally free of worries. At her house, her and her family were all smiles. It was as if she didn't know what worries were. I'd only embarrass myself if I talked about mine. Sonja was different. She was sensitive. And she recognised things. Me.

PLUCKING A DAISY

SONJA WAS WAITING at our new meeting point – where the end of my road met the grassy path that meandered alongside the railway to her house. She turned up with her bike. It was proven: her father was nicer to her while giving her mother the silent treatment. I hurried back home to get mine as well, and we rode to school. I showed Sonja the bike shed and we locked ours up. There was still time before the first lesson, and so we went into the schoolyard, strolling around. For some reason, Mrs Motte came up in our conversation.

"Do you remember what Mrs Motte talked about yesterday? In religion class?" I said.

"No?"

"The ten things. The comments. Rules that came down to Moses."

"Ah. The *commandments*!"

"Yeah. There was one about parents. That you should honour them," I said.

"Hmm."

"I wonder what that means. I mean, how do you honour your parents?"

Sonja didn't answer.

"Is it like loving them?"

I saw Sonja from the corner of my eye. She shrugged her shoulders.

I turned to her. "Well, do you love your father?"

She didn't answer. She watched the ground as we were strolling, scratched her head in awkwardness. Had I made her nervous?

We were silent, but then she said, "No, I don't love my father."

"No?" I was shocked.

"No, not really." She blushed; ashamed of the truth.

"So, him fixing your bike still doesn't make you love him?"

"No, not really." She unzipped her jacket.

There was more silence. We kept strolling.

"And you? Do *you* love your father?" Sonja said.

I got hot all of a sudden. Lots of little stings on the skin of my arms and back. I hesitated, thinking.

Then I said, "Um, yes, I love my dad."

Silence again.

Did Dad actually love *me*? He'd never told me he did. Never. I spotted some daisies growing among the grass, and in my imagination, I picked one. *He loves me, he loves me not. Dad loves me, Dad loves me not.* I was plucking the petals. I couldn't work out if my daisy finished with 'loves me' or 'loves me not'.

At 7.55am, the school bell rang. I forgot about the daisy, and Sonja and I went inside the building.

Dirty Number Twenty-Four

July 2014

THE LITTLE CLOCK radio beside my bed shows 9.30. Time is going slowly. At least tonight. According to Sonja, 9.30pm is a good time. A clean one.

Six minutes ago, the time wasn't clean. Nine-twenty-four is a time I shouldn't speak out loud, because twenty-four is a bad number. A dirty one. If I mistakenly say it, Sonja tells me to say another number afterwards to 'clean' my mouth, her ears, and the atmosphere around us. She also cleans her mind of the number twenty-four. Even if she only thought of it without hearing, seeing or saying it, she still needs to think of a different number. The more she tries not to think of the number twenty-four, the more it will assert itself.

The reason why the number twenty-four is dirty is far-fetched. Sonja chose it during her stay at a clinic for therapy. There was a patient she felt needed to be regarded as dirty. I'm not really sure why. It didn't seem one hundred per cent logical. Some sort of randomness must have been involved. She argues that the patient's problems were very similar to hers, and so she feels she must avoid being linked with him.

His birthday is the 24th of April. Thinking of twenty-four therefore links her with him. Thinking of April does, too. The entire month of April is as dirty as twenty-four. Every other month's twenty-fourth day is dirty. We can't celebrate Christmas Eve. But then we don't celebrate any day of Christmas because the whole event is dirty, simply because it contains the number twenty-four. For us, Christmas does not exist. I must not mention any words related to Christmas, or definitely not when Sonja and I are together. When people decorate their houses with Christmas lights, I don't even put a candle up in my room. And I don't dare to eat a single chocolate Santa.

This arbitrarily made-up, life-restricting corset has existed ever since I've known Sonja, though it 'changes colour' depending on our circumstances. When we lived in England, the words 'German' and 'Germany' were forbidden. Dirty. If we needed to talk about Germany, we called it 'the Wrong Country'. I struggled whenever somebody asked me where I was from, at least when Sonja and I were together. If I accidentally said, "Germany," or had no other choice but to mention that country, she told me to clean my mouth, her ears and everything around us by saying out loud, "England," "France," or "Poland," for example. Switzerland couldn't be used as a clean-up country, because it had been contaminated by Germany.

When we watch football, no matter which teams are playing, I must pay attention to the players I talk about. Mentioning the name of a player who has the number four or twenty-four on their shirt is a problem. Four stands for April, the fourth month. Sonja wants me to say a different name as soon as possible. It can be tricky when we watch with Roger or other people. I certainly don't want to appear to be talking nonsense when I deflect from a 'wrong' player to a 'clean' one for no apparent reason. I try hiding Sonja's demands to spare myself from embarrassment.

These days, Sonja can use the word 'Germany' again. But she's introduced the forbidden numbers – a different colour for her corset.

Now that it's 9.30pm, a good, clean time, she won't stand still or stop whatever she's doing. But at 4.24, she would. It's the worst time possible, since it means the 24th April to her. At 4.24am, she's normally asleep. But at 4.24pm, she's not. I've told her 4.24 in the afternoon is actually 16.24, but she doesn't care. She still stops everything. If she didn't, those actions themselves would become dirty and she wouldn't be able to do them at any clean time any more. Shame, though, that she makes an exception for breathing at 4.24!

SEXY, AIDS AND GREEN

August 1987

IT WAS CLOSE to the end of the summer holidays. My family and I hadn't gone away. We stayed home and enjoyed the hot weather in the garden. Mum and Grandma made and bottled jam using our own cherries. I helped Grandma remove the stones. She used a manual machine fixed to an old table to punch out the stones one by one until there was a huge cherry-juice mess. That was why it had to happen outside in the garden.

I also played with Sonja during the holidays, since she didn't go away with her parents either. Sometimes we played at her home, sometimes at mine. The good thing about playing at mine was that we never needed to 'play around' any glass bottles or rubbish. Since the day I met Sonja, I hadn't played with Susanne any more; let alone gone to hers. Whenever I was at her house, there were also a couple of other girls from school. With Sonja, everything felt more intimate – just her and me. Maybe Susanne and I had never been real friends, given how easily we let go of each other. What actually makes a real friend? Mum and

Dad didn't have any; not that I knew. Mum had colleagues. Sometimes she chatted with a neighbour. And she had two brothers. Dad just had colleagues.

As it was only a few days before the first day of the new school term, I got excited. Really excited. I was going to go to high school, like my brother. In Germany, after four years of primary school, every child must choose one of three types of secondary school: *Hauptschule* (a basic kind of school that finishes at age fifteen), *Realschule* (an intermediate type of school that finishes at sixteen) or Gymnasium (high school that finishes at nineteen). I was supposed to go to high school for the next nine years and take the so-called Abitur in the final year – the exams that are the licence to enter university.

I looked forward to travelling on a school bus to Dabendorf every day. I couldn't wait to start using my shiny new schoolbooks, my new and bigger exercise books, and my new loose-leaf folders in A4 instead of A5. I also had a new, more mature-looking school bag. It wasn't so box-shaped and made of leather.

Mrs Motte had been great and I was going to miss her, but I was excited about getting new teachers. Also, I wondered about the subjects. My brother had said they did English, for example. And biology – including sex education.

I labelled all my new school supplies and went to Sonja's to see how she was getting on with her stuff. She was also going to go to high school, in the same class as me. I loved that.

A big pile of cardboard and papers 'greeted' me in her bedroom. Sonja hadn't done her current job, which was taking the waste paper to the recycling container at the end of Fessdorf. I was used to this kind of thing by now. I'd been at hers often.

"Oops, what's that?" I jumped up from Sonja's bed and checked the duvet.

"Oh sorry, I forgot to warn you," Sonja said. "I haven't removed them yet."

"What is it?"

"My breakfast crumbs. My father put them there."

We took the duvet, each of us holding one end, opened the window and shook the crumbs off outside.

Sonja was lucky that no other girl from our former class was going to be in our new one. They were all either going to a lower secondary school or to a high school in a different village. No need for The Rule any more. The problem had disappeared. But there was a new one; only I didn't know it straight away.

Her new school supplies were arranged on her desk. I saw the same books that I had, and exercise books of the same size, as well as loose-leaf A4 folders. I saw all the colours demanded on the high school's equipment list except for one.

"The green one is missing. For biology," I said.

"Err, yes. I'll take the brown one instead. It's the spare colour on the list."

I raised my eyebrows.

*   *   *

THE FIRST DAY started with an introduction and a ceremony with parents and teachers in the school hall. Then I had plenty of new faces and names to learn in my new class. I'd rather have learned everybody's birthday – I wasn't very good with names.

Sonja and I were pleased to have been seated next to each

66

other again. Nothing very much happened on that first day other than the students getting to know each other, and before afternoon came we were released from school to go home. However, we were warned that the next day would start as a normal, full day.

I didn't sleep very well during the night. Mum had assured me she would wake me in the morning in good time to make sure I caught the bus. She never wanted me to be stressed about anything.

I left the house at 7.15am to walk to the bus stop. On the way, I met Sonja. She was as happy as I was to go to school and start our first proper day there. She had one concern on her mind, though.

"I saw the news last night when my parents were watching. Have you heard about that new illness? It's been on for the second time. *At least.*"

"No. Which illness?"

"It's called AIDS."

"Ah, yes, I've seen that," I said.

I had heard about it – that recently discovered illness. I'd also heard it was deadly. Mum seemed to know about it as well. But given how worried my mother generally was about illnesses and her children, I found it comforting that she was rather unconcerned about this new one, despite it being deadly.

"It kills people!" Sonja said.

"Are you worried about it?"

"Yes. Very! Aren't you?"

"Hmm, a bit, maybe. But my mum says there's nothing to worry about, because there is no way *we* would get it." I said, soothingly.

"I know. But, somehow, I'm still afraid."

"Really, you don't need to be. Children don't get it. It's for adults who use the same syringe to take drugs, you know," I said.

"It's the blood," she said.

"Yes, but you'd need to hold your own blood right next to someone else's. That never happens to you."

"I know. It's a virus that only lives in blood and dies after some seconds when it's in the air."

"You see. You don't need to worry about it at all!"

* * *

MRS KRAUSEL WAS our new tutor and gave us our first proper lesson: German. Nothing too difficult, but also nothing too exciting. I tried to pay attention, however it proved difficult. I was constantly distracted by Mrs Krausel's nipples. She seemed to have two Smarties, sized XXL, inside her bra that were poking through her jumper. Mum didn't have breasts like that. I didn't have any myself yet, and certainly didn't want to get some that looked like Mrs Krausel's. I even hoped I wouldn't get any! I'd said to Susanne, one day, that I'd want to cut them off if it were actually possible. She had laughed. I didn't think boobs would suit me. I was too boyish. Not that I wanted to be a boy, no. I just believed I appeared and behaved like one. Dad had always told me to be brave and tough. He hadn't wanted me to cry in front of Mum during our last skiing holiday, when I'd hurt my arm after a little accident. He had pressured me to not even tell her, although I wanted to so badly. Dad said I was too big to cry.

My brother always encouraged me to play rough boys' games with him and his friends. He also taught me how to carry out pepper pranks to give people sneezing attacks. How to mix Mum's cleansing agents and shoe polish together in a big pot of water, tie a big cloth handkerchief against the stench around my nose and mouth, and then 'be' doctor and nurse of some kind. He was the doc, of course.

The only times I had been a girl were when I played with Sally. By myself.

After the German lesson, we had English. I was curious about it. My brother had said I would be given an English name by the teacher. Timothy was my brother's. I was keen on one without 'th'. My brother and his friends said it was sexy when girls stuck their tongues out through their teeth! I'd watched carefully when he showed me with his tongue and was unsure if I'd be able to manage that without spitting.

"You'd better get used to it quickly. Otherwise you'll start saying, 'ze'," he had warned me.

I didn't like that exercise. It was embarrassing. I thought adults used their tongues when they kissed on TV. "He's got his tongue wrapped around hers!" my brother always commented.

It was bad luck when Mrs Krausel read out the list of English names for everybody.

"Katherine," she told me. "That's your English name."

Damn it. There was no way I wanted that; no way I wanted to have anything to do with 'th' and 'sexy'.

"Mrs Krausel, can I please have a different name?"

"Don't you like Katherine?"

"No," I said, hoping she wouldn't keep repeating it and putting her tongue out right in front of me, while her Smarties were only an arm's length away from me. They were *frightening*.

"Well, do you have one in mind?"

"Anne. Can I have 'Anne', please?"

Anne, a name I had heard on a children's cassette, came to save me. I got her unsexy and spit-free name instead.

After the experience of that very first English lesson, we had a break of twenty minutes. Sonja and I went into the schoolyard. It was big. I saw my brother with some of his friends and smiled at him. He quickly turned away when he spotted me.

At primary school, in my first year, he had approached me in the schoolyard during my first break. He came to show me around. Or maybe to show off, but at least it did feel like he was my big brother when he was seven and I was six. Now, he was almost twelve. Was age the only difference? Or was it something to do with me in particular? He seemed embarrassed about me!

"Are you disappointed?" Sonja said.

"A little," I understated.

*   *   *

FOUR LESSONS LATER, school was out. We went home by bus: Sonja and I were at the front, and my brother stood at the back. He saw me and then faced the other way, not wanting me to approach him. He raced home a few metres ahead of Sonja and me when we got off the bus.

I told Mum about my first day at high school and that I was Anne in English. I also pointed out that she was much prettier than Mrs Krausel. She didn't know I was talking particularly about her breasts. I also liked that Mum wore no lipstick. Mrs Krausel's lips had been bright pink. Mum never wore lipstick. And the *one* time she had sat topless in a sun lounger on our terrace during the summer break, I freaked out.

After lunch, I went into my bedroom to do my first high-school homework. Then I practised 'th'. According to my brother, I would sound silly if I only used my teeth with no tongue, and would end up saying, "ze". I didn't want to sound silly. The problem was, I didn't want to sound sexy, either.

*　　*　　*

IT WAS ALMOST time for bed. Almost! The sun had set and clouds made it very dark outside. I needed to find out if it was only at school that my brother wanted to avoid me. I stood outside his bedroom, the door not fully shut. There was no light inside when I slowly pushed the door. He was sat on his little stool in the darkness, in front of the window. The shutter wasn't closed. He was staring outside, elbows on the windowsill, comfortably resting his face on his hands.

"What's out there?" I asked.

I stepped all the way into his room. His window faced the neighbouring house – Step-Grandmother's. He was staring straight into her dining room.

"There you go. Look, you can see it live now. Not just on TV. He's got his tongue wrapped around hers!" he said.

I stood next to him. "Huh!"

Bertha sat on the lap of a man who was in a chair at her dining table. His arms were tied around her back and sides; almost like an octopus. She had her arms around his neck and shoulders, their faces close together.

"They call this 'foreplay', I think. And then there should be some more stuff in a bit," my brother said.

"They're having sex?"

"Not yet, but let's wait and see. Just get your chair and sit down if you don't wanna miss out."

Yes! I'm allowed to join him! He's inviting me to stay! I hesitated for a moment, because I wasn't sure if I wanted this: watching the kissing next door. If people kissed in a film that my parents were watching, and it so happened that I had walked into the living room, I couldn't handle the silence between my parents during that hot moment. Mum and Dad would lounge close to each other on the sofa, seemingly finding the intimate scene normal – they never appeared to stiffen in their seats and that led to *me* doing it. I was even worried they might start kissing like that themselves.

Still, I just had to pounce on my brother's invitation; regardless. I nipped to my bedroom, got my chair, and came back to take a seat next to him. We leaned with our arms on the windowsill. With his bedroom still in darkness, we could easily see the show at the table in Bertha's dining room.

My brother picked binoculars up from the floor. He held them in front of his eyes, then handed them to me. "Here, you'll see even better."

"They're really kissing – and with tongues!"

"See. I told you." He sounded proud.

I gave him back the binoculars. "And is this randy, then?"

"Hmm, I don't know. But *I* wouldn't stick my tongue even a millimetre into the mouth of any girl in my class."

"Me neither. I mean, I wouldn't kiss a boy."

I had actually seen our parents kiss each other, but not with as much passion as what we were watching now.

Bertha had a boyfriend we knew quite well. Bernd came twice a week to stay at her house; every Friday night until early Monday morning, when he left for work. He was also allowed to come on Tuesday nights, and then had to leave again on Wednesday mornings. I say allowed, because he would have liked to live with her permanently, but once when they had planned to do so and moved all his furniture into her house, she spontaneously changed her mind and asked Bernd to keep his flat in Gadburg. He had to take all his stuff back with him and stick with the accustomed four nights per week at hers.

"And who's that man?" I asked.

"No idea, never seen him before," my brother said. "Maybe she fancies her old job back."

"What old job? She's always worked in some store!"

I'd only seen Bertha leaving or returning to her house wearing a short-sleeved, hip-long white overall. I knew she'd go to a supermarket, then use a handset to stick price labels onto products before putting them on the shelves.

"Don't you know? She's been a hooker!" my brother said.

"A hooker? What is that?"

"You can also say, 'prostitute' if you want."

"Prostitute?" I watched Bertha change her position. Now she didn't have her back towards us, but faced away from the man.

"Yes, prostitute. It's a bit more formal than 'hooker'. But it's the same thing."

"But I still don't know what her old job is."

"You really know nothing, Finja!" I almost thought I could hear my brother's eye-roll. "She had sex with men and they gave her money for it."

"Really?" Although surprised, I wasn't shocked. Bertha couldn't shock me. Not even with the things I was just seeing now with my childish eyes – I didn't love her; and she didn't love me. I knew she had fled the DDR (=GDR; German Democratic Republic; East Germany) many years before and left her then-toddler girl behind. I understood, as a ten-year-old, that the DDR and its regime was something the people who lived there didn't like, and that they were all forced to stay in their country. I knew people tried to flee, and some had lost their lives while attempting it. I had understanding for Bertha wanting to live in West Germany, but not really for her leaving her little child behind. She didn't know whether or not she would ever see her again.

"That's what she did before? She had sex with lots of men? Like those women Mum says they have in that road in the city where they stand around in short dresses and bras?" I asked.

"Yep. Bertha used to live in the red-light road," my brother said. "I thought you knew that. And it was Grandad Ernst, Dad's father, who got her out of there after Dad's mum died. But don't dare say anything about it to her. Mum says Bertha shouldn't know that we know!"

"How did Grandad Ernst get her out?"

"He was one of her clients. And then she lived with him."

I felt my blood surging through my veins. A myriad of questions rushed through my brain. It almost hurt.

I didn't know either of Dad's parents, since they'd died before I was born. But now I understood my grandfather had bought sex from women, I had a different image of him all of a sudden. I'd only known he'd married Step-Grandmother because Grandma Gerda, Dad's mum, had died, and that was why Bertha lived next door.

The new man behind Bertha's window became more and more engaged in the act. His octopus arms creeped all over her body. Just as he was attempting to get them underneath her top, she stood up from his lap and left the table. Maybe the man didn't know Bertha used to be a professional. He found himself dropped like a hot potato.

"Oh, she's gone," I said.

"No worries, she'll be back soon. She's probably going into the kitchen, getting him another course."

"You been watching this for long?"

"For a while." My brother grinned.

"Why did Mum tell you this? She didn't tell me!"

"Oh, I came into the kitchen when Mum and Dad were talking about Dad's parents. And Bertha. So I asked. A while ago." He shrugged.

I wanted the binoculars again to have another closer look at the new lover. He was having a drink. He sipped from a glass and then glanced into it, seemingly enjoying what he had in his mouth.

"I don't like him," I said. "He looks greasy."

"Yeah, but it doesn't matter. As long as his dick is big. That's the most important thing, they say." My brother took the binoculars out of my hands and looked through them himself.

"Dick? That's the penis, right?" I tried to make sure I got it right this time.

"Yep."

"And who are 'they' who say that's important?"

"At school. It's talked about." He shrugged again.

"Aha. And why has Bertha not put her shutters down?"

"She thinks her white curtains are fine. She doesn't get that we can still see them when it's dark outside but bright inside."

Bertha appeared again. She had a tray in her hands with some dishes on it.

"Looks like she's brought dessert," my brother said.

Bertha placed one of the desserts in front of the man. He smirked but didn't seem that interested. Instead, he reached out for her. She bent down, as he was still sitting in his chair. She kissed him on his mouth again.

"Come on, sit on his lap!" My brother sounded impatient.

"When did Grandad Ernst see her? Was Grandma Gerda still alive?" I asked.

"Yes, she was. He cheated on her."

I felt my blood starting to boil. I was in need of an Imaginary Comfort Bubble, but my brother was right next to me. I wasn't convinced he would understand the state I was in. *His* blood seemed cool and calm. "Come on now, Bertha. Sit on his lap!"

"I'm sad now," I said.

"Eh? What about?"

"Grandad Ernst. That he cheated on Grandma Gerda."

"But Mum said he wanted to divorce Bertha again. Only then he died and couldn't do it anymore."

My head was spinning – so much news. Also, even if Grandad Ernst had divorced Bertha again, he'd *still* cheated on my real Grandma! Had he at least regretted it? Badly? So was it okay to like the image of Grandad Ernst again?

At that moment, the door to the bedroom opened. Mum came in.

"What are you guys doing?" she asked.

"Mum, don't switch on the light. You're spoiling everything!" my brother said.

Mum came close. "Oh my God, what's going on over there? Have you been watching this for long?"

"Only for a little while," he said.

"Yeah, I can tell." Mum saw we both had something to sit on.

"Here, look through the binoculars," my brother said, holding them towards Mum.

"No, thanks, I can see enough without. So Bertha's got herself a new lover. Poor Bernd!"

Mum didn't tell us off for spying on Bertha – I knew she didn't like her either! But she still made us move from our seats at the windowsill, putting an end to the show. She switched on the light and closed the shutter. I returned my chair to my bedroom. Then I searched for Dad to say goodnight to him. Dad never came into my bedroom to say goodnight to *me*, except for once when he'd had a fight with Mum in the kitchen about something. I'd been so confused by his appearance on the edge of my bed that I froze in his hug like a girl in her kidnapper's arms. I mean, Dad hardly ever set foot in my room, let alone sit on my bed! The only real reason for him to be there had been when he changed my wallpaper from yellow to a white one with lots of tiny blue spots. He didn't know my schoolbooks; or the homework I had to do. He didn't know which of my toys I liked the most. Most likely not that Sally's name was Sally, even though she'd sat with us at the dining table hundreds of times.

Once I'd hugged Dad on the sofa and pressed a kiss on his face while he'd still looked at the TV, I went back to my room and slid into bed. Tucked up, I waited for Mum to come and sit with me. Saying goodnight would now feel mutual.

* * *

WITH THE LIGHTS off, I lay in the dark, my eyes wide open. I thought about Bertha and the new man. But I couldn't let go of the fact that Grandad Ernst had been her client, and that he had cheated on my Grandma Gerda. I didn't know her, but I still felt for her. Grandad had been bad to her. And suddenly, he appeared in my mind. He was walking down a road that was lined with lots of street lights. They were all red. Women in short dresses and with Smarties inside their bras came out from the houses, approaching him.

"What's your name?" Grandad Ernst asked each of them.

They all answered, "Katherine."

He smiled as they put their tongues between their teeth. I only observed the scene from a distance, but when all those Katherines formed a circle to enclose my grandfather, I went closer. I needed to rescue him from what he was doing. Only then, his face actually became clear to me, and I recognised the man the prostitutes had *really* ensnared: Dad.

I started to run. I wanted to get to him as quickly as possible. I needed to save him! But I didn't gain any ground. I kept moving in the same spot, as though I was on a conveyer belt that moved in the opposite direction. Even when I tried harder, I couldn't get close enough to Dad to save him from the danger.

"Take your green jacket off, throw it away, and rub your sleeve against the wall while you run. That creates safety. It'll rescue him!" Sonja shouted from somewhere.

"Using your techniques? Like at primary school? During choir class?" I asked.

There were a couple of nods, somewhere, and so I took off my jacket and threw it away. I rubbed my arm against a wall until the sleeve was ripped open. My entire jumper unravelled, exposing my torso. The bunch of Katherines threw their gazes at my immature nipples and then disappeared into the darkness just as the bricks of the wall had scraped my skin to bleeding point. Then I opened my eyes.

My God. What happened? I sat up in bed, breathing heavily, soaked in sweat. Did Dad go into that road as well? Did he see a woman for sex other than Mum? Did he take after his dad? Was he cheating?

I was desperate to talk to somebody. Mum wasn't the right person, because Dad might indeed have taken after his father. But Dad wasn't right either, and I never talked to him about my worries, anyway. Not even Sally was around. She had recently moved away from my bedroom and now lived up in the loft in a big cardboard box of old toys.

I blew up another Imaginary Comfort Bubble, slipped inside and stayed in there for the rest of the night. Only the next morning was I able to talk to somebody, when I met Sonja by the railway track on the way down to the bus stop. And she listened to me until I had nothing more to say.

No Green!

WE HAD OUR first biology lesson. I got my biology book and my green loose-leaf folder out, putting them onto my desk. Sonja also got her book out. And her *brown* folder. I checked – only green folders on the desks of everybody else in the class. Why had Sonja chosen brown?

My brother's warning about the upcoming sex education was in my head. The most embarrassing occasion about sex so far had been several years ago, when I was eating supper with my family and Grandma. I had asked out loud how Mum and Dad knew how to have sex, and my brother explained that, of course, Grandma would have demonstrated to them. I had never seen Grandma's face as red as on that evening. She'd have been glowing in the dark.

Biology on this day was not about sex, really. We only heard the first things about how a flower of a cherry tree was fertilised. Nothing too embarrassing. No dicks. No octopus arms.

* * *

IT WAS A school-free Saturday. I went to Grandma's place for a sleepover. It was such a great thing to do. I was allowed to do everything – play Rummy and Ludo as long as I wanted, eat whatever I fancied and watch television right until I fell asleep.

Grandma refused to heat her entire place, only turning the radiator on in her *Stube*, a word for the living room used by older generations who grew up in big families that gathered around the only oven in the house, which was inside the *Stube*, to keep warm in the cold season. The temperature in her kitchen fell so low in winter that she was able to switch off her fridge. She put the saved money into special ingredients for the cakes she baked for her children and grandchildren, as well as directly into their bank accounts.

My brother regularly went to Grandma's for business reasons. She gave him ten Deutschmarks each time he stayed over. I had been rather offended when she offered the same to me and told her I didn't come for money. Grandma must have been very lonely at times.

This weekend, I even brought another guest with me: Sonja. I was convinced that watching unlimited TV would be particularly fun for her, since the brown family meeting folder only allowed her to watch twice a week. She had to make crosses in the weekly TV magazine, next to the two things she wanted to watch.

Mum had taken us to Grandma's and was chatting with her in the kitchen, before leaving for home. Sonja and I were in the *Stube*.

"Well, sit down on a sofa, we're playing something with Grandma when my mum has left," I said.

"Hmm, I prefer sitting on a chair."

"What? Why? I mean, a chair isn't very comfortable. You know, we'll be playing cards and Ludo and then watching TV all afternoon."

"A chair is fine for me."

"But I'd like us to be comfy. Otherwise it's no fun!" I was disappointed.

"But I have a problem with the sofas."

"What problem?" I couldn't see any problems, just a blanket on one sofa and a few cushions on each of them.

"The cushions," Sonja said.

"The cushions? How can they be a problem?"

"They're green."

Huh? I didn't see why green cushions were a problem.

"Don't you like green?" I asked.

She shook her head.

"Why not?"

"It's complicated. I can't touch green things."

Complicated? Then I remembered her brown loose-leaf folder. She had used it to replace the green one for biology.

"Why not? Is it a new rule?" I said.

"No, not a new rule. But it could be dangerous."

Grandma came into the *Stube*. "Would you like some cake?" she asked.

"Yes, please, Grandma!" I was desperate for her to leave for the kitchen again. I wanted my friend to be comfortable but didn't know if I was allowed to talk about her problem with anyone else. Maybe she didn't want Grandma to know about it, because not wanting to sit down because of some cushions being green sounded weird. I didn't want Grandma to think I had a weird friend!

"I'll remove the cushions from the big sofa. Then you can sit on it, next to me," I said.

"No, please don't touch them. It's no good. They might give you AIDS! Let me do it."

"What? AIDS? What are you talking about?"

Without answering, Sonja took the tea towel she spotted

on one of the chairs around the dining table and used it to remove the green cushions from both sofas. She didn't touch any of them directly. I watched her frantic movement.

"Well, is everything fine? Can you sit down on the sofas?"

"Um, not yet. I need to wait two minutes," she said.

"Two minutes? Why? Come on now, Grandma will be back. Sit down!"

"I have to wait until the virus has died. Then it's safe. Don't you want to be safe?" she said.

Err. Well. Yes. Of course I did. Sonja sounded as if she knew that doing this routine meant being safe. Admittedly, I liked the idea very much. I wasn't sure about the techniques she used, though – *how* they created safety. But what did I know?! And who else made me feel safe? Mum? Yeah. Dad? No!

Sonja was counting to 120. That was two minutes. I wondered how serious that AIDS-phantom was. Sonja almost frightened me with it. But there was something there that fascinated me at the same time: her conviction. She appeared so confident about her beliefs. Even about herself, unlike me. I was rather doubtful of myself – whether I was able to impress Dad, or whether I was weird. Sonja had self-esteem, and I was definitely fascinated by that.

At 122, Grandma came in with a cake and hot chocolate. Sonja and I rushed to sit on the sofas. Grandma put the cake and the mugs on the tea table in front of us. She sat in the armchair and then cut the cake.

"You don't need any cushions?" She spotted the pile by the wall on the floor.

"No, there's more space for playing without them," I said.

Grandma bought it, and I really wanted to know why Sonja believed they could give us AIDS. But I had to wait until we could speak privately again, since all three of us played, ate and watched TV until Sonja and I fell asleep.

* * *

"Mum, should I be frightened of AIDS?" I strolled up and down in the kitchen. She was making lunch.

Mum once again explained there was no danger for me, and that I wouldn't belong to the groups of people at risk. Neither would my brother, nor my parents. She also explained where the virus originally came from.

"It's from Africa. Far away. It comes from monkeys that have bitten humans and transferred the virus to them," she said. "Scientists believe it's a certain kind of monkey. They're called vervets. Green vervets."

"*Green?*"

"Yes, small green monkeys. I guess they actually look cute," Mum said.

I didn't care whether or not the monkeys were cute. I cared only about their colour. Oh, Sonja! Did she really believe it was possible all green things could give her AIDS? Didn't that appear as nonsense to her? Unfortunately, it did not. Not at all.

* * *

After lunch, I went over to hers. Just when I'd rung the bell, I realised it was Sunday afternoon – family meeting time. The door opened and Sonja's mum appeared. Her face was wet. Bluish traces of tears were running down her cheeks, as they had smudged her eye shadow. She took a hanky out of her pocket and wiped her face.

"Sorry about this," she said. "Come in."

"Err, is it family meeting time?" I was suddenly grateful I had come at the wrong time and was supposed to go home again.

"No, no, don't worry, it's not. Come in!" She forced a smile onto her face and pulled me inside.

Sonja turned up in the corridor. "My father isn't speaking to her," she said.

It was the second time that I had seen Sonja's mum crying. Her father not speaking to her again was the reason why there was no family meeting.

We stood in the kitchen. Sonja's father wasn't around; not even in the garden. He had left something on the kitchen table, though: a newspaper opened at a page with adverts for apartments to rent. I looked a bit closer. Some of the studios and two-room apartments were highlighted in red.

"Are you moving?" I was surprised. They had only recently moved into this house.

"No. This is my father trying to get at my mum," Sonja explained.

"So *he's* moving out?" I asked, although I suddenly thought that this shouldn't be a reason to cry.

"No, he isn't either. He's *pretending* he is. He's left the paper here for my mum to see. He wants her to think he's leaving," Sonja said.

"It's just his mind games. He's not serious," Sonja's mum sobbed.

I didn't like her statement – it's *just* his mind games – as if it wasn't that bad. As if she could play a joker from her own cards and easily defeat him. She couldn't.

"But why are you so upset then, Mum?" Sonja asked.

"Because he's said to me I was the lie of his life."

I was struck. And I could tell Sonja was, too. I now wished her father *was* actually serious with those red circles around the adverts. I would even have helped to find him a place to move to on his own!

Sonja's mother got her hanky out again and blew her nose. She also wiped off some more bluish traces from her face.

"It's okay. I'm okay. Don't worry. I should be tough and stop crying. I'm too big to cry," she said, trying to brush things off.

Ha, what a coincidence – it hadn't been long ago that I had heard that very same sentence from Dad.

Sonja sighed. Then I sighed, too.

"Really, I'm okay now. Go upstairs and play a little," Sonja's mum said.

And so we did. But it was difficult to switch to playing.

* * *

IN SONJA'S BEDROOM, I spotted a pile of clothes on her sofa. Some were green; others only had green in them.

"Please don't move the clothes!" she said. "Don't even touch them!"

I knew why.

"It's the green monkeys, isn't it?" I asked.

"Yes, the vervets. How do you know?"

"My mum told me earlier when I asked her some more questions about AIDS."

I wondered what Sonja planned to do about the clothes. "So you won't wear them any more? How are you going to explain that to your mum?" I said.

"Um, maybe I'll blame fashion. They're not my style," she said.

"But you can't do it like that," I said. "I mean, you can't just leave them here and never wear them. There's nothing wrong with them. They won't make you ill. A colour can't give you AIDS, Sonja!"

"I know. But they still feel bad to me." She sounded as if she admitted the ridiculousness of her thinking. But the problem was her feelings. "I find them dirty. Infectious. Something like that."

"That's too strange, Sonja. Really. It makes more sense to worry about those groups of people who could give you AIDS. Not the colour green."

"But *still*," she said.

"Still what?"

"The clothes feel bad to me."

What else could I say now? Nothing.

* * *

SONJA PAID ATTENTION to all green things. At school, Mrs Krausel's pencil case was green, and Sonja stared at it as though it was actually a real monkey that would jump at her face. The blackboard was green – Sonja wouldn't go close to it. The more I watched out for green, the more I noticed it. It was everywhere. The grassy path to her house was bright green. Sonja must have hated it. However, whenever I walked down it with her, she seemed okay. Was she not consistent with her thinking? There was no way that she could avoid the path! Did she feel it was fine to walk down it *because* she had no other option? And this was the point: it was about feelings; not logic. It was completely arbitrary.

HE LOVES ME, HE LOVES ME

July 2014

IT's 22.52. OR 10.52pm. Both are good times for Sonja – no problem to speak them out loud. And no problem to do anything at this time, since no action can be spoiled.

I'm expecting her knock on my door. It should happen within the next few minutes. I admit to feeling nervous. It'll be the last time we speak with each other. Only she doesn't know. And she mustn't!

I'm bored here by my window. It's dark now, and the yard outside is totally quiet. WHWM-Dad is home, though nobody else has appeared. The chair I'm still sitting in isn't very comfortable. My back hurts, so I'm going to lie on my bed. Sitting worries me anyway, because most of the time I feel jumps in my chest. And pains. Dr Google says it could be heartburn. It may be trivial, but it could also be a more serious stomach problem. Dr Google might be right with his assessment, but of course he isn't one hundred per cent sure. He says the little jumps could also be extrasystole – some contraction of the heart that happens additionally to the normal rhythm. It can be harmless or actually increase the risk of mortality. I find that worrying. Very worrying.

I'd love to consult a real doctor but then I'd have to pay. I have no money for that. To be honest, Sonja is the one who should pay for it. I blame her for almost all my symptoms. But she's broke herself. I don't want money anyway. There's only one thing I really, really want: to get away from her. Please, Lord, that's what I need. You do know. I know.

Since I left Germany, I have no health insurance. I tried to get some but the French state would need to give me a so-called *Numéro Sécurité Sociale* – and I can't get one of those because I don't have a proper job; not one that I'm paid for. The advice bureau I went to told me that without that number I can't even get private health insurance. No matter how rich I am.

Roger helps me out financially. He is so kind. I know if I asked him, he'd give me money to see a doctor for my chest pains. But I have qualms. I don't want to take so much from him.

My mother should be glad. Glad that I have him, that he's there for me. That he's saved me. She should pray for him, light a candle when she goes to church as she does for other people sometimes. If she loves me, she should be thankful that he takes care of her daughter. And tell God about it. Maybe she even does, I can't say for sure. All I know is that she used to do such things when I was a kid. But she didn't practice her faith that much. Not visibly. My father was too anti-church; and he didn't like it when she'd put her ceramic angels up. When I was baptised, I was already ten; my mother had to wait until my brother and I were old enough to decide ourselves if we wanted to become Christians. Then I started talking to God under my duvet like my mother told me she did. Maybe she is grateful for Roger; maybe she does tell God. But I find it hard to imagine since she has criticised Roger for contacting her using a mobile phone that isn't his – he once texted my mother using my phone, asking how she could let me down the way she did.

Roger does love me, doesn't he? I suppose if I picked a daisy and plucked its petals, it would finish with *He loves me*. Only I haven't got a daisy!

Ten-fifty-five pm now. Come on, Sonja, knock on my door. Please. The sooner you bring me the key and ask me to lock you in, the better. And of course I will turn it twice.

LACK OF AFFECTION

1989

IT WAS SPRING. I was in Year Six at high school and twelve years old. My brother was thirteen and a half. Despite him distancing himself from me at school and in public, I was still emotionally attached to him. It was almost like with Dad – I loved and admired him. And I wanted him to like me back. Reciprocating *love* felt like asking way too much.

It had been like that from the day I was born. Mum had told me that when she brought me home, wrapped up in my carry-cot, my brother raced to slap me in the face. First things first: *he* was the boss. He also hurried not to miss the moments that I tried to make my first steps – each time he'd shove me over, resulting in me only being able to walk at the age of almost two. Whenever we played together in the small paddling pool my parents put up in summer, *he* sat in the water… and I fetched the toys he tossed around like a dog. I *was* like a dog – I loved my brother unconditionally… no matter how far away he threw the toys; no matter how commanding he sounded. I fetched, regardless.

We always played his games. Never mine. If we played inside, we played in his room. Never in mine. If we watched TV, the remote control was his. Never mine. This way, he liked me. And when, one time, he started a flea market in his room and succeeded in making me buy a bouncing ball for five Deutschmarks, he must have been the closest he came to ever loving me back. At night, under my duvet, I would pray for him to become the next Boris Becker – he also played tennis.

Now, playing together was very difficult. My brother's games had become too rough for me, the boyish girl. He loved to construct flour bombs, and go around with his friends putting firecrackers into dog poos before setting light to them. The boys regularly went out into the fields and the nearby forest to play 'North and South'. They crawled in mud with warpaint on their faces, as they tried to steal the opposite team's flag. I had practised throwing grenades (pushing the tips of long, bendy tree branches into apples, then swinging and hurling them over the fields), but I didn't want to smoke the cigars the troops had stolen from their dads and suffer that horrible diarrhoea my brother got one day after he came home.

My parents had never taught me the importance of a family. I guess they didn't teach my brother either. Was it their fault that he had started to look down on me now? Or was it simply a character thing?

He made comments about me that were far from complimentary. I wasn't needed as a playmate any more. Sometimes, when I asked to join him and received his answer, I could tell he was annoyed by me.

Dad was similar. "Daughter, you are *so* annoying," he would say when I talked at him. *At* him, because he wouldn't engage with me. When I tried to sit on his lap as he was at his desk, he moved me off. Dad didn't always accept me on his lap. Sometimes he did, sometimes he didn't. When he did, I was happy enough to be allowed there. He never cuddled or rocked me, though, so an Imaginary Comfort Bubble had to do. God, how I would have loved it had he helped me out of them.

I was desperate for attention. Affection! Particularly from Dad. My hunger for it forced me to search for a way to get some. A way that wouldn't only earn me his affection but also recognition: I had given up playing tennis almost a year before, since my leisure time had decreased now I was going to high school. I'd had to drop one of my hobbies – piano, ballet or tennis. I chose tennis, because I'd lost interest. The same was true for piano, but I'd always been unable to ditch it. Mum and Grandma really needed it every Monday afternoon. But now that I was searching for a solution to increase Dad's affection for and recognition of me, I had no choice but to sacrifice my piano lessons for a new tennis career. It was a real heartbreaker for Mum and Grandma, and frankly also for Mr Fink. He didn't get Mum's cakes and coffees any more. I hated hurting Mum and Grandma, but I so much needed to earn myself something more from Dad. I wanted him to be better than Sonja's father; not cold, not nasty. Dad also played tennis, and I pretended I liked it, too. He seemed pleased.

"Well, that's a good idea," he said.

See, he loved me. Didn't he?

January 1990

I WAS ABOUT to enter puberty. My body was changing a lot. I worried I was an unusually early developer, because I was the tallest girl in class at thirteen. I was prepared, as much as that was possible, and had paid attention in the sex education lessons. In reality it was more difficult, though. I just didn't feel comfortable growing breasts. Baggy T-shirts were my best attempt to cover them up, and I walked with a bent back whenever I was outside. No neighbour was supposed to see I was getting tits!

When Mum took me to the hairdresser, I ordered, "Short all over, please."

"Wow, that's a huge change. Are you sure?" The hairdresser raised her eyebrows.

"Yes, like a boy's cut."

"Are you really sure? Really, really?" The hairdresser almost seemed scared.

"Yes, I'm sure. Really!"

Throughout my life until then, I'd had typically girly long hair. It was the most, if not the only, girly thing about my appearance. It didn't take very long before my long blonde hair was on the floor.

"Not too bad!" A big smile suddenly stretched across the hairdresser's face. I could see it in the mirror as she took the bib off me.

I viewed myself in the mirror. "Yeah, not too bad."

I smiled, too. And avoided glancing at the floor.

* * *

AT HOME, I bumped into Dad.

"Oh, that haircut suits you, better than before," he said.

See, he loved me. Didn't he? And who would ever have imagined Dad would speak a whole sentence to pay me a compliment? It was music to my ears.

I wondered if Dad would have preferred me to be a boy?

DAD WAS RIGHT

As far back as I could remember, Dad was right. He was even right when he was actually wrong.

Dad was a teacher. At a high level: high school – every year he marked Abitur exams. That entitled him to be one hundred per cent right. Always! Nobody around him would have dared to doubt him. Not while he was there.

"The problem with your father is he's always right," an uncle once said to me.

Dad was right about politics, attitudes, German grammar, history, money, how to do things, and what he remembered as fact. He was also right about other people and their personal opinions. Sometimes, it felt as if two plus two wasn't four. But Dad always knew best.

When he redecorated my brother's bedroom, putting up new wallpaper, he mixed the remains of several old packets of paste together. Only a few hours after he and Mum had stuck the wallpaper to the walls, it came down again. Mum, who always helped with spreading the paste, had warned him about his odd mixture. He went to buy new paste, but while redoing the whole renovation, he insisted he would only need half of the powder indicated on the packet to mix with water. "They only want to make more money! You don't need such a high concentration!"

Dad wasn't just right, he was also *very tight*. One day

later, the wallpaper came down again.

On another occasion, during a skiing holiday in the French Alps, Mum hadn't managed to make pancakes in the flat we rented. She assumed the altitude made a difference, but Dad claimed she was incapable. Mum was a teacher at a lower level, and so Dad took over. To Mum's satisfaction, he ended up with the same gooey mess.

Dad had the need to tell people when they were wrong. He regularly wrote letters to the editor of the local newspaper, letting him know how incorrect and bad their German was, and how embarrassing he found that. Dad was a teacher of German. Unfortunately, he didn't realise he actually embarrassed me and Mum, and possibly my brother and Grandma, when neighbours commented over the fence, each time they had read his complaints printed in the paper, "He couldn't hold himself back again, could he?"

SONJA'S EXTREME BEHAVIOUR...

I HAD CALLED Sonja after breakfast one Sunday, asking if I could come over in the afternoon. I left my house for hers at 4pm. Her mum answered the door and told me Sonja was in the bathroom.

Before I reached the upper floor, I heard Sonja crying. *Screaming*. I pushed down the handle of the bathroom door and, since it wasn't locked, slipped inside. Sonja didn't hear me coming in. Her screaming was too loud. She was lying curled on the small piece of carpet in front of the shower, naked, half on her front, half on her side, holding the sides of her head with her hands. Her face against the carpet. Her skin and hair wet.

"No, no, no!" she screeched, hitting her hand on the carpet.

"Sonja," I said softly, not wanting to startle her too much.

I kneeled down on the floor. She didn't react to me, just cried.

"No, noooooo!"

"Sonja!" I repeated louder, and closer to her head.

She stopped and mumbled something into the carpet.

"What did you say?" I said.

"He's switched off the water. This time, he's switched it off completely!"

97

She resumed her screeching and rolled her head left and right over the bathroom carpet.

"Bloody hell, he's really done it?" I said.

I knew that Sonja, by then, was only allowed to shower twice a week. Her parents had noticed her strange habits, like cleaning herself and her belongings. She didn't succeed in keeping everything secret. She didn't care about green any more but, instead, her corset had changed colour and she worried about something new – a person. One particular boy in our class: Goran. She had picked him seemingly out of nowhere. He hadn't been a problem during all our previous years at high school, but since Year Eight he had. From one day to the next, she felt she needed to avoid any contact with him. We were now in Year Nine.

Goran had long, blond, greasy hair. He drank beer with older teenagers. Whenever he walked past me, he carried a cloud of smoke around himself. I hated that stench. For Sonja, Goran most likely had AIDS, because he fitted the image of a drug addict. At school, she made every effort to avoid him. She also tried not to touch anything he had. But Goran was a fidget! She and I sat towards the front of the class, not too far from the blackboard. Goran sometimes cleaned the board using a dry sponge. Sonja then felt contaminated by the chalk dust being dispersed in the air. Goran had infected the chalk through the sponge.

After school, Sonja washed herself and changed her clothes. She took fresh ones out of her wardrobe, and if she found a fair hair on them, she couldn't tell whether it was hers or Goran's. She then dumped the clothes straight into the dirty washing and took new ones out. One afternoon, her mum told her off after finding seven fresh T-shirts in the laundry.

KATJA SCHULZ

Sonja saw contamination from Goran everywhere in her home, although the boy had never been there. Sonja's father made the connection: he went, one evening per week, to a sports club in Dabendorf, not far from our school. Goran's father went to the same club. They knew each other. Sonja's father's sports bag, containing his kit and towel, was an object she despised. She couldn't stand it when it was moved away from its place in the cellar, next to the laundry room. Her father always put it down in the hallway before leaving for his sports club, and so she had to walk around that spot on the carpet when the bag was there and when it wasn't. He'd come home a gazillion times, still in his sports kit, and sat down on the sofa or in a chair in the living room. Sonja always ate at the desk in her bedroom, and stood if she watched TV. Goran was everywhere. Even on the light switches. Sonja reached up to them with her foot, keeping a shoe on. She pushed down door handles and turned on the taps in the bathroom in the same way.

And that wasn't all. Sonja's father regularly went into her bedroom, wearing his sports clothes. He did so for only one reason: to put down her window shutter at night. She always tried to be quicker than him, but sometimes she didn't manage. He contaminated her room by walking across it and closing the shutter. He spread bits, fluff, dust, hair, and whatever else that might have transferred from Goran via his father onto Sonja's at some point while they were at the sports club. She had asked her father not to come into her room dressed in his kit. She had also explained the problem with Goran to her parents. Her father had agreed not to step into her bedroom before he'd changed and taken his usual shower, and yet he didn't stick to it. It happened over and over again. Sonja was left furious and devastated, since she couldn't hold him to any punishments in a brown-family-meeting-folder way.

To be able to carry on living in her bedroom, she needed to decontaminate it. She cleaned it to an extraordinary degree, spending hours vacuuming. Everything her father had touched, and everywhere he had passed, had to be cleaned. She vacuumed her window, the window frame, its handle, the band of the shutter, and the box the band was rolled up in. She cleaned the carpet, the little glass table that stood by her sofa, her chair, her desk and everything on it: books, exercise books, folders, note-pads. Her hole punch, ruler, eraser, pencil sharpener, scissors, pens and pencils, as well as the in- and outside of their case. Then she decontaminated herself by changing her clothes and taking a shower. A nightmare.

* * *

I DIDN'T KNOW if Sonja had performed one of those big cleaning sessions in her bedroom on this Sunday afternoon. But whatever it was, it seemed very serious. She was desperate about the shower not working.

For a while, her father had allowed her to shower only twice a week. More recently, she was also restricted to twelve minutes' duration for each shower.

"And for the other five days of the week you will have to stand by the sink and use a fucking pile of facecloths!" I was there when he had shouted at her.

Her father never forgot that agreement of twelve minutes – that order. If she showered only one minute longer, he presented her with a bill afterwards. He calculated the water costs and she paid from minute thirteen onwards. She had been invoiced many times before this Sunday. Only when her father was not at home was her mum able to take the risk and allow her daughter an additional third shower without the twelve-minute time limit. Risk, because she would have been punished, had her husband caught her out. A good week of silent treatment.

But Sonja's father was still unhappy with his own regulations. Because Sonja paid and paid, not stopping her showers early. She didn't care where her pocket money went. So instead of financial punishment, he turned the hot water off after twelve minutes, flipping the main switch in the cellar. Each time, Sonja suffered a shock when the water became ice cold. Driven to continue until she was clean enough, the water tightened her skin so much, she said it felt as if it would burst.

Now, as Sonja was screaming on the bathroom carpet, I assumed a similar position to hers, lying next to her beside the shower. I reached out to put my arm around her back. But as soon as my hand touched her shoulder, I pulled it away. Her skin didn't feel human. Sonja was an ice block. She was so cold I thought her blood was frozen. I forced myself to place my hand on her.

"Sonja, calm down. Sit up if you can." I rocked her slightly.

She hesitated but then sat up, resting her face in her hands. Still crying and sobbing. "I want to die!" She cried for relief. She was helpless. I was helpless. Or was I?

We were completely used to each other. We'd been so close for five years. At times, we'd shared the same Imaginary Comfort Bubble. So was I lost with her?

"No, come on, please, don't say that. Don't even think that! Please!" I said. "You'll get through this. I'll help you."

She wiped the wet hair out of her face. We both stared at it in the mirror on a shelf. Her face was covered with tears, her nose was running. Her lips were a deep purply blue.

"He's turned the water off. Completely. Even the cold," she said. "I haven't finished rinsing myself!"

"You need to dry yourself and warm up, Sonja!"

"But I'm not finished. And now I'm mega dirty from the floor."

"Why did you lie on the floor, then?"

"I don't know. Just because it's all terrible. He's switched the water off." She burst into tears once again, throwing herself back down on her front, on the floor.

Someone scurried outside the bathroom. I hadn't locked the door, but nobody came in. I thought it was Sonja's mum, stopping right in front of the door and then moving away again. I wondered how she felt. I mean, she was her *mum*. It was clear her daughter had a problem, but nobody was able to identify it. Not even the youth psychologist Sonja saw regularly. She actually took sessions together with her parents, but her father wasn't really up for it. Sonja was convinced he attended reluctantly. Her mum was behind them and must somehow have persuaded her husband to go. *She* tried to get help for the problem their daughter suffered from. *Help* – switching off the water and leaving Sonja 'unfinished' on the floor outside the shower; was that perhaps her father's idea of help? Maybe. Maybe he seriously believed this cruel way was the only one to help his daughter. Did he simply want the best for her? Had he also wanted the best for her when he had shouted at her, "And for the other five days of the week, you will have to stand by the sink and use a fucking pile of facecloths!"? When he had *shouted* at her? I doubted it.

I wouldn't reproach Sonja's parents for not knowing what her problem was. It wasn't very well understood at the time. And if it was, it stayed undiscussed, hidden from society. Sonja's father was ignorant, which made him partly innocent. But not fully, because it was mean that he used a comment from the psychologist: that Sonja's problem would bring her a lot of – if not too much – attention from the family. Her father felt that this allowed him to point things out to her again and again. He said he would help by noting down his thoughts about her and the development of her psyche and being. He drew Sonja in the centre of a sheet of paper and named her 'Glow-Worm'. She was the glow-worm of the family who attracted, and enjoyed, most of the attention – too much, in particular from his wife.

He'd written the names of other family members on the same sheet of paper, such as Sonja's grandmother, who lived in a mountain range. All the people were connected with Sonja – arrows pointed from them towards her. Funnily enough, he left out one person from his presentation: himself. Wasn't it actually *him* who tried to attract all the attention of the family; of his wife? Wasn't it *him* who was sulky and angry, punishing her for those occasions when she didn't put him first? Wasn't it *him* who couldn't stand it when his wife didn't do what he wanted? It was *him* to whom the biggest arrow on the paper should have pointed! But Sonja believed what was drawn. And she wasn't proud at all of being the glow-worm of the family.

"Come on now, you really need to warm up," I said.

I took a towel from a nearby pile and put it over Sonja's back. She grabbed it and sat up again.

"What shall I do?" she asked.

"Can't you tell yourself you've simply tried hard and

done your best in the shower? And that trying and doing your best is good enough?" I suggested.

She seemed to think for a moment. I was pleased she didn't say no straight away. She probably knew that, unless she actually died at that moment, she had to move on and live with the situation. Somehow. No more water came out of the shower; the main switch for both hot and cold water had been flipped by her father.

"You have to carry on, Sonja. He won't switch it back on for a while. Try and tell yourself it's not your fault that you aren't one hundred per cent clean, if that's what you think. I think you're clean enough, anyway."

Wrapped in the towel I'd given her, she stood up and pulled a tissue from a box on one of the shelves. She blew her nose several times, took another tissue, and wiped her face. As she used another, smaller towel to wrap her wet hair, I heard more steps in the corridor. Once Sonja's mum seemed to have walked away from the bathroom door again, I heard her father in the distance.

"She *needs* pressure. It's good for her!" His voice was so calm and confident, it churned my stomach.

Again, he might have thought he was doing his daughter some good, but why did he always use the rough, cold and cruel way? Why only harshness? There was one thing he left out of all his 'help' and treatment: love.

No Self-
Confidence

AT FIFTEEN, I had already completed the first two courses at a dancing school in the city. I was able to dance nicely and pleased to have found a regular partner for my third course. It had been horrifying whenever it was the girls' turn to choose a partner for the next dance, instead of the usual boys'. There were slightly fewer boys in the class than girls. If it was the girls' turn, I was 99.9 per cent guaranteed to end up with no one to dance with. All the other girls threw themselves greedily at the boys, like a bunch of starved vultures hunting a fresh carcass. They couldn't wait to be tango-bent-down in their arms. The anticipation of sexily swinging their rumba-ing hips around the young, horny waists of the boys was exciting! Not for me. I was too scared of a 'no' to my question: "Shall we dance?"

With my regular dancing partner, that problem was removed. He was a good dancer. So was I. Together, we passed all the tests with full marks.

My hair had grown back since my short, boyish haircut. I looked more like a girl again with my ponytail, but I wasn't keen on the boy (or boys) I met at the dancing school. I just fancied the dancing.

My brother also went there. He had more influence on

me than he probably knew. At seventeen years of age, he'd lost all interest in me. Now he lived in a different world: he was attractive, and his brown eyes and thick dark hair had earned him a modelling job at a hairdresser's. At school, he did well and was rather popular; not an introvert like me. And, he was in love. Jennifer was his first girlfriend. She was nineteen and even had her own little car. My brother seemed proud and happy when he walked down the road with her, holding her hand and swinging his arm. He was connected with her, clear for everyone to see as a smile stretched across his face. I was convinced he enjoyed wrapping his tongue all around hers.

Jennifer had long brown hair. She was also good-looking and a very nice girl. I liked her. My parents did, too. She was welcome to stay over at our house at the weekends; otherwise, my brother went to hers. The two came across as a lovely couple. I liked to be around when Jennifer was in our house so I could talk to her.

My brother had a small TV of his own in his bedroom. Sometimes, I was allowed to watch with him and Jennifer. And one day, when I'd just come in, my eyes fell upon a soft toy that sat on top of the set.

"Where did you get that goat from?" I asked him.

"It's Jennifer's," he said. "I got it for her because she's a nanny goat."

Jennifer grinned and tweaked him playfully on his leg.

Wow! My brother had bought his girlfriend a nice, cute present with real thought behind it about how much it would suit her – the person he loved – even if it was meant playfully.

I had never got a present like that from him. Nothing which I felt he'd put real thought into, browsed for.

Whenever I got a little something from him for my birthdays, it was purchased by Mum. I'd like to allege he didn't give it proper thought. And it seemed clear, all of a sudden, that he didn't love me. Did he?

It hurt. Because I loved him! I definitely did, and remembered the cake I once baked for his birthday. It was in the shape of a train. The carriages were filled with gummy bears as passengers – I'd sat them in their seats with icing sugar. And then there had been those white shorts I tailored for him, using old linen. Okay, he never wore them, because I 'sewed' them with Dad's Pattex super-glue and mistakenly stuck the legs together… but I was only five!

"Oh, that's very nice. Really," I said, commenting on the goat for Jennifer.

Neither of the two responded. My feelings bubbled out as if something in my soul had burst, making a mess.

"I'd also love a goat like that," I said, meaning I wanted it from my *brother*. Not to buy it myself.

As soon as I'd said it, I didn't know why I had done so. Why I hadn't kept it to myself. I was wary but hopeful that my brother would say something nice, like he would be getting a similar present for my next birthday.

"*You?* But you're only a stupid cow," he said.

I took it as it was meant: I was downgraded. The category of soft-toy animals he had filed me under was second class, maximum. A lump in my throat grew big within milliseconds. I couldn't dismiss his words. I was unable to rise above them. How could I, when he was seventeen and no longer a little boy? I just had to take his comment seriously.

The tiny nobody-me immediately needed to blow up an Imaginary Comfort Bubble and slip inside. I left his room and went into my own. Tears ran down my cheeks as big as those of a crocodile, only mine were real.

*   *   *

A FEW DAYS later, I had to endure my brother's arrogance again. I now knew I was a stupid cow, but I had never heard his opinion of my looks. He was gazing at himself in the mirror on the wall in his bedroom. Jennifer was there again as I stood in the doorway, being nosy and wanting to chat with her.

"You look fantastic," my brother said into the mirror, a grin on his face.

I couldn't really disagree. I had always liked his full hair, which he had inherited from Mum. It was me who'd got Dad's – fine, blonde and boring.

My brother stepped away from the mirror, which was right next to the door. I bent to the side until I saw my own reflection.

"You too," I said about myself, attempting to be funny.

My brother coughed. I turned around and stared into his face. A comment was being formed rapidly behind his eyes, and then delivered hot and fresh from his brain to his mouth. "*You?* You only have an ordinary face!"

His words were as staggering as a conviction. A conviction for life. And, my God, *how* he had given it to me – callously!

Yep, there I was again, thank you very much: in my Imaginary Comfort Bubble. Shut and closed.

I let the door go and went into my bedroom. I fell onto my bed and watched the ceiling, while tears trickled from my eyes down the sides of my face, dropping onto the sheet next to my ears.

Fait Accompli

May 1993

It was towards the end of Year Ten. Almost six years at high school had gone by, as well as six years since I had met Sonja.

I was deeply involved in her problems. It had become impossible to put them to one side whenever we were together. In her bedroom, I followed her instructions about what I was allowed to touch and what was contaminated. It was all about AIDS and Goran. She'd abandoned her school bag and used a rucksack instead. Goran had somehow stepped over her original bag, and Sonja discovered a long blond hair on top of it. Now, she was on her third rucksack and running out of bags.

Doing homework was a problem. Sonja had become unable to complete any, since she needed to get rid of all traces of Goran as soon as she got home from school. She dumped her bag in a corner of her room and wouldn't touch it again until the next day. She changed her clothes and washed herself, if not by taking a shower, then by using a fucking pile of facecloths. Once she was clean, she couldn't touch anything to do with school any more. The world of school was separated from the one at home. She faced questions from our teachers about allegedly having forgotten to do the homework. Not only did she not do her homework, she also didn't prepare for any exams. She suffered a five in geography and just about managed fours in politics, biology and history – marks she could definitely have avoided by looking into her books at home.

Things became so difficult that her stress even washed over to me. Our close friendship – partnership – didn't let me stay away from her troubles. My class at the dancing school was the only time I could recover from all the fuss with Sonja. I loved going there.

One morning during that May, as Sonja and I walked to catch the school bus, she announced she had some news.

"I've decided to change schools," she said.

I was rattled. "What? You mean you're leaving high school?"

Sonja's recent exam results hadn't been very good, but I didn't think she should drop down to a lower school.

"Yes. *This* high school. I'm not going to a lower school, though."

"Where, then?"

"A school in Gadburg. Away from the villages around here," she said. "Are you coming with me?"

I felt odd. Almost empty. Something was aching around my heart. I had just been presented with Sonja's decision without being asked for my advice or opinion. How could she come up with such a change and not mention it to me earlier, when she had first thought of it? I was her best friend, for God's sake! I was offended.

"Is it because of Goran?" I asked.

"Yes," she said, making no bones about it. "So, you coming with me, then? Sure you are."

She had made a real decision, a proper plan. By herself.

And after having presented me with it, she expected I'd say nothing other than yes and follow her. Now I was outraged. Did she think I had nothing else in my head than her interests, her needs?

The bus arrived, and we went to school. We entered our classroom and sat down. Goran buzzed past. I pictured Sonja's heart pumping at full speed. I didn't want her nervousness to influence my own feelings, and opened my school bag, putting book after book on my desk. Even those I didn't need for the first lesson.

I felt an elbow nudging my side. "Finja, are you coming with me?"

The urge to leave overwhelmed me. I stood and pushed my chair back with my calves, making it screech over the floor. Outside the classroom, I paced down the corridor. Only a few metres further on, Sonja grabbed me by the shoulder. "Hey, don't let me down. I'm your friend! Your—"

I turned abruptly, and felt how my arm wanted to swing; how my hand wanted to slap her. But I restrained myself, and saw our teacher appear in the corridor.

I sat back in my seat inside the classroom. During the entire lesson, I struggled to pay attention. All I did was glance around class; at my classmates. And then I knew what Sonja had wanted to add: *only* friend. And she was right – I had not made friends with any of the others within *six years*.

I did not want to lose Sonja. I was suddenly worried I would. My anger softened. Vanished completely.

The bell rang for the end of the lesson and Sonja turned to me.

"Please," she said.

I took a deep breath.

"All right then," I said, and within an instant I had her

arms wrapped around me; her head rested against mine.

*   *   *

I HAD TO get my parents' green light first, though. I was sure they would be as surprised as I'd been. But I already had an excuse: pretending I wanted to join some others from the dancing school, and convincing them that the other school would offer more options for my Abitur subjects.

Two days later, I could tell Sonja I had my parents' permission. It hadn't been difficult – Dad didn't really care, and Mum found my reasoning plausible. Done.

From then onwards, Sonja and I prepared our project. We visited the new high school, made an application by handing in our former school reports. We figured out how to get there every morning for eight o'clock. Time was the only struggle with it: getting daily from sleepy, secluded Fessdorf into town. Bus and further tram connections were complicated. The most straightforward and fastest way was going by bike – over six kilometres every morning starting at 7.15am, and then back again.

From late August 1993, after the big school holidays, we made that long return journey to our new school – twelve seemingly never-ending kilometres. Even though my frequent dancing had kept me fit, I found the daily ride to be a real struggle. In winter, the trip was particularly hard as we cycled through snow and frost.

In Control

July 2014

It's 11.04pm.

I have the key. Sonja's key. And I have turned it twice!

It went okay. The locking in, I mean. She didn't suspect anything. We didn't really talk; no asking of questions. No nothing. I kept my thoughts to myself. All is fine now. I'm in control.

I saw Mr Stumble-Late, my neighbour, on my way back to my room. He came out of his door, not stumbling. We traded the usual nods before he went down the corridor and stairs – going out, I suppose. To drink.

Bzzz, bzzz. My mobile phone vibrates. Another text message?

Will you call your father tonight? Roger asks.

I turn the phone a few times in my hands, press it against my chin, turn it again.

I'm not sure, I text back.

A few seconds later, Roger replies: *I'm proud of you!*

Proud of me? What for? For not being sure? Or because I've turned the key twice and locked Sonja in? Because I'm in control of her now? No, that can't be what he means. He doesn't know.

My father has never said he's proud of me. Never, ever. And he probably isn't. There's no reason for him to be. Not in his view. But he'll be rather proud of my brother – the better child; the successful one.

When my father last made contact with me, some years ago, it was via text message: *Happy birthday and all the best.* A standard message. Nice, but unemotional in my opinion. He cannot have been truthful with his words, because if he wished me all the best, why would he not change his behaviour towards me? He still hasn't spent a cent on calling me. Not even once.

When he was in his late fifties, he told me he wanted to enjoy the evening of his life, but I was in the way. I expressed my pain at this to my mother, and the only comfort she had for me was "He's said that about me once, too."

That 'happy birthday' message didn't make sense; responding and thanking him didn't either.

If he's proud of anybody, it will be himself. He'll also be proud of how he's always treated me – the non-princess way. He won't regret a thing he did to me, or others. Or that he was wrong at times when he insisted he was right. I guess he hasn't the slightest problem with me being afraid of him. Am I? Still? Roger thinks so. Despite me having nothing to do with my father any more.

What's left inside my head? Is my father mentally in control of me? Is that why I hesitate to call him, to tell him the truth? If he was asked, he'd maybe say he didn't know I was afraid of him. But I wouldn't believe that at all. Surely he does know. He'll even know that his wife is, too. And he might be proud of that!

Sometimes Roger compliments me. Then I struggle to respond, because I'm both flattered and ashamed at the same time. I'd definitely diagnose myself with an inferiority complex. Whenever I've done something and somebody tells me I should be proud of myself, I'm unable. I don't want to be wrong or too much in love with myself. I certainly don't deserve pride; I belong somewhere lower than that.

If I had something to celebrate – my birthday, my wedding, an achievement – I'd hesitate to invite people like the occasion of my confirmation. My father once said I had too much liking for putting myself up 'on stage'. He knew I loved going to pubs and meeting people – possibly men. He told me that was my stage, how I tried to get attention. I was bad, going to pubs, wasn't I? I still am. My father doesn't go to pubs himself; neither does my mother. Pubs are for working-class people, lower ones. My mother said I wouldn't find a decent man in a pub. I met Roger in one...

Once, I managed to lure my father into a pub. I told him how nice it was to watch football in a group, for atmosphere. I soon regretted inviting him – he behaved as if he felt contaminated by where he was; the people around him.

These days, if I celebrated something about myself, whether in a pub or elsewhere, wouldn't that still be me on a stage? Glow-worm-like? I'm fed up of doing the wrong things, so I'd rather not dare.

Is my father mentally in control of me?

I press the reply button to answer Roger's text: *I'm proud of you*. Again, I only put a smiley face. Send.

Goodnight, and don't forget that I'm thinking of you, he texts back.

Goodnight, sleep well, I reply, adding another smiley, and my eyes glisten.

Roger is such a good guy. Sonja must not be allowed to send that damn photo of the embrace and take him away from me. She just *mustn't*!

I put my mobile away and lie down on my bed. Now I'm really on my own. WHWM-Dad went home a long time ago. Roger will be asleep in a minute, if not already. He always sends his last text from under the duvet. Mr Stumble-Late is out. Sonja is locked away – my *former* best friend. Listening to music on my little radio will help the next four hours to go by quicker, until she's in bed. Peculiarly, she actually did *not* ask me tonight to turn the key twice. How strange… she's only forgotten to say it once before. But I've turned it twice, anyway.

When Sonja's World was Rocked

1995

Sonja and I were in Year Thirteen – the last one. At our new high school, there was no Goran. Her mother had urged her to watch out and not go and find a new one. Sonja didn't. However, instead of forgetting about him, she exacerbated the whole effect he had on her: she stopped eating the food her mum bought in Dabendorf; the village where our former high school was, which Goran went to. The village he also lived in. Its supermarkets were far too contaminated. *His* mum went to buy food there, too!

Sonja's corset had become crushingly tight, preoccupying her so much, I now doubted she was going to manage the final big exams. I was actually worried for her.

In late September, Sonja's parents went away alone during a short school holiday. She preferred to stay at home. On their return, they dropped a bomb: they told Sonja it was best if she moved out into a place of her own. Anywhere. *Boom!*

It splintered far and wide. It took me days, if not weeks, to come to terms with that explosion. The shock was so huge that not only Sonja, but also I, had to cry over it. I didn't understand her parents. I particularly struggled to understand her mum. Mums didn't suggest to their children that they should move out, for crying out loud! But indeed that was what had happened, and I wanted to scream about it. I wanted to run around Fessdorf and scream long and loud until every single inhabitant came out onto the streets and realised that something was wrong. I wanted to scream in protest, in defence of my best friend. Like a rioter that the police would take into custody. I wanted to scream until I lost my voice.

"Dad and I didn't like coming home from our trip. Because of you!" Sonja's mum had told her, reasoning that it was down to her fuss about Goran.

It felt like injustice, or as if a judge had mixed up some files and been mistaken in their ruling. I couldn't believe this was supposed to be true. Was Sonja really such a hassle for her mum? Did this mean she didn't love her daughter any more, or not strongly enough? It was logical, wasn't it?

To me, there was no excuse – like Sonja standing a lot in the house instead of sitting down – for a mother to want her child to leave the nest at the very young age of eighteen. And while she was still at school! Or had her parents seriously tired of Sonja? I mean, *I* was the one dealing with and supporting her, really.

I wasn't shocked by her father though, although he was as involved in this decision as much as her mother. It didn't feel like he had been dozy and made a mistake in his ruling. Not at all. The whole thing fitted him perfectly. He had given little to no love to his daughter, whose soul was surely now scarred. He was able to be cruel.

Questions were penetrating my mind and wouldn't go away. It was unbearable, because I knew that whatever the answers were, they would carve the scars even deeper. Who of Sonja's parents had first had the idea of her leaving? Was it really only down to her difficulties in the house? Or had it been manipulated, somehow?

"Well, maybe there is at least one good thing in all this," I said to Sonja.

I was almost expecting a slap in the face.

"*Good?* How can it be good?"

"Perhaps we should try and make the best of this situation. Find the positives," I said. "If you don't live with your parents any more, you'll be able to shower whenever you like. More than twice a week. No more ice-cold water, and nobody to switch it off."

I saw a change in Sonja's eyes. Suddenly she understood – no more glass bottles, rubbish, or crumbs in her bed. "True. And my father won't come in and contaminate everything with his sports kit," she said. "I won't need to vacuum everything in my room."

But despite recognising that she could get some relief by moving out, she didn't really appear happy. And why should she? The fact that her mother had asked her, in the name of both her parents, to leave home was not something that could be forgotten. It was hurtful, regardless.

"Maybe your mum actually wanted to relieve you of your struggles. I don't know, but could it be like that?"

Sonja hesitated. She seemed not to want to admit much that was positive about her parents' decision.

"Maybe. Maybe, yes. My mother said it would be best for all of us, including me and my problems."

Still, her mother's raw words – *We didn't like coming home from our trip. Because of you!* – kept floating in my mind. She hadn't even tried to phrase them less cuttingly. I don't know when I actually lost sight of them. *If* I did.

RELATED?

THE PARENTAL BOMBSHELL brought some risk: Sonja had to live by herself while still at school. In just over three months' time, the final Abitur exams were due. The mess she was in could affect her marks.

Sonja's parents were going to give her a fixed amount of money per month. Her mother explained she had to use it for her rent, food and everything else she needed or wanted. Her father would calculate how much she had to have to live. I trusted he was able to do so accurately; I knew him well enough to know that. God, I'd seen it. He had done it when Sonja had taken her showers twice a week. He had known exactly how much it cost per minute to let water run. And, when Sonja was even younger, there had been a price to pay to her mother for any leftover food – that rule from the brown family meeting folder. And suddenly I realised, oh my God: he wasn't so different from my own dad! Dad was also very precise when calculating money. Whenever I made a call from my parents' phone, I had to place twenty pfennig next to it afterwards. If I hadn't just made a local call but one to relatives in the country, I had to note the time for which I talked. Dad then presented me with the costs, according to the relevant tariff. At eighteen, I got one hundred Deutschmarks in pocket money per month. He handed ninety to me in notes, and the remaining ten in the form of a hundred-coin roll. I never used up that heavy and bulky thing, because I had no friends to call. Sonja was living nearby! Grandma was the only one I phoned regularly. She lived in the city centre of Gadburg. If Mum called her first and then handed me the phone for some minutes, I got away without any payment. Dad couldn't charge me for that. But nothing appeared too trivial or ridiculous to him, as he once even wrote me a bill for DM 1.20 at the end of a month.

Now it occurred to me: Sonja's father and mine were more similar than I had realised. How could that be? I hadn't heard of any other father who was so keen on calculating costs for his children. There were at least two girls and one boy in Year Thirteen that I knew had been given cars for their eighteenth birthdays; one was a brand new BMW! I had heard a girl telling another how her dad had installed her own phone line into her bedroom so she could chat privately with her boyfriend. I wouldn't have dared ask my classmates whether their fathers did any silly calculating of costs. Too embarrassing! Wasn't it odd that Sonja's father and my own dad both had such a strange and rare habit? Were they related somehow?

I had never met a relative of Dad's; not a close one at least. He had no family really. Nobody. Honestly, that was pretty sad. His parents had died young, and he was an only child. But was he? Really?

LEAVING THE NEST

FOR ABOUT A month, Sonja looked for somewhere to live. I was the only one who helped. She didn't want her parents to. She now wanted to take advantage of what I'd pointed out: showering whenever she wanted; warm water; less time pressure. Besides, she had to leave all the Goran contamination behind her, in her parents' house, otherwise the advantages would have been too small. Her parents would contaminate her new place, had they interfered in her move – her father was still in the same sports club as Goran's father, and her mother still went shopping in Dabendorf where Goran's family lived. The chance that her mother used a trolley Goran's had touched before was real!

Sonja's parents agreed when she asked to get new furniture to replace her old and contaminated stuff. All that time that we searched and viewed places in the afternoons, she appeared distracted at school. She didn't listen to our teachers any more. She just stared through the window, her mind gone. Sometimes I nudged her with my elbow to try and bring her back into the real world. Biology, geography and maths were our main subjects for the Abitur. Our teachers asked Sonja simple questions that she had no answers to. Her lack of participation in biology became that grave, our tutor needed to be involved. Sonja's problems at school were really serious now.

I, too, had to pull myself together and not get distracted by Sonja's struggles. I even had to give up my dancing to focus a hundred per cent on school.

One grey morning in November 1995, Sonja didn't meet me outside my house to cycle to school together. We had found a room for her, and she moved into it on that day. Her new place was halfway between Fessdorf and school. It was handy – I only needed to cycle the first three kilometres by myself.

The room was small and within a flat shared by three other young people who studied at university. The dilapidated house was the last of six on a dead-end path leading into a wood at the edge of Gadburg. Sonja's two little windows faced trees to the north. I worried it could get depressing. At eighteen, Sonja was the youngest in that flat.

While I was at school, I hoped all day she would do okay. She wouldn't let me help her move out from her parents'. She wanted to be in full control of everything. Her new furniture was going to be delivered in the afternoon. She hardly took anything from her former bedroom; only a few clothes, her school bag and books. She also took her bike, but that was all. Her music system was too dirty, too contaminated; she had to leave it behind. God, it *was* actually depressing in her new room!

Sonja now had to handle everything – be independent and self-sufficient – while focusing on the big exams. I didn't want to be in her shoes. But maybe she wouldn't have been able to do any better had she not moved out from her parents'.

SERIOUSLY

December 1995

SONJA AND I arrived at her new place. I'd been there often by then and now it was December with its dark days that didn't let much sunlight through. We locked our bikes by the side of the house and went inside. It was a foggy day and my jacket was slightly damp. Dark December, and the trees didn't let much sunlight through.

I was heaving my bike basket with the food we'd just bought on our way home from school, wrapped in my arms, school bag on my back. She was hauling two bags up the stairs in front of me when I spoke. I dumped my load onto the kitchen table.

"Do you miss your parents?" I blurted out.

I knew it was a sensitive subject for her. I knew I could, maybe *should*, have avoided it. And still, I didn't hold myself back.

Sonja shrugged.

"Your mum? You haven't seen her for three weeks!" I just couldn't keep my mouth shut.

She didn't answer but started to put food item after food item onto her shelf in the kitchen. Packets of spaghetti, jars of ready-to-eat tomato and cheese sauce, two bananas, an apple. A bar of Kinder chocolate, and a family packet of crisps.

Sonja's mum called every second evening on the flat's phone. At times, it was difficult to get hold of Sonja as the other tenants used the phone, too. She liked it very much whenever her mum called. Of course she missed her! Her father never phoned. And neither of her parents came around to the flat, although it was only three kilometres away.

"I'd be nervous if my mum came. Her clothes would contaminate everything," Sonja said.

I nodded knowingly – the Goran contamination stuck to everything. We fell into silence while I handed Sonja her shopping, and she put it onto the shelf.

I twitched. Sonja's body jerked too, and the milk carton I had passed her slipped through her hands and tumbled onto the shelf.

"Oh, who's that?" I asked, despite knowing Sonja couldn't tell.

The phone was ringing. I hadn't noticed before how shrill it sounded.

Sonja stared at me. "No idea. Nobody normally calls at this time. The others are still at uni."

"But don't you want to pick up?" I had the feeling she hesitated for a good reason, though the phone didn't give up.

"All right, I'll go."

Sonja went into the hall. I watched.

"Hello?" She spoke into the handset, looking towards me. My wide eyes stared back at her.

"Oh, hi!"

My eyebrows rose.

"*Now?*" Sonja said. Her brows shot up, too.

Then there was silence in the hall. Sonja listened, but I

126

was bursting to know what was going on. Who was Sonja talking to? I slowly approached her, and, as I came closer, I could hear the voice at the other end. Sonja looked anxious.

"Okay, if you really think so," she said, her tone matching the expression in her eyes.

She placed the phone on its cradle. Frozen.

"Was it your mum?" I couldn't wait.

"Yes."

"And?"

"She's coming. Right now!"

"But she'll contaminate everything?!"

"She said she knows how to handle it. That I shouldn't worry but trust her."

Something struck me. *Trust?* Trust her mum who had recently not behaved like a mother, saying, "We didn't like coming home from our trip. Because of you"? I was sceptical.

* * *

THREE KILOMETRES WAS so close, it wasn't long before the bell rang. Sonja rushed to press the buzzer to unlock the main door downstairs. I stood by her side, then peered closer at her. Her pulse beat hard in her neck. The back of her mum's head became visible as she walked up the spiralling stairs. Her shoulders, back, legs and feet followed. She turned around and halted as soon as she spotted Sonja and me. We were standing at the top like two soldiers, ready to fend her off – well, fend off the Goran contamination at least. But then, both Sonja and her mother smiled. Goosebumps crawled up my neck. It was clear: despite all the previous pain and upset, Sonja still loved her mum, and she still loved her daughter.

"Hey," Sonja's mum said, her smile even bigger.

"Hi, Mum," Sonja said.

I smiled, too. Sonja's mum still didn't move further up the stairs. She seemed to keep a safe distance from us. She knew she was too contaminated to come closer.

"I now know what you have."

Sonja looked puzzled. I didn't understand either.

"I mean I know what the problem is. What you suffer from."

'The problem' had always been the term used for Sonja's struggles. It made it sound like an alien thing.

Sonja had seen her first therapist as a girl of eleven. As a teenager, she and her parents regularly went to see the woman, who never recognised what 'the problem' really was. Another psychologist Sonja later consulted on her own also had no idea what was going on. Instead, it was her mother who had to 'do the job'. She had gone to different health services within Gadburg and gathered information about certain mental struggles, combined with odd behaviour.

"You have OCD. Obsessive-compulsive disorder," Sonja's mum said.

"Huh?"

"Yes, that's what you have. It's a real mental illness!"

"A real mental illness?"

"Seriously, your problem is an illness!"

The look on Sonja's face was reminiscent of a wall or a mountain.

It did make sense. Sonja's problem was so grave and affected her life that much, it was clearly more than just a problem. And so, finally, she found out. It had taken *nine years*.

However, knowing that Sonja suffered from a real illness

didn't mean she would now simply be able to go and see a doctor who'd prescribe a pill to solve everything. That was impossible. The good news was, though, that the new knowledge seemed to have changed things for her mum, who was still standing some steps down on the stairs.

"Look, I've bought a paper table cloth. It's clean, in this plastic." She pulled a wrap from her handbag that had a cloth sealed inside. "And I can open it and put it onto a chair in your room to sit on. So I don't make it dirty."

Another smile flashed up on Sonja's face. She nodded, and her mum climbed the rest of the stairs. She was aware Sonja's OCD didn't allow her any contact with her clothes. The material was too textured for OCD-imagined Goran hair and bits attached to it to slide off. She moved her sleeve up and stroked Sonja's face with her bare hand. It was heart breaking that they couldn't embrace each other. Painful. I still needed *my* mum's hugs, even as an adult!

MOODY CHRISTMAS

IT WAS CHRISTMAS Eve, and it was going to be a sad time. The very first sad Christmas – that was what I thought back then. But only because I had done well in pushing so many others to one side. They'd all been sad due to Dad. He never appreciated Christmas. He was a party pooper. Maybe, as a committed atheist, he wasn't emotionally touched by Christmas. Although nobody is obliged to believe in the religious part of the festival, he didn't bother about the pressie one either. But he could have done. He should have – for the sake of the family. Instead, he spoiled Christmas by being moody. Every. Single. Year.

Moody every single year. Moody just in time. Moody on purpose? Hang on – Sonja's father was also moody every year, just in time, on purpose. Sonja had warned me about it, when Mum and I had been invited for cake and coffee on Sonja's mother's birthday. Her father lounged in his seat, poking his piece of cake with a fork. When her mum asked him, "Would you like some more coffee?" he replied with a death stare. In front of everybody. *Humiliation!* There'd been no rule in the brown family meeting folder that would have forced him to shit on the kitchen floor for such disgraceful behaviour.

Now, again, I saw a resemblance between my dad and Sonja's father. I had to force myself to stop thinking about the possibility of a connection between the two, fighting off my fanciful ideas.

Dad didn't like Christmas. And that extended to spoiling it for me. He took it away from me; stole it by being moody. The only thing he participated in was putting the presents under the Christmas tree when Mum asked him to. Yes, he and Mum put them there. Santa had never existed in my world. Neither had the so-called *Christkind*, who is also an option for bringing gifts to children in Germany. I'd never believed in those guys, because I'd never been told either story. Well, I had been told *about* the stories – that they *were* stories – that they were believed by all the other children. When Santa brought small gifts and chocolates into our class at primary school, I had to swallow the truth in order to not destroy the fairy tales the other kids were living. And I could barely stop myself from bursting out laughing when Matthias – my classmate and Mum's colleague's son – came around to our house with his mother one afternoon. He was confused. "You're wearing the same jumper as Santa!" he said. I too had seen Mum's sleeves inside his heavy coat.

I had known, days before, that Mum had agreed to play him that year, as she practised speaking with a deep voice.

I'm sure I would also have loved to live the fairy tale. It would have made Christmas much bigger and better. What I would have given for Dad to take me to meet Santa, sit me on his lap, and explain that I must write to him and let him know what I wished for. For sure, I'd have written one of the most beautiful letters, and Dad could have enjoyed observing his little princess living the fairy tale.

But I wasn't his princess! And Dad never enjoyed things, it seemed. The only excitement I ever observed from him was when one of his favourite songs was played on the radio.

Then he'd wiggle his toes to it.

* * *

ON THE AFTERNOON of that Christmas Eve in 1995, shops had already closed and people were at home, preparing for the evening. But I just couldn't get excited about it. Not this year. I couldn't stop thinking about Sonja and her parents. She didn't want to go to them for Christmas, and went to visit other relatives instead, somewhere in a different city hundreds of kilometres away. Her parents were set to spend the festive season without their daughter. I was convinced it would be a sad Christmas for her mum, just as I was convinced it would be sad for Sonja herself.

TRAPPED

Spring 1996

I HADN'T SEEN Sonja for a while. It had been another school break. She'd gone to visit relatives again, taking books and notes with her to study for the upcoming Abitur exams. I wasn't convinced she really had an idea about photosynthesis or functional plant anatomy by now. Both were complex. But I hoped she'd achieved a miracle and crammed it all in; not just biology, but also geography and maths.

For the big exams, we were supposed to sit at the grindstone for five hours, from 8am till 1pm for each subject, on three different days. Big gaps between the students' desks were obligatory, to prevent cheating. Only small and individually taken pauses were allowed. During the first five-hour exam, whenever I looked up, my view was the same: Sonja's back with her head down. She'd been seated in front of me and was zealously scribbling, seemingly non-stop. Now I believed she had no real difficulties working out the tasks. She was so busy I thought she'd better come up for air. Had I been allowed to make a joke, I'd have asked if she needed a snorkel. Had she really achieved a miracle?

Yes, she had. Weeks later, we got our results for the first exam – biology. Sonja definitely impressed me. And our teacher: not only had she managed to score twelve out of a possible fifteen points, which was a good result in itself, but she had also landed the best mark in our class!

When we received our results for geography and maths, I wasn't thrilled about my merely satisfactory eight points in geography, but very much so about my thirteen in maths. That was close enough to a distinction. Now the only part of the Abitur outstanding was the oral one, which wasn't going to happen for another few weeks. This time period was odd, because we still had to attend lessons and sit some small exams that impacted our overall Abitur grade.

* * *

ONE THURSDAY MORNING, Sonja didn't show up at our meeting point by the wood. I was slightly late, so I carried on cycling to school on my own and expected her to be there already. But when I arrived in the classroom, she wasn't there. I had *not* missed her.

After school, I cycled down the path to her accommodation. I rang the bell and opened the main door as the buzzer sounded. Lucas, one of Sonja's flatmates, stood in the doorway as I walked up the stairs.

"Hey!" I said.

"Hi, Finja! Come in."

Lucas studied electrical engineering. He was doing his diploma thesis; mostly from home. I had found it cute when he'd told me he would feel the need to fully dress each time before calling his tutor. "I shouldn't be naked on the phone to my professor," he'd said, and now he stood there in the doorway, his black hair damp from his shower, shoes laced up. Even a tie around his neck wouldn't have surprised me.

"You having another phone meeting?" I asked.

"Yeah, in ten minutes."

He was nervous. Sometimes he was nervous, even anxious, about the well-being of his sisters – he would have rolled up his sleeves, ready for a fist fight, to protect them. Gabriele often came to the student flat.

Lucas was sensitive. He knew that Sonja had OCD. She had told him, since she now had a name for her struggles. And Lucas didn't seem to mind. Nobody in the flat did. Now and again, there was a little issue between the students and Sonja about using the bathroom in the morning. She took a bit too long getting ready, despite things being a lot easier than in her parents' house. But because she had come out about her mental illness, the others could deal with her behaviour. I was glad she didn't have to hide everything like she did at school.

After Lucas had let me in, I knocked on Sonja's door.

"Come in."

She was lying in bed, covered up to her chin.

"Are you ill?" I asked, closing the door of her room behind me.

"No. Not really." She hardly moved; she just stared at the ceiling.

"What do you mean, 'not really'?"

And that was a good question: was Sonja only ill if she had something physical? If OCD was a proper illness, then she was actually ill all the time. Mentally ill.

Now she sat up. I grabbed the chair from beside her desk – her only other thing, apart from the bed, to sit on.

"Yesterday, I left the house, went down the path, and into the road," she said. "I was on the way to the bus stop, going to meet my mum in the city centre. I just looked at the people around, and guess who was ahead of me?"

I shrugged.

"Lasse – Goran's brother!"

She didn't need to explain any further. I knew what the problem was.

"I was so shocked. Thankfully, it was very windy and the wind came from behind me, towards him. I didn't get contaminated. I just ran away back home," she said.

She considered micro particles blown by the wind. Her thinking happened in a world like that of a forensic scientist – how had the blood splattered at the crime scene? She'd been like that ever since I had known her.

"I get it. But that was yesterday. Why didn't you come to school today?"

"I couldn't."

"Because the road is dirty now? Lasse has contaminated it all?"

"Yes. I can't even cross it any more."

Fucking hell! The road was now as dirty as Dabendorf – Goran's village. Problem: we needed to cross it to get to school. Sonja was trapped.

"Are you telling me that you won't ever leave this place? Never go to school again? Throw it all away? The Abitur, I mean," I said.

"I've been struggling with it all day." Her eyes dropped to the floor.

Sonja was a master at avoiding things by finding ways around them. No matter how strange they were, no matter how hard. Using her feet to switch on the lights in her parents' house had been one of her easier solutions. Avoiding eating the Goran-contaminated food her Mum bought in the dirty shops had been more difficult. At times, she went hungry. Changing schools and taking on a daily bike ride was exhausting, not just for her but also me! Now that she couldn't cross the road any more, she presented me with another way of getting around things – literally.

"Well, I will have to take a different route," she said.

"Huh? There isn't one. The path into the wood is a cul-de-sac. There are only trees behind this house!"

"But still, a few small trails lead through. Then there's a proper road on the other side."

Now I understood. Sonja was going to take a long detour, including a very bumpy ride through the wood on her standard city bike. It would add about three kilometres, so she would be back at the original length of her journey to school, when we had cycled together from Fessdorf. I had nothing to say. I had known her for long enough to be sure it was a done deal. However, I wasn't prepared for her to top the whole thing.

"You know, there's something else. Um, I don't really want to ask you but—"

"But what?" I cut in, as if I couldn't wait but didn't want to hear at the same time.

"But I just *have* to." Her tone alerted me. "I need you to cycle the same way with me. From tomorrow onwards. To keep you from being contaminated too."

There: that was what I hadn't wanted to hear.

"You must be joking?! Do you realise what you're asking of me?" I said.

"Yes, I do," she said quietly, lowering her head.

I did not want to cycle those extra kilometres.

"No, Sonja!" I shook my head in disbelief, frustration, defiance – just everything.

"But—" she tried.

"No! No 'but'! It's too much!" I thought this was the moment to put a spanner in the works of Sonja's plans. Cycling through the wood in the early mornings, over tiny, bumpy trails, would be a nightmare. Enough was enough!

"Let me just suggest something, please," she said, trying to calm me down.

"There isn't anything that will make me agree to this!"

"You could stay here and not have to cycle from Fessdorf. You've already done it a couple of nights. There are only three weeks to go until the oral part of the Abitur. Then school is over."

Sonja was good at this: having the last word. And she used it so well. I hated it. It was like when she had decided we would move from our first high school to our second – a fait accompli. Now she forced me into thinking about it. She knew I had tried to make friends with Pia over the last two years or so. She knew it was hard, because Pia and the other girls at our new high school had been in cliques since Year One; maybe kindergarten. Sonja used the fact that we were close to the end of our school career. And that she was my only friend.

But what about Mum and Grandma? Wouldn't they miss me? Dad? My brother? My twenty-year-old, arrogant brother? Even though he was often at home again, since Jennifer had broken up, there was no sibling love from him for me. He had no interest in me whatsoever.

I stared at Sonja. She stared back, awaiting my response. And she knew that she had me.

WHAT NEXT?

I GAVE IN. I stayed at Sonja's for three weeks, and we cycled her detour. Mum had to get used to seeing me only at the weekends.

When we took the oral Abitur in art, we were given our results straight away. I got nine points out of fifteen. Not great, but not horrible either. I was happy with my overall, final Abitur score of 2.3 – not bad for a stupid cow, particularly given that Arrogant Brother had only achieved 2.4 the previous year. (The smaller the number, the better the score; pass marks range from 1.0 to 4.0.)

Now that school was finished, a change of life was approaching. Having graduated meant that Sonja and I were ready for university. But did I want to go? I wasn't sure. I wasn't a hundred per cent sure about anything. Dad had said when I was sixteen and expressed interest in studying biology, "You won't do that. It won't earn you money." Mum now recommended I go and see a career adviser. At the job centre I scoured the folders and watched numerous videos. But I remained undecided.

"Sonja, what's happening? What are *you* going to do about further education or training?" I asked.

"I must leave. Move to a different city. I can't stay here any more."

It sounded like another fait accompli was rolling towards

me. It was so familiar – first the lightning… and then you knew you just had to wait until the thunder arrived. But of course, it was obvious why she had to leave: she was imprisoned in her student flat! The only places she went to were the little glade and the tiny supermarket on the other side of the wood. She was far from living – she was restricted to existing.

"Where to, then?" I was prepared for almost anything.

"Maybe Würzburg."

"Würzburg? To do what? Study?"

"Yeah, maybe. Or maybe not. As long as I'll get out of here… " She shrugged.

"Würzburg is hundreds of kilometres south of here!"

"I know."

"So you've decided already?!" I threw my arms aside.

"No, I haven't. I wanted to talk to you about it."

Huh? No thunder after the lightning? This was against the laws of nature. No fait accompli? Did she also care very much about us not going our separate ways, now that school was over?

I actually liked the idea of leaving Gadburg. I lacked any interest; neither of us had real friends there. Lucas and the other two students probably came closest to that. I did love Mum and Dad, and Grandma. But, naturally, I'd untied myself from my parents' home, having been staying in Sonja's flat, exploring the independent way of life. I had done all sorts of self-catering with her.

"Okay, I'm happy to leave. But not Würzburg. I want to go to Munich," I grabbed her idea and stepped it up.

"Munich?"

"Yeah. It must be great down there!" I imagined Würzburg being a little too dull. Munich, however, had over a million people; and was even further away from Gadburg. Close to the Alps, not far from Austria – a whole different world.

"Okay," she said, with a hint of disbelief; maybe baffled I didn't resist leaving.

* * *

IN THE END it was decided: we would move to Munich. Of all the big cities in Germany, it was the furthest possible away from where we'd grown up.

For Mum, I guess it was a heart-breaker. She may not have been surprised when I presented her with my choice of place to live. Whenever we'd been on holiday, I was sad on our return home. Mum knew I loved being out and about in the world. But she would certainly still be sad to see it happening. And very soon, it did.

I bought newspapers containing ads for accommodation in Munich, made several phone calls, and after one week of hard work I found myself an internship with an interior architect. Sonja also went for one. She'd seen an ad from a law firm. We found two single rooms in a big student house – a Catholic institution for girls only.

Now we had a good three weeks left to prepare for our move to the far south of Germany. Sonja sold her furniture, which she'd only had for eight or nine months. She got next to nothing for it. I had to leave my own furniture behind, too, because the student rooms in Munich were furnished. It wasn't worth transporting it anywhere, anyway, and for Sonja this came in very handy. The fewer things we took with us, the lower the Goran contamination. She launched a debate, almost negotiating, on personal things I wanted to take, asking me to leave as many things as possible behind. All my clothes were made out to be older, and more worn, than they actually were. I hesitated before throwing certain things away, as I went through my bedroom.

I would miss Mum and Grandma. Grandma hadn't been around at my parents' house to help Mum with the household as often as she used to when my brother and I were younger. She had aged quite a bit and wasn't able to manage everything any more. She was now seventy-five years old. Because I saw her less often, I phoned regularly, and still felt very close to her.

Then the day came when I had to give Mum a big hug. I also embraced Dad. Things were ready for our long journey. I'd had a driving licence since the previous year; driven Mum's car every now and again. Now I prepared the car I had hired, making sure I didn't forget my Abitur certificate. It was evening by the time I sat behind the steering wheel and put the key into the ignition. I took a deep breath, started the engine and with a lump in my throat, I drove away.

I went to pick up Sonja. When I got there, she was waiting for me outside. For her last few days in the flat, Lucas had let her stay in his room, because hers was empty. She had slept on his sofa.

I switched off the engine and got out of the car. Sonja's hair was wet. She'd washed herself last thing before coming out of the house. I struggled to breathe when I stood next to her – a pungent smell of shower gel pinched my nostrils. Now she was Goran-contamination-free – ready for a new and clean life in Munich. All she handed me to put into the car was her own Abitur certificate and a round biscuit box made of metal.

"Snacks for the trip?"

"Don't open it, please! It's clean," she said hysterically. "My old CDs are in there. Without covers. Just the discs. I washed them with soap and water. And the box. Everything is decontaminated!"

No snacks, then. I briefly imagined her cleaning so thoroughly that there were only notes and lyrics left as the discs had vanished. I put the box in the back of the car without lifting the lid, as requested. Regarding clothes, Sonja took only those that she wore. She planned on buying new stuff in Munich.

We sat inside the car. I thought perhaps Sonja wished I had come by helicopter to fly her out of her isolated place. She still couldn't cross the dirty road, but it was impossible to get through the wood by car. Flying her out would have been a hundred per cent clean. But unfortunately I only had a driving licence. She had to accept that we needed to head down the dirty road for a short while, and content herself with the idea that all the bits from Goran would hopefully be blown away as we sped down the motorway.

THE GIRLS' HOUSE

WE DROVE SOUTH through Germany, all night long, only taking a couple of breaks, including forty-five minutes of dozing in the car. At 8.12am, we passed a yellow signpost for Munich. We'd made it.

We dropped the car at the rental place and took the Underground to get to the house. Three middle-aged ladies managed it, all Catholic. One of them, Mrs Lange, welcomed us. I was embarrassed as she checked us out, her gaze scanning our bodies.

"Where are your suitcases? All your stuff?"

Sonja really looked stupid, stood there clutching a biscuit box!

"Err… umm… at a friend's for the moment," I lied.

Mrs Lange showed us the building and explained its rules. Most remarkable were the attached church with a nunnery, and the rule that said no boys were allowed in after 11pm, anywhere in the house.

Standing in the doorway of my room, she assured me there would be new furniture for all the rooms sometime soon. I'd opened the doors of a cupboard, and because it was empty, the doors shifted the thing's balance, making it tilt towards me on its overly long, thin legs. The desk, chair, bed and wardrobe had a few years under their belt, too. The newest things seemed to be the sink and the mirror by the wall next to the door.

"And don't worry, when you decorate with your personal belongings this afternoon, the room will definitely look cosy," Mrs Lange said.

"Sure."

She had no idea! And I was lacking conviction that this room would *ever* feel like home. Mrs Lange left and I was by myself in my new twelve square metres. There was no way I was able to go and buy anything to decorate them on the same day. I was knackered from driving. I crawled onto the bed and curled up. I didn't even have a duvet to cover myself, but fell asleep instantly.

*   *   *

DURING THE FOLLOWING days, Sonja and I bought clothes, duvets, covers, and a few cheap pots and pans to cook with. I had saved up those bulky pocket-money coin rolls Dad had given me for making phone calls, and now they were all in my bank account. But they weren't enough to decorate my new room just yet. When Sonja opened her Goran-contamination-free biscuit box, the inside was covered in rust, and so were the thoroughly washed CDs. None of them was useable any more.

Sonja still received a monthly allowance from her parents. Rather than food, she spent it on new, contamination-free clothes and everything else she had to replace. She went a little hungry for a while until the next month's payment came.

My parents now also paid me maintenance. It wasn't just a random amount. Dad had done his research: the German state provided students with a maintenance, if it had to stand in for parents who couldn't afford to pay for their children at university. Dad had decided to take this average amount as guidance. I guess it was to justify his 'minimum pay'. He now put a thousand Deutschmarks into my account each month. My parents were both teachers and wealthy, enabling them to have private health insurance. Since I wasn't trained or a professional of some kind yet, I remained insured via them. It wasn't expensive to add children who were still in education to the policy. Dad therefore deducted the monthly fee for insuring me from those thousand Deutschmarks and gave me DM 972.34. He embarrassed me with that ridiculously precise amount when I applied to be exempt from paying to watch TV, as I had to disclose it on the form. "Why thirty-four pfennig?" the woman at the desk had asked.

Sonja and I got to know the girls on our floor; floor six, the top one. At first, I was expecting a bitchy atmosphere but it turned out different. At the weekends, they went out to party, and I joined them. We explored discos on Friday and Saturday nights. However, the tarting up in preparation wasn't for me. I was an ordinary girl with an ordinary face, according to Arrogant Brother. I barely owned any make-up, and my mouth stood open when Tatjana scattered hers over half a sofa in the common living room, searching for the right eyeliner. I didn't follow any of the girly protocols, and couldn't see why I needed to ask one of them to rub and peel my back in the bathtub. Or, even worse, sit on a sofa, expose my legs and let another girl torture me as she tore out the hair with an epilator. Tatjana was always the loudest screamer during that treatment. She was also the one who had the most exciting stories to tell, on the mornings after the disco nights, when lots of girls, including me, sat side by side on all three sofas, reporting on their nocturnal activities. Girl after girl talked about how good, or bad, their previous night's boy had been.

"You're still a virgin?" Tatjana asked, her bangles jangling from her wrist as she put her hand to her chin.

The spotlight shone on me. I froze, desperate for it to move on, knowing I stood out as naive, possibly cloistered and unworldly. Heat suffused my cheeks. My poor attempts and subsequent failures in my haste to snatch a boy at dancing school flashed through my mind. How would I catch a man when I hadn't been able with boys?! I was hopelessly inexperienced at nineteen.

"It's also nice to still be a virgin," Tatjana continued, smiling at me.

My cheeks cooled a little. Phew.

Despite my lack of experience with boys, I was no outsider in this group of girls. It felt amazing to be among them; so very different to how it had been for our years at school. Even Sonja was included. Her OCD symptoms in our clean new world remained limited. There was no Goran contamination in Munich. That was, until things changed.

LIFE IN MUNICH

I LOVED IT – life in Munich. It was great… until Sonja came up with a way to spoil it. Although Goran was far away, his hair and skin particles – his *touch* – still reached her, like some creeper stretching after us.

Sonja created it, in her head; her view; her opinion. She simply widened the reach of the Goran contamination. I wondered if she sat down and drafted her thoughts, or if they popped up in her mind automatically, intrusively. It seemed her brain searched to be filled with that old fear again, unable to remain free from anxiety.

She defined new contaminated areas, and the seven-hundred-something kilometres separating us from Goran didn't count for them. They turned into real danger zones, and she needed them. Sonja needs the presence of both danger and fear. She is an addict. OCD is an anxiety-linked mental illness. Whenever she senses danger, she is able to produce the feeling of security and safety with a compulsive action. She needs to create fear so that she can feed her *real* need: that for reassuring safety. The cycle works like a drug!

"Hey, Bayern Munich are playing on Saturday." I waved two tickets at Sonja. "You coming with me to the stadium? Klinsmann now plays for them!" I'd been a huge fan of Jürgen Klinsmann since the World Cup in 1990.

"Huh? Where did you get the tickets from?"

"Someone sold them to me outside the merchandise shop. They weren't expensive."

Sonja flinched. "You went to the merchandise shop?"

"Yeah."

"You shouldn't go there!"

"Why not?"

Sonja's face turned red, gleaming with sweat. "There are too many tourists in that area!"

I didn't understand what she was talking about, but I knew Sonja by now. It was obvious there was a problem that was going to restrict me. I tried to ignore it.

"Are you coming to the game, then?" I asked.

"Who are they playing?"

I glanced at the tickets, and suddenly didn't want to say who.

"A team from the north?" she asked.

Damn. I stared at Sonja. "Yes."

"No! I'm not coming. And please, I ask you not to go either. Not when they play against teams from northern Germany. Please!"

"You're afraid there'll be people from Gadburg amongst the other team's fans?"

"Yes. Or nearby. I must stay away from them."

"Are they all contaminated?"

She nodded.

That's how Sonja produced her safety – after creating the danger. I threw the tickets in the bin in the toilets, hoping that Bayern Munich would face a team who weren't from the north next time they played at home.

Sonja was afraid of physical contact with northern tourists. *All* tourists, effectively, because she couldn't tell where they were from. Bits of Goran might have stuck to their clothes. She was also concerned about the small chance of bumping into Goran or Lasse themselves, wandering in Munich as tourists. The beautiful city has lots and lots of places tourists visit…

*　*　*

SONJA UNLOADED HER shopping bag onto her desk. A jar of honey was amongst the items inside it, and accidentally ended up upside down. It was bad luck that she could now see the label on the bottom, showing the name of where the honey was made: Dabendorf. Without hesitation, she rushed to the bin in the toilets and threw the unopened honey away. The other items had to be thrown away, too, including her cloth shopping bag. Everything was contaminated.

She washed her hands for nine minutes with soap and hot water. As hot as she could stand. Her desk needed cleaning. She went back to the supermarket to buy a pair of rubber gloves, together with some detergent and a sponge, to decontaminate it. Then she washed her hands again. For nine minutes. Just in case… there may have been a tiny hole somewhere in the gloves.

From now on, before she bought anything, she carefully investigated where it had been made. The honey from Dabendorf became taboo, of course. And to make sure that she avoided any cross-contamination between honey producers, she neither bought nor ate honey at all any more. She asked me to avoid it, too. We didn't even go near the shelves of jam and honey when we visited supermarkets.

*　*　*

October 1996

OKTOBERFEST HAD STARTED a while ago. I'd been constantly itching to go; I wanted to experience it. Badly. But I didn't. Because Sonja didn't. Too many tourists.

I imagined it being mega fun. I wasn't necessarily longing for the beer, no. I was keen on the party, with people from all over the world. Yes indeed, I was keen on the tourists. Not particularly on those from northern Germany, but all the others, at least. I had heard that even people from Australia and New Zealand made their way over.

Quite a lot of the girls from our floor went and I had to listen to their stories when they came back. It hurt. And I could only be part of the laughter when they brought back some boys to our house. Boys who weren't allowed in after 11pm. I helped squeeze them behind the sofas in the living room whenever Mrs Lange & Co. were checking up on the noise.

When all my colleagues from my internship went to the Oktoberfest as a group, I feigned a stomach bug and went home. So did Sonja. Everybody else in Munich went to the Oktoberfest, at least once per year. It was a must-do thing. Like a religion.

THE SECOND SAD CHRISTMAS

23rd December 1996

IT WAS EARLY evening, dark outside. I was strolling around the Marienplatz – the square in front of the town hall. A tourist trap. Sonja didn't know, and I didn't plan to tell her. It didn't feel like breaking the rules, because I was careful not to touch people's clothes. So close to Christmas, I assumed not many tourists would be there anyway. Surely they were all at home.

December hadn't been very cold, but the temperature fell gradually throughout this day and it started to snow. I watched snowflakes landing on my sleeves, on my hands, my chest. I looked up into the sky, brightened by street lights, and saw millions of flakes coming down, their touch cool on my nose and cheeks. It fitted the bright, flashing, glowing huts of the Christmas market around the town hall, the *Jingle Bells* that pealed in my ears, and the gingerbread smell that filled my nostrils. Christmas was almost here – the second sad Christmas.

Sonja didn't want to go home for the festival. Well, she actually considered Munich her home by now. So did I.

We loved it there. I had suffered no homesickness at all. Talking to Mum, Grandma and sometimes Dad on the phone was good enough. However, during the previous days, with Christmas just around the corner, I did feel the need to go back to northern Germany to see my family. I'd become sadder and sadder with each day that passed. Now, I was hurting.

"How am I going to explain this to my mum?" I'd said to Sonja when she'd begged me to stay.

She had no answer.

I told Mum my boss had asked if I was able to help with a special project on the afternoon of Christmas Day in return for some good money. She knew I normally didn't get paid as an intern. Maybe that convinced her. Maybe not.

On the morning of Christmas Eve – the first main day of Christmas in Germany – the last few girls on our floor left for home. Most had gone days earlier. There were over twenty rooms on each floor in the house – that was how many girls were normally around. By midday, our corridor was empty. No one left except for Sonja and me. I walked down the stairs to floor five. I checked its common kitchen and living room, opened the doors to both wings and glanced down the corridors. No other girls. I walked further downstairs, checked the kitchen, living room and corridors of floor four: no girls. Same on floor three. I carried on walking down without really looking any more, and as I passed the phones on each floor, I noticed none of them rang. No chatty, high, girly voices. Silence everywhere. The whole house was dead. It felt surreal.

On the ground floor, Mrs Lange spotted me. She hadn't closed the reception desk yet and she invited me to join her and her colleagues later in the day to celebrate Christmas.

I felt another of those lumps in my throat and hoped it wouldn't result in tears. An invitation from three old ladies and their priest was the best that could happen to me at that moment.

When I made my way to the attached nunnery and church, Sonja came too. I was convinced she'd also be welcome. Father Winfried held the Christmas Mass. After that, we sat around a big round table that was mostly surrounded by nuns, and overloaded with steaming Bavarian food. Sonja's and my street clothing stood out like scarlet macaws in a green jungle. Mrs Lange and the other two ladies who managed the house weren't wearing nuns' habits, but their mousy outfits almost qualified. It was then that I couldn't withstand the pressure of that lump any longer and I burst into tears. I was missing my family – Mum and Grandma, at least.

The nuns and Mrs Lange turned to me. I was fortunate that they were understanding. They helped me to dry my tears and cope with my first Christmas without my family.

*   *   *

At 11pm, the food was eaten, Christmas carols sung and gifts unwrapped. The party was over. Sonja and I were stood in front of the main entrance to the house when my chest, my head, my whole body suddenly wanted to explode. Like something had to be freed; to get out of me. Sonja was waiting for me to open the door with my key, as she had left hers inside her room. She had accidentally dropped it near a touristy road, and it was contaminated and hadn't been washed yet. I looked up at the tall, wide front of the building. Windows were everywhere, but no light came from them. I assumed all those facing the back garden were just as dark. Because nobody was there. It was a unique thing during the course of a year.

I stared at Sonja. She was tucked up in her coat. It was freezing cold. Snow hadn't stopped falling since the previous evening. White stuff everywhere. She was shivering, and I was happy to leave her in that state for a while.

"You know what?" I shouted.

She pressed her lips together. Because, yes, she knew.

"We're the only ones in this damn house for the next night and day. It's not that I'm scared, but it's fucking sad that everybody else is at home, just as they're supposed to be. And *us*, we're lonely by ourselves! Well I am, if you aren't!"

Sonja still said nothing.

"This is *t-e-r-r-i-b-l-e*!" I yelled.

Something clicked inside my head. I realised how much I had given in to her demands already in my young life. As if I was dependent on her. Was I? Nobody, not even she, had ever really forced me to cater for her or do her the favours she'd asked. I'd just done them voluntarily. I'd taken her detour through the wood, avoiding the contaminated road. I'd left my belongings behind, giving her the chance to start over in Munich. I'd missed out on going to the Oktoberfest, because she needed me to. And here I was standing outside a darkened house at Christmas, being lonely. I did all that because I needed her. The childish Imaginary Comfort Bubbles from when I was younger weren't good enough any more. I had outgrown them. Sonja was my friend and the only one I felt I would want comfort from in case something didn't go well. She knew me. And I craved comfort and security. But was she really my only option? There were *plenty* of girls on our floor. I had social contacts now, unlike at school. Some of them were funny and made me laugh. But none of them was like Sonja. None had heard my stories about Dad, when he'd removed me from his lap, when I'd dreamed about him cheating on Mum. None had confided in me, trusted me with the painful rules of a family meeting folder. Nobody would ever be as close to me as Sonja. That's what I believed, at least. Yes, she was my only option! And she knew it.

She stared at me with big, sad dog eyes, and I started to fumble with my key.

"I'm sorry I got you into this," she suddenly said. "But— at least I love you."

I felt an arrow hitting my heart. Out of nowhere. Warmth streamed through my veins; head to feet. So strong, it could have melted the snow around my boots. I turned the key a couple more times in my hands and then opened the door to the house.

*　*　*

I PULLED UP the shutters, and bright light blazed into my room. I squinted, then glanced out. The view was fantastic. It had stopped snowing, and the surrounding roofs were all covered in 'icing sugar'. The sun was out, not a single cloud in the sky. I opened the window and stuck my head out. After only one breath, I coughed – the cold had reached inside my throat and punched me all the way down into the depths of my lungs. I pulled my head back and shut the window. Then I heard it on the radio: −22°C.

After breakfast with Sonja in the deserted living room, I decided to talk to Mum. I went downstairs to the phones since those on each floor were only to receive calls. I

pretended Christmas Eve had been nice and that there was
no need to worry. Then I made my way to the architect's
office. A hat on my head, a scarf around my neck with the
collar of my coat turned up, hands in my pockets and still
shivering, I walked to the Underground. Moisture froze in
my nose, reminding me of the temperatures from when I
was a child, back in the '80s.

During the evening of Christmas Day, I confronted
Sonja. It had bounced around in my head all day, so I
knocked on her door.

"Come in!"

"Sonja, are you ever going to return to Gadburg?"

She stared at me.

"Am I, at least?" I asked.

She kept staring. Just staring. With her big, sad dog eyes.

CELEBRATING 25 YEARS

Spring 1997

SONJA AND I sat on a high-speed train, travelling from Munich to Gadburg. Sonja's parents' silver wedding anniversary was coming up, and her mother wanted Sonja, her child, to be there; her grown-up child – twenty years old now. A big party had been planned. I was invited, too. So were my mum and dad.

I enjoyed the journey, although it dragged on quite a bit; six hours. But I was looking forward to seeing my family for the first time in eight months. Sonja sighed every few minutes. I heard her, even though she only sighed softly. I knew she was nervous about coming back to Munich after the silver wedding. She didn't want to make our new, clean world dirty with Goran contamination.

The switch between worlds – dirty northern Germany and clean Munich – would be crucial. Sonja had prepared for it well: a plastic bag containing a few items of clothing hung on the outside handle of the door of her room in the girls' house. A bottle of shower gel and her house slippers were also in the bag. These were to be used as soon as we returned, when Sonja wanted to have a shower and wash away all the Goran contamination from her body and hair. She made sure she wouldn't need to go into her room before she was clean. The clothes and shoes she wore during the course of our trip up north would be thrown in the bin in the bathroom. And me? I had to do the same. A similar bag hung on my door.

It was my mum who came to the train station and welcomed us when we arrived. Sonja had asked her own mother not to come, because both her parents' cars were far too dirty. Her mum would come and see her in her old student flat, which was where Sonja stayed for the three nights we were there. Lucas had invited her. I promised Sonja I'd keep away from all the contamination of her parents' house, while I stayed with mine.

My parents had converted my former bedroom into an office. They now used it for doing their school marking and lesson preparations. It was strange when I walked in and saw a mattress with a duvet and pillow on the floor for me to sleep on.

A couple of hours later, I went to the city to visit Grandma. Mum let me use her little brand-new car. Grandma opened her arms when she saw me coming up the stairs to her flat. She screamed with joy and I flew into her hug, pressing my cheek against the side of her head.

"Grandma, it's so lovely to see you!"

"Nice to have you back, my poppet!"

I rocked her body slightly, before leaning back and glancing at her. My hands kept running up and down her arms.

"Ha, Grandma, you're getting shorter and shorter. But you're still as cuddly as ever!"

I wrapped my arms around her once again, squeezed

a tiny bit and realised how old she appeared. God, I was going to lose her one day.

"Come in, my dear. Come and eat something," Grandma said.

God, oh God, thank you for that! Despite her having aged, inside she'd stayed my same old Grandma: always concerned about her children and grandchildren being hungry.

"Thanks, Grandma, but I've eaten at Mum's," I said as we walked into her *Stube*.

"Then have some of my fruit juices. They've got lots of vitamins. You can even take a bottle with you."

"Okay, if it makes you happy." I couldn't resist a smile, and stroked Grandma's head; I'd been able to look down on it ever since I'd reached my full height.

* * *

I drove Mum's car again, picking up Sonja and Lucas. The party took place in the ballroom of a hotel. The closer we came to the venue, the sicker I felt, as if I'd swallowed poison. Flashbacks flitted through my mind. They weighed heavy on me. I saw Sonja's mum sitting on the carpet, sobbing, hardly able to speak as she was devastated by her husband ignoring her. I saw those long blue traces of smudged eyeshadow running down her cheeks, from when he had played mind games and told her she'd be the lie of his life. But now we were all driving to their silver wedding – the jubilee of *twenty-five* years of marriage – as the poison reached my head.

When I entered the ballroom, I spotted garlands, flowers, and tables with white cloths everywhere. A delicious smell of warm food wafted past me. I saw staff laying out a buffet, and a DJ in the corner. Sonja's mum sashayed between the tables, dressed in a long, elegant gown that didn't make her look like herself, placing nameplates next to each dessert spoon. Her happy movements and the huge smile on her face were disturbing. Surely she wasn't thinking of all those sessions at her therapist's office, when she cried about the difficulties with her husband; when she wanted answers and advice about how to deal with him. This party could be thrown because she'd always dismissed the option of divorce. Whenever that had been brought up, she'd played down her husband's mind games. They became *just* games. His threats of leaving her with no money always worked. She kept convincing herself that sticking with him was the only way. Her blind spots helped, and she bent herself around his whims until she fitted. Today, we were actually celebrating twenty-five years of adaptation. It was sickening. And even more so because she would carry on bending herself around him until the next big anniversary.

Neighbours and relatives I remembered from Sonja's mum's birthday parties rolled in, followed by faces I didn't know. Mum and Dad arrived, too. They had decided to drive separately from me. Nobody knew how long the kids or the oldies would want to party. But was I in the party mood? Everything appeared so hypocritical. I rather fancied protesting. Unfortunately, it wasn't my business to go to Sonja's mum and ask her how she could possibly have wiped all those years of mental abuse from her mind.

I spotted Sonja's father, also spruced up. He seemed false, like a display dummy in his suit. An exaggerated smile stretched from one ear to the other. His upright posture annoyed me – not the usual lounging in a seat, as he greeted guest after guest and even guided them to their respective tables. And the party began.

Ha, what a farce. What a show, with Sonja's mother and father as the main actors. When someone introduced the first silly game – one of those people do when they actually get married – I was disgusted by having to observe a husband I hadn't seen before. Sonja's father had never smiled at a party, for crying out loud! I'd always seen him pulling a face when it was his wife's birthday, in front of everyone. Every single year.

Tonight, though, there was no sign of his shitty behaviour. Tonight wasn't just about his wife; it was as much about him. So hold on, was he in fact acting? He appeared authentic! He really did enjoy himself as one of the two main characters in the movie – err, at the party. What a stage he set himself up on, what a glow-worm he was!

It was true, he was authentic right now, but for the whole act – the pretence of those twenty-five years of marriage being worth celebrating – he deserved an Oscar for best actor, with his wife best supporting actress. Congratulations!

Nobody seemed to realise the fake. Nobody, except for me, seemed to feel that the whole thing was wrong and rotten. Really? *Nobody?* If only I could have peered into the heads of those guests and relatives that I remembered from Sonja's mum's birthdays, when Mr Moody didn't act, but was the real him.

I wasn't sure any more *who* was acting. Was it really Sonja's father, given he was being authentic tonight? Was everybody else acting instead, or at least those guests who knew him well enough to understand that a show was going on? Those who knew about the decades of trouble Sonja's mum had endured with her husband? Were they all attending the event in walk-on roles, helping to stage the show? Including me?

The poison took over my entire body. My brain turned

in circles, and I couldn't see clearly any more. I left the
ballroom, needing some fresh air, and walked around the
hotel to get away from it all.

* * *

SONJA APPEARED. LUCAS was with her. Tonight his neatly
laced-up shoes, black trousers, shirt and suit-jacket were
fitting, rather than when he was just at home working on
his thesis.

"Finja, what are you doing here? Is something wrong?"
Sonja said.

I almost couldn't believe she'd asked that question. "*Is
something wrong?*"

"Yes – why have you come out here?"

"Don't you see what's happening in there?" I said. "Are
you not bothered? About your own parents play-acting, as
well as everybody else who knows them, including you and
me?" My blood was simmering.

Sonja was silent. Her gaze dropped to the ground.

"You've told me so many times how much your mum
has suffered with your father. And here we are celebrating
them?!"

She didn't move her head. Just one leg, drawing lines in
the dust with her shoe. Lucas didn't speak either. He stood
still, rooted to the spot. Hands in his pockets, glancing at
Sonja. Some pain in his face; pity for Sonja.

"You know, one day – ages ago, when we were ten years
old – I came into your house without ringing the bell. The
door was open. I saw you and your mum sitting on the
carpet in your bedroom. Your mum was crying. Then your
father came upstairs. I hid, so he didn't see me. And I'm

convinced he heard her pain. And then, instead of going into your room and making peace with your mum, he fucking turned away again! I've seen everything with my own eyes and I won't ever forget, Sonja!" My blood was reaching boiling point.

Sonja finally looked up and into my eyes. "You sound as if you're traumatised."

What? *Me* traumatised? *I* wasn't traumatised.

"No, not me. But you must be!" I said.

And then a theory pounced on me, so heavy and uncomfortable that it hurt: was Sonja's OCD covering up something else – a *real* problem; a trauma? Was her mental illness a self-constructed way, a *crutch*, to survive?

"I know what you mean about play-acting," she said. "I've thought about it, too. And if I could, I'd go inside, take the DJ's microphone and let everybody know. I'd shame them for participating in this lie. But nobody would want to hear it. I'm telling you: *people live lies!*"

I wasn't able to respond. She carried on. "Nobody would ever dare tell my father what they think of him. They're all too fearful. He's a powerful man, you know."

Yes, I did know. And Sonja's mum was weak and paralysed. Other members of her family were, too, at least partially. I knew that Sonja's maternal grandparents hadn't wanted her mum and father to get married in the first place. It was a fact: people were living lies.

"I'd have liked my parents to get divorced a long time ago," Sonja said.

But this would never happen. Instead, the pretence and the lies would carry on, without interruption – Sonja's father was right when he'd told his wife she was the lie of his life. But he was hers, too.

THE SECRET

BACK INSIDE THE ballroom, I distracted myself from my heavy feelings, the dark memories, trying to cope with the evening as well as possible. I talked to guests, ate from the buffet, spoke to Lucas about his ongoing studies. Lucas, in fact, had a confused look on his face. Did he feel out of place? He was no walk-on, he'd had no experience of the true life of Sonja's parents.

I didn't chat much with Mum and Dad. They were busy talking to the other oldies. Dad was engaged in conversation with Sonja's father. They were shoulder to shoulder, at the same table, when the next brain-wave hit me. I stared, unable to keep my eyes off them. They didn't notice my focus; my realisation; my shock: *brothers*. Bloody brothers! I'd had that thought before but ignored it. I'd seen similarities between the two but played them down. I'd even fought off my idea of them being related. This time, I couldn't dismiss it any more. I couldn't stop comparing the two: both calculating stupid costs for their children. Both behaving unacceptably at times. Both moody on purpose – one at his wife's birthdays, one at Christmas. Such irrational behaviour from two men. They *had* to be related.

I'd never met my paternal grandparents – Grandad Ernst and Grandma Gerda – because they died before I was born. I knew Sonja didn't know her father's parents either. I'd heard a few stories about my paternal grandparents, including the one about Grandad Ernst cheating on Grandma Gerda with a prostitute – Bertha. So was Sonja's father Dad's half-brother? Was he sort of my uncle? Did Sonja and I have the same paternal grandfather, and were we therefore half-cousins? Was it all just coincidence that she had moved with her parents to Fessdorf, so very close to my parents' house, back in 1987? And that she was seated next to me in class at primary school? And that her name ended with 'ja', even 'nja'? Had everything happened just by chance? I doubted it.

But why was it not mentioned that I had a half-cousin? It was a family secret, right? It had to be kept hidden that Sonja's father's mother was a prostitute. That Grandad Ernst was a cheat.

My eyes remained on the two brothers. They were talking in a very relaxed way, still not noticing my shock, my outrage. Or that I had discovered their secret.

"Hey, come on, let's all go to the dance floor." I heard a voice next to me. Sonja nudged me. Then she pulled me by the arm, Lucas right next to her.

"Huh?" I said, not really knowing where I was. My head span when I got up from my chair, not feeling like dancing at all, but my cousin kept pulling me.

Going Through Transformation

Mum waved goodbye to Sonja and me from the platform. We were sitting on a high-speed train down south. My throat tightened as I waved back through the window to Mum, who I knew was suppressing her tears too, despite the smile on her face.

The longer the journey and the closer we got to Munich, the more restless Sonja became. She fidgeted in her seat. All Goran contamination had to be removed before entering the 'good' world, otherwise it wouldn't be a good and safe one any more. I considered discussing us being half-cousins but because she was getting more and more uptight, I gave up on it. Perhaps another day.

Instead I talked out of the blue, wanting to ease her mind. "My dad let me dethatch his lawn yesterday afternoon. I loved doing that as a kid."

Sonja's brows went up, eyes wide open. She stiffened in her seat. "What? You dethatched? That job people only do once a year?"

"Yes. It was fun. I used a machine my dad got from a neighbour. They share a few they only use rarely."

"Nooo!" Sonja's hands flew up to her head, pressing against its sides as if she suffered a sudden pain in her temples. "A nightmare! A catastrophe!"

And there it was, rolling straight and fast at us. I didn't know it was her father who mine shared that machine with.

"It's kept in my parents' cellar, right next to the bag with my father's sports kit. The machine is highly contaminated!" Sonja's face turned pale, her healthy colour chased away by the de-thatcher I had used the day before.

And so I knew: I was highly contaminated. So was she, because I had deposited Goran-bits all over us, top to toe, inside out. Touching the de-thatcher that was stored next to the sports kit worn by Sonja's father whenever he went to the same sports club as Goran's, was equal to shaking Goran's hand – in Sonja's world.

I was so angry now. I didn't know who with, though. Sonja, because of her made-up rules she imposed on me? Or Dad, since he hadn't told me he shared that machine with Sonja's father? I could hardly blame him for that, could I? Was I angry with myself? I hadn't anticipated the whole situation before taking on the garden job!

I didn't know my anger. I couldn't work it out. I just felt like... I didn't know. Like a victim. A victim of fate. Or a victim of Sonja. It wasn't fair. Nothing was fair. Because her OCD wasn't even *my* problem, *my* business.

Sonja told me we were now far too dirty to enter the good world of Munich, and that we must go through an even stricter cleaning process to get in. I defended myself. Yes, *defended*, because it felt like I couldn't let her see me as so dirty. I had just behaved like a normal person, not permanently remembering her rules. I had spontaneously asked Dad to let me do the dethatching. I didn't want to have to do what she now demanded of me: to wash myself in the same way she was going to.

"I can't deal with you any more if you don't do it like me."

She meant being friends. We'd been friends and gone through things together for an eternity. Of course I needed her and would never find a substitute. That's what I must have thought. I was too stupid to understand how much she needed me too. That she wouldn't have come far without me at all. That I had some power over *her*. All I knew was I didn't want to lose her. I didn't want to risk anything even close to that and end up alone in Munich. And she knew that. I gave in and made myself a slave to her rules.

*   *   *

WE ARRIVED IN Munich Central Train Station and made our way to the girls' house by Underground. Neither of us sat down or grabbed hold of a post to avoid contaminating anything. We had to balance ourselves with just our legs as the Underground sped on. And neither of us had any luggage. I was supposed to throw away the clothes I was wearing in the bin of the bathroom back at the house. For the silver wedding, I had worn some of Mum's evening wear which I'd given back to her.

It was late in the evening as we walked down the corridor on floor six. It was a Tuesday, so we saw no one. The girls were all in bed. This was the reason Sonja had wanted us to arrive back in Munich at such a late hour. She didn't want to bump into them and so risk contamination.

The plastic bag containing the fresh clothes, slippers and shower gel was still on the handle of my door. So was the one on Sonja's. I made sure I didn't touch the handle itself as I slid off the bag. We disappeared into the bathroom, locked the main door. In fact, it was one bathroom behind the other, but when someone locked the front one, the second was unavailable, too. We left the door between the two bathrooms open so we were able to communicate. Sonja was going to shower in the back room; me in the front. All the other girls of our wing were now blocked from these facilities; only the individual cubicles in the toilets were accessible.

I copied Sonja, everything she did, undergoing *hours* of torture. I undressed and stuffed my northern-Germany clothes into the bin. I washed my hands and then soaped the key to my room, before rinsing and repeating. Doing it twice was safer! I placed my clean key next to Sonja's on the shelf below the mirror. Then I started scratching Goran contamination away from underneath my finger- and toenails, using Sonja's file once she'd finished with it herself. She watched, and I was only allowed to stop when no more skin came off.

One hour must have passed, *at least*, when we stepped into the tubs to shower. I followed all of Sonja's instructions – rubbing shower gel everywhere – into my skin, my hair. I rinsed my body assiduously, for minutes on end. Then I poured shower gel onto my flattened palm, mixed it with water and sucked the froth up my nostrils. I needed to cough and make awful noises. The gel was pinching and biting the inside of my nose. My inner tracts burned up into my head. It felt as if my brain was being attacked but couldn't escape from my skull. I had so much pressure in there. I rinsed my nostrils in the same way with plain water.

Now I had to clean the inside of my mouth. Sonja had already poured shower gel directly from the bottle into her mouth, caught some water from the running shower, and was about to gargle the mixture, bending her head backwards. Everything was going deep into her throat, as far as possible. I forced myself to open my mouth and squeeze my shower gel bottle for the gel to flow onto my tongue. It tasted so bitter. I caught some water, bent my head back and gargled just before I would have swallowed the stuff. It wasn't easy not to spill it all out as I made abominable noises. Then I spat it out into the tub, soapy bubbles around my mouth. I retched for some seconds. Thoughts of abandoning this horrible routine throbbed in my head. I wanted to ask Sonja, beg her. I couldn't go any further. I didn't want to.

"And now the eyes," she said.

"No. Sonja, I can't do this. *Please.*" I actually did beg her.

She turned, her head slightly bent so she could see me fully from the back room. "But you promised. So keep going. It will be over!"

There was no abandoning. How could she be so disciplined? It was unbelievable that she was able to do all this against every natural reflex and reluctance. I had to coerce myself to keep my eyes open as I rubbed shower gel into them. Once I felt the burning pain, I was allowed to rinse with water.

After that, everything needed to be repeated. Long and thorough soaping of my body and hair. Rinsing, for minutes. Then washing my nose. I was already disgusted simply by the look of the green shower gel, pouring it onto my flat hand. I hated its smell, although I knew it was nice. Shower gels normally aren't horrible.

I sucked the froth I had made all the way up my nose, and I heard my own noises echoing off the tiled walls. I rinsed. Tears wanted to make their way out from behind my eyes. But Sonja pushed me on to the next step. So callously demanding.

I pulled myself together and poured shower gel into my mouth, added water and gargled deep down into my throat. Just before swallowing, I again heard the echo of my noises as I spat the whole shitty cocktail out around my feet, followed by retching. It was murder! I rinsed with water. The insides of my cheeks were sore, burning from the alkaline shower gel.

We finished the second round of the procedure by washing our eyes, and then started the third one by soaping our bodies again. Washing of noses, throats and eyes followed. I was lucky Sonja hadn't invented a technique to wash deep inside her ears.

During all of this washing, I thought it would never end. I almost didn't believe I'd ever get to the point where Sonja could pronounce me, and herself, clean enough. But then, *finally*, we reached the finish line. Thank goodness, the torture was over.

* * *

SONJA PROTECTED HER fingers with a piece of tissue to unlock the door. The lock and handle were far too contaminated since she had touched them with her dirty hand before washing herself. The tissue was the last item left in the prepared plastic bag from the handle of her bedroom door. I had nothing left in mine, since putting on my Munich clothes that were now glued to my limbs and body like a second skin – wet, as I had pulled them on without drying myself first.

"Leave your shower gel behind. The cleaning lady will clear them away," Sonja said.

Our bottles were pretty much empty anyway.

I was allowed to enter my room, having successfully managed the switch. *Welcome back to the clean Munich-world, me!* On the way into her room, Sonja didn't forget to thank me for my effort. I peered at the time displayed on my alarm clock: *4.03.* I turned the heating on and brushed my wet, matted hair. My skin was softened, my fingers wrinkled. Like those of a washerwoman. I glanced into the mirror. My face was white. My eyes red, making me think of Floppsie, the albino rabbit I used to have as a kid. They were smarting! I didn't bother brushing my teeth; the insides of my cheeks were still burning. I unpeeled my damp clothes and spread them over the radiator, then rubbed my skin with the towel from next to the sink and slipped into my pyjamas. Crawling into bed, I just wanted to close my eyes.

It was cosy in bed. Very cosy. I was happy to be back in Munich. Very happy.

* * *

WHEN I WOKE, my eyes felt bizarre. I got up, felt my way across the room. By the time I reached the mirror over the sink, I still couldn't move my eyelids. They were stuck! I splashed water from the tap over them. Eventually, I was able to see myself in the mirror and looked closely into my sore eyes, pulling long threads of slime out of them.

I felt harmed. Harmed by Sonja's routine. In fact, I didn't just *feel* harmed, I *was* harmed. I left my room, wanting to tell her off for what she had done to me. For what I had *let* her do to me. For what I had done *myself* to me.

But that was the point: I'd given in to her inhumane demand voluntarily. I had allowed it.

So what could I now accuse her of? Blackmail, maybe?

She'd said she wouldn't be able to deal with me any more if I had said no. The problem was that it was too late, because I had made the decision to suffer the torture. Because I didn't want to risk losing my best friend.

And still I knocked on Sonja's door, but when I saw another two red Floppsie-eyes, I just turned around, marched back into my room and banged the door closed behind me.

So Does Dad Love Me, Then?

Summer 1997

I WAS IN the ladies. Yellow walls. I was facing a white toilet bowl. The seat was up, and somebody was holding my hair back.

I heard a voice. "Stick a finger down your throat!" I thought I'd understood.

"Jessica?" I burbled.

"Come on now, stick a finger down your throat. *Please!*"

Though I didn't understand why she wanted me to do that.

"Or shall I do it?" she said.

No, she shouldn't. I didn't want *any* finger down my throat. I just wanted peace, and to close my eyes again.

I was out with a group of girls from my floor. Rebecca and I had been bingeing: one Bacardi, one vodka, two whiskies and *four* tequilas. All within an hour and a half or so. All well shaken inside our bodies, since we were at a disco. The Bacardi and the vodka had been mixed with Coke. Whiskies and tequilas we drank neat. The shots had changed from tasting totally awful, to tasting all right, to tasting of nothing. I had decided to retire when I'd found a bench somewhere inside the disco and laid down.

Now I noticed straps around my arms and shoulders. I was lying on something. I heard some diffuse voices around me but barely understood a word. Then a man spoke loudly at me. God, he almost shouted.

"How are you insured?"

He was so annoying. Such a trivial little matter. I told him to ask me another time; I was unable to remember anyway.

Then I was being lifted, I guess on a stretcher, and taken to an ambulance. I had a blurred vision of Rebecca, some distance away from me, as she crawled on all fours around the carpark. Good girl, she was fine. She was about twice as heavy as me and could handle her drinks better. I could fall asleep again, reassured.

I'm not sure why I drank so much. Why I drank at all. I normally didn't. Sonja didn't either, and going out wasn't her thing. But it was mine. I could have done it without the alcohol, though, because its taste really wasn't for me. But all the other girls loved to drink, and I couldn't be the only one not to.

*　*　*

I HAD QUIT my internship. I didn't want to become an architect. And Dad wasn't happy I was still not in real training. He demanded I start something proper. Unfortunately, I remained undecided, not convinced of anything that I really wanted to do or become. I'd applied for a university place to study nutritional science and hoped there was a chance the German central application system, which allocates places according to family situation, would give me one in Munich despite my family living in northern Germany. I had to wait several weeks for a response. In the meantime, Dad stopped giving me maintenance and told me I had to make money myself, since I'd been wasteful with my time and decisions for training. I didn't feel good about that. I hadn't been lazy. Dad hadn't said I'd been lazy, but still. I had tried hard. He'd only start paying maintenance again if I were in training or studying.

I'd found a job at a factory, sorting and packaging different kinds of food. It was such a boring job, but I worked up to twelve hours per shift at the conveyer belts for two months. It earned the money that Dad didn't pay me, and more: about twice as much as he'd have given me during the same period.

Now this job was over, and I had gone out to party with the girls.

* * *

WHEN I WOKE again, I was in a strange kind of bed. I sat up. Lots of white furniture around me. Glass partitions divided the big room into smaller sections. Tools, test tubes and kidney dishes on a trolley next to me. I spotted a woman in a sky-blue uniform, but she disappeared. I looked down at myself. The cloth that covered me seemed to be a single-use sheet. I was attached to some cables. A drip stood next to the bed, its needle inserted into my right arm. Where was I? Never mind, because I was actually faced with a much more pressing matter. Literally: I desperately needed to pee.

"Hello?" I didn't recognise my own voice. It sounded deep and rough.

"Hellooo?" I croaked again.

Nobody answered. Maybe I didn't shout loudly enough, but that was all I was capable of.

Once again: "Hellooo!"

Still, nobody replied and nobody in a hospital uniform turned up. I was sitting in this neon-light-bright room by myself, needing a pee.

I climbed out of the bed, grabbed the metal drip stand to make sure I didn't tear out the catheter, and started pushing it along next to me. Down the corridor, I found a bathroom and stumbled inside. I had to support myself with both hands. I was still drunk.

Then I peed; for a whole minute or so. When I emerged from the bathroom, a hospital uniform was already approaching. She took me back into that bright room and asked a few questions. Without really knowing how I was answering, I watched her removing the drip from my arm. Then she escorted me into a proper hospital room, pointed to a bed, and told me that the breakfast next to it was for me. She left as I was supporting myself on the railing of the foot end of 'my' bed. Unsteadily.

A woman was sat in the other bed in the room. Big eyes. I felt her stare at me, piercing my body as she was checking me out. I saw thought bubbles popping up above the woman's head; she was wondering:

Where have you *come from?*

What's your *health issue?*

And why the hell are you barefoot?

She was entitled to be shocked by my appearance: I was tottering despite holding on to my bed, I wore a summer dress that barely covered my knickers, my hair was a mess, and I had lost my stilettos!

I followed her gaze: my dress was stained, my legs smeared with mud. My feet dirt-black rather than skin-coloured. No doubt she thought I was a bum who'd been drinking too much, hanging around in a car park all night.

I heaved myself into bed and tried to eat the breakfast. My hands and fingers were like rubber. I couldn't open the chocolate drink. There was no place to stick the straw, so I skipped it. I did manage to open the biscuits and a yogurt with my teeth, though.

Then I wanted to go home. I couldn't stand the embarrassment; the legitimate stares and unanswered thought bubbles from that woman. I slid out of bed again to ask the nurse if I could please go home. She had further questions.

"How're you feeling now?"

"Fine," I lied.

"Use the phone over there by the wall and call somebody to pick you up. You cannot go home alone."

I tried to concentrate on my walking to the phone. Steady, steady. *The nurse mustn't see I just lied.* I struggled even to get the handset up to my ear. It was so heavy. Thankfully, I remembered the number of the phone on the sixth floor of the girls' house. I dialled, and heard several rings.

"Hello?" a girl said.

"Hi, it's Finja. Is that Marina?" My voice was so croaky.

"Yes. But, sorry, who are you?"

I repeated my name. "Can you please wake Jessica and tell her she should pick me up from the hospital?"

Marina didn't seem to know I was in hospital. I explained briefly how I had ended up there.

"And which hospital are you in?" she asked.

I hadn't thought about the fact that there were loads of hospitals in Munich.

"No idea. I really don't know where I am," I said. "But Jessica must know. They told me she held my hand all the way inside the ambulance."

Less than half an hour later, Jessica turned up. As soon as I saw her coming down the corridor, I smiled. She opened her arms. God, was I happy to see her.

*   *   *

Once back in my room, I didn't want to do anything but go to bed. I wanted to sleep and have some peace. From everybody. But it was a Saturday, and I expected a phone call from Mum. She called every Saturday.

Recently, I'd had my own landline installed in my room. Every girl who wanted one, and was willing to pay the necessary installation fee, could get one. I was lying in bed and reached for my phone. I decided to call Mum straight away, so I could sleep for the rest of the day. My parents would find out about my binge, and where I'd stayed the previous night, because I was insured through them. Dad was going to see the bill. There was no point even considering hiding anything from them.

I dialled the number, pulling myself together, hoping my voice wouldn't give away the terrible state I was in. Eventually Dad picked up and said Mum wasn't at home. I confessed to Dad and prepared him for receiving a bill, possibly with some strange remarks on it.

"And why did you do that?" He spoke with an unusually soft voice. He wasn't angry at all.

"I don't know," I said. "Rebecca and I just wanted to try

a little bit of everything. It was spontaneous."

Dad laughed – in a nice way. "Well, we've all done that. But I hope you've learned from it!"

Had I heard right? Was I *still* drunk? Dad being understanding, even caring? I was pleased about his reaction, but it didn't feel like the real him. He sounded so warm. *Too* warm.

"I'll tell Mum about everything when she gets home and call you myself in about half an hour if she's not back. See how you are. I guess you're alone in your room?" he said.

It was un-be-liev-able: Dad really seemed to be worried about me.

"Yes, I'm alone. But don't wait too long before you call. I'm so tired, I'd like to sleep," I said.

Dad understood.

*   *   *

I WAITED TWENTY-FIVE minutes. Twenty-six, twenty-seven, twenty-eight. It was a struggle. Dad had charmed me with his desire to know how I was feeling. He wanted to make sure I was fine. But, as hard as I tried, I knew I couldn't stay awake much longer, though I wanted to avoid being startled by the noise of my phone.

I waited twenty-nine minutes, thirty and thirty-one. Then, I couldn't wait any more. I figured Mum hadn't returned home, so Dad must have decided to wait for her a little longer. I didn't mind not speaking to her; Dad could report everything back to her. I just wanted to sleep.

Thirty-two minutes passed before I pulled my phone cable out of the socket for some undisturbed sleep. I would call my parents later. I turned around in my bed and managed to take off my dress and bra, without bothering to put on any pyjamas. It was going to be another hot day anyway. I fell asleep instantly.

*　*　*

KNOCKS ON MY door woke me. I opened my eyes, glanced at the ceiling and blinked two or three times. I lifted my head slightly. Two tall and solid men in uniform, with guns, truncheons and handcuffs hanging from their belts, stood in my doorway.

"No need for alarm, it's just the police!" one of them said.

Just the police?

I sat up, not forgetting to hold the duvet in front of my body.

"My God, are you arresting me? I've only been drinking slightly too much," I said.

"Don't worry, miss, don't worry!" the other policeman said, making a calming motion with his hands.

His colleague closed my door. Who would have thought that I'd find myself dressed only in underwear with two fully armed police officers in my room telling me not to worry? I really wasn't going to be arrested, was I? Who knew what I'd done while blacked out? I didn't!

"Your father called us. He's worried about you. He couldn't reach you on the phone. You haven't had the best of nights, he told us," one of the officers said, and winked.

The policemen's eyes turned to the floor next to my bed, noticing the unplugged phone cable.

"You need to call your parents right now, please. Or would you prefer us to do it?"

"Err, um, yes. Err, no! I mean, no, you don't need to call

182

them. I'll do it. Right now. Promise!"

"All right then." The officers nodded and left.

I pictured Mrs Lange & Co. when the police had asked to pass through reception and enter the house. When they had told them *who* they wanted to see, and why.

I plugged in my phone and called my parents. After only one ring, Dad picked up.

"Everything is fine, Dad, I was only sleeping."

He let out a sigh of relief as if my life had been saved.

So he *did* love me, didn't he?

Although I hardly ever felt his affection, I believed he had just shown some. Maybe Dad and Sonja's father were not brothers, then.

LOYALTY

It took two days to recover from my alcohol binge. Whereas Rebecca had slept for one afternoon, I'd needed two full days of just sleeping and eating. I reached out for bananas, chocolate and biscuits directly from my bed. Water was also on the shelf. I only left my room to walk down the corridor to the toilets.

Now I was myself again. And so was Dad. He'd recovered from his show of emotion, and announced the arrival of two bills for my special night out. One was for my stay in hospital, which was luckily paid by my parents' health insurance. The other, however, wasn't. It listed my journey to the hospital. The ambulance ride from the disco's car park had cost a thousand Deutschmarks. And, of course, Dad wouldn't have been Dad, had he not made me pay that bill myself. He would give me a hundred Deutschmarks less each time, over ten months, once I was in an apprenticeship or at university and he'd resume paying maintenance. And so I now had to be even more careful with my money.

*   *   *

In late August, I received the news that I was being offered a place to study in a small city in northern Germany. Sonja didn't need to worry – there was no way I wanted to go

184

there. Dad wasn't enamoured of my refusal to take my place at university. He pressured me to become something. One year had gone by since we moved to Munich, and I didn't want to leave any more. I applied for an apprenticeship as a lawyer's assistant in Sonja's law firm – a job I couldn't imagine I'd ever like – just to do what Dad asked of me. He resumed maintenance payment. As I earned a bit of money as a trainee, he reduced the amount he paid me. Law and order – rules and punishments as a profession – had never interested me, but I was simply so happy in Munich and with the girls there that I had to hold on to that with the first apprenticeship that I could get.

The only thing spoiling my happiness was Sonja increasingly checking up on me and my whereabouts. Her obsession about tourists from the north and the places they went to turned into a real strain. Also, I couldn't stand the phrase 'Goran contamination' any more.

September 1997

"WHERVYUBIN?" I HEARD a voice from somewhere in the corridor. *What?*

I was fiddling with the lock of my door, narrowing my eyes to try and focus. My key just didn't want to slip into the lock; I kept hitting the woodwork of the door with it. Lydia, Helen, Rebecca and Jessica were probably trying to get into their rooms, too.

We'd come back from the Oktoberfest, which had started on that day. Yep, it had only just started, and I had gone there… along with tourists from all over the world!

"Whervyubin?" Sheesh, it was so loud, so shrill, it almost blew my head off.

I couldn't work out for certain what I was being asked. Because I was pissed. Lydia, Helen, Rebecca, Jessica and me – all five of us were bloody well pissed.

Since my night in hospital with alcohol poisoning, I hadn't drunk any whisky, vodka or Bacardi, and not a single drop of tequila. Just a whiff of the stuff would have made me vomit. I carried on drinking beer, though, because everybody else did. I'd only had two, but a standard glass of beer (the Bavarian Mass) at Munich's annual Oktoberfest was one litre. And some beers were brewed extra strong. Too strong for a normally teetotal flower like me.

Was it Sonja speaking to me now, asking me, *Where have you been?* Was there even a tone of reproach in her voice? It was true I had eventually done something against her rules.

"Sonja, I was… was… I was atthOktoberfest with Lydia, and Heln, and Rebecca, 'n' Jess… Jessica. Theryugo, I didit. 'N' now, I'm goingtosleep, g'night," I mumbled.

"Why did you do that? You *know* I have a problem with it!" she screamed.

God, my ears, my brain – all my senses quivered. And maybe those of the other girls on the corridor, too. I turned and faced her, holding on to the door frame.

"Thersnoproblem. I've just done what everybodyinMunich does atthistime. I'm not dirty now, Lydia 'nd the others aren't dirty. Yuvnever had a problem with them meeting tourists, now I'm just thesame asthem. Fullstop."

"Eww… ffff, you stink of beer when you speak." She waved her hand in front of her nose.

"Sowhat? Yushould go 'n' smell Jess… ica. Sheedabout *four* Mass!"

I went back to searching for my lock, and finally the key

went in. I slipped into my room but couldn't shut the door. Sonja had her foot in it.

"Whatthef… aryudoin? You freak'n' me out, Sonja! You damnfreak'n' me out. Stopit! I'm just livin'mylife. Acceptit or I'll have to——"

The door shifted. I'd pushed it against Sonja's foot, but she removed it. Bang – the door was shut, with Sonja outside.

I fell onto my bed. I couldn't even remember what I'd wanted to say, but it felt like a warning was still hovering inside my head. A warning to her. About her. About her restrictions on me.

*   *   *

AFTER SLEEPING OFF my two Mass, I knocked on Sonja's door and stepped into her room. No response; she ignored me. I closed the door – from the outside!

When later I bumped into her on my way to the toilets, she didn't acknowledge me either. As if I was made of air. I tried to see the positives in this. Not having to face another discussion about this and that and this and that, and Goran contamination here and there, and blah-blah-blah, was a good thing. I was so tired of it.

Back in my room, I brushed my teeth. A hint of bitter alcohol still lingered on my tongue. I ate breakfast and then rolled back into bed, chilling out, watching TV, and enjoying my day off before another week at the law firm.

Five minutes later, somebody knocked on my door. I reckoned it would be Sonja, ready to give me another round of Goran-contamination discussion, looking at me with either sad-dog eyes or I-can't-deal-with-you-any-more ones.

"Come in," I sighed, and my door opened.

"Hey, Finja, how's it going? Are you coming out with us?" Jessica asked, a huge smile stretching over her face.

Oops, I hadn't expected *her*.

"Err, out where?" I asked.

"To the Oktoberfest of course!" Her eyes flashed.

She occupied most of my doorway. She was a solid girl. Her smile definitely pleased me. Her whole body language did.

And then Rebecca joined her. "If *you* don't come, I'm not going either."

My God, I was wanted! Jessica and Rebecca flattered me.

"Why not?" I said. "Yeah, yeah, I'll come with you again."

"Cool! We're setting off in half an hour. Meet us in the living room," Jessica said.

Goodness-beer-gracious-me, it was only 10am!

*　*　*

I WAS LYING on my bed, thinking. It was Thursday night, and I hadn't spoken to Sonja since the previous Friday. Nor had she spoken to me. It was an unprecedented situation. Whenever I'd seen her in the corridor, she'd not only refused to meet my eyes but pretended not to sense me at all. It was the same at work. There at least it was easier to forget about it, because we weren't on the same floor. But we usually set off in the morning together. Not for the last four days.

The whole thing bothered me. I knew I'd been the cause of it. I'd ignored her rules, her needs. Maybe it was legitimate that she punished me. I left my bed, went to her room, and knocked on the door. She answered. As soon as she saw it was me, she turned away.

"Sonja, can we talk? Please?"

No response. She was sat at the desk, eyes fixed on a sheet of paper, fingers scribbling.

"Hey, *please*, speak with me. I know you're angry. I'm sorry. I'd like to talk about it," I said.

No reaction.

A wave suddenly broke over me, over my head, my heart, flooding me with rage. "Okay, you're angry, I accept that. But what I do not like is that you keep ignoring me. Even when I say I'm sorry," I said.

This should have been so familiar to her. It should have *alerted* her. Rang all the bells in the world, pulled the emergency breaks. But it didn't.

I had to shake her mind, rattle her, rub her nose into what she was doing to me. "You know who you remind me of?"

Now her head turned in my direction.

"Yes, Sonja, indeed: you act like your father! And let me be clear: I will *not* kneel down before you and beg you to speak to me again!"

I left her room, marched back to mine and banged my door behind me. One minute later, Sonja stood in my room.

"I don't want to take after my father!" she said, almost panicking.

"Well, you just behaved like him."

"Sorry I ignored you. Sorry! Sorry! Please, I'm really sorry." She paced up and down, hands frantically fiddling with her hair.

"Okay, it's all right. Sit down now," I said.

She flopped down onto my bed. "You know, I see why you enjoy this drunkenness, the euphoria at the Oktoberfest. You love to party with the others. With me, you don't get that. But remember this: how long have we known each other? How long have *we* been friends, and how solid has our friendship been? One day, the life in this house with all these girls will be over! They'll finish their education and move out and on from here. Then it's bye-bye! How many of them will stick with you? Who will still be your friend after all this?"

A prickly shower of goosebumps mounted up my shoulder blades. My neck. My scalp. She'd got me. I understood what she said. Her point – her warning. She was right. The others would all go their separate ways. None of them would remain my friend; would still want me. Sonja was the only true one. She was like a guarantee. A life insurance. Total safety. That was what she was talking about: loyalty.

"Okay, I won't go to the Oktoberfest any more. Promise."

THE ORDINARY FACE

SONJA ALLOWED ME to carry on going to discos – but only as long as they weren't in a tourist area. I stopped drinking. I didn't like it anyway. But I loved the dancing. One of the girls, Antje, had said my dancing was so sexy. My dancing, sexy? Me, sexy? Ha!

I'd never had anything to do with sexiness. My primary school plan of chopping off my breasts once they'd grown obviously hadn't come to fruition. I'd definitely got tits by now. Still, I wouldn't have liked to put my tongue to my teeth, had I had to speak English with its 'th'. Good God, I had no need to.

Now, I was being told my dancing was sexy. I liked that a lot. I'd become much more girly. A bigger make-up set sat on the shelf above my sink. Short skirts hung in my wardrobe. The tops I wore were tighter than ever before. I was okay that they enhanced what I carried inside my bra. And my trousers hugged my bum and thighs. I now *wanted* to be girly. And why not sexy? Hopefully more people would find my dancing sexy. *Boys, please!*

On a night in November 1997, I'd been on the dance floor for three hours already, when one boy attracted my attention. Every time I looked over, he smiled at me. I normally didn't dance with guys; only by myself or with Antje. But this guy had me glued to him. His brown hair, his dark-cherry eyes, his straight white teeth, and his six-pack showing through his skinny, sweaty T-shirt, were simply too enticing. My goodness, was he handsome. So very handsome. He pushed through the crowd and stood right in front of me. I let him dance with me. I let him touch my hands, playfully flick my hair. I let him dance around my body, grab my arms, make me move around his body until we were entangled and gliding like the spaghetti I had stirred in the boiling water some hours before going out. And it was then, when I sensed a tingle in my tummy I hadn't known could exist.

At 5am, I gave Florian my phone number and left with the group of girls. The first Underground train would leave soon, and we decided to head home.

Less than twelve hours later, I got a call.

"Hello?" I said.

"Hey, Finja! It's me, Florian."

The tingling in my tummy was back. "Hey," I said.

First, I was so nervous. And then, I was *very* nervous. My whole body felt like melting butter. Marina always used something to help in her own nerve-racking situations: she sipped from a little bottle of sparkling wine she kept especially for the minutes leading up to when she called her Markus. She'd told me it worked wonders. But I didn't have that kind of potion handy and had to go through the conversation totally sober.

Florian invited me to a party at his friend's house on the following Friday. I couldn't believe it. I just didn't understand why such a good-looking man as him would ask me to go to a party with him. To go *anywhere*!

Suddenly, my door flew open. My brother marched in, hands on his hips.

"What on earth are you doing here?" I whispered.

He didn't speak properly. He only moved his lips without making a sound. But I was able to read them. *You? You only have an ordinary face!*

My brother in my room, in Munich? That was *impossible*.

"Sorry, what did you say?" Florian asked, still on the phone. "Are you coming?"

"Err, err, um… " I stuttered. "Um, yes, okay then. I'm coming. Looking forward to it."

My hallucination passed.

In reality, I was very shy about meeting Florian. I'd never touched a man before. Not even with the tip of a finger. Okay, at dancing school back in Gadburg, yes. But not in that way – the real one. And why was Florian interested in me anyway? I didn't understand how he could possibly be attracted to an ordinary-faced stupid cow. Why not one of the other girls from our group? There had been plenty.

* * *

AND THEN, IT was Friday. I was about to get ready for the party, standing at the sink in my room, staring into the mirror.

Mirror, mirror on the wall, who has the fairest ordinary face of them all?

No response. Not from the mirror. Not from the reflection in it. I just shrugged.

I brushed my long blonde hair, put some spray in, highlighted my eyes with some colour and put a touch of lipstick on my lips. Done.

Florian was twenty-three years old and had his own car. He lived just outside Munich and picked me up at the train station where we'd agreed to meet. He greeted me with a quick kiss on my lips and then another on my right cheek. It was overwhelming. I was aware, though, that it would be really naive to expect him to greet me with a handshake. But still, I didn't know how to respond to his sweet kisses. Fortunately, he didn't wait for me to do so as he guided me around his car to the passenger door. He opened it and I slipped inside. What a gentleman he was. I was charmed.

After some minutes of driving, we parked next to a big detached house. I heard loud music even when I opened the passenger door by a small margin. I'd never been to a party at somebody's house. Never.

When we walked in, I saw lots of young men and women, and assumed they were Florian's fellow students. I didn't know anyone. Although Florian introduced me to some people, I knew I was the stranger at the party. Everybody else was slightly older than me, and they all spoke with strong Bavarian accents. I would have a tough time understanding them.

The music was good. Florian danced with me. I was aware of the others watching all the time, and I loved it. It made all my tingles even stronger.

When I was sat on a sofa, taking a rest, Florian came from the kitchen with some drinks. I'd asked for a soft drink, and so he brought lemonade. He sat next to me, smiling. God, was he *handsome*! His chest hair was slightly exposed by the undone top button of his white shirt. I only had two gulps of my lemonade before he lifted it out of my hand and put it on the floor. I didn't complain, and he turned to face me fully. Looking at me. Into my eyes. My ordinary face! My heart was beating so fast, because I knew it was going to be *the* moment. The moment I couldn't avoid any more.

I'd been dancing non-stop, attempting not to get into this situation. But now I was sitting on the sofa, with his eyes on me. God, it was going to happen. My back slid further and further down the sofa, trying to move away from him. But no, I was trapped. His hand stroked my hair, before holding my neck. I remembered Mum's warning about the first time. She'd said people sometimes hit their teeth together instead of their lips. I was afraid of that.

I'd moved all the way down the sofa when Florian pressed his lips to mine. He held them tenderly with his teeth, putting his tongue a little way into my mouth and then asking for mine. I was dizzy, as if I was riding a carousel. Without drinking alcohol! Spinning. And then I copied everything Florian did. Nibbling his lips. Asking for his tongue. All without hitting teeth. I loved it. I hoped it would last forever, including all those tingles.

* * *

THE NEXT DAY, butterflies fluttered inside my tummy. I was back in my room in the girls' house, floating on cloud nine, as I picked up the phone to call Mum. I had to tell her I had a boyfriend.

"Ah, at last," she said.

Um, *at last*? Did I hear relief?

Well, whatever, I just had to call Grandma too and break my news to her.

"Grandma, guess what – I'm in love! I've got a boyfriend!"

"You? In love? I thought you'd not even look at a man. Does that mean you're not a lesbian?"

What?! What was Grandma talking about? Had I given the impression I was a lesbian? How? Was it my ordinary face? And who was I supposed to be with? Sonja?

I fumbled with my hair, eyes darting left and right, searching for what to say. I hated to be thought of in that way.

"Grandma, I'm in love with a man, all right?"

"Oh, my poppet, I'm so relieved," she said.

SHATTERED

FLORIAN AND I rarely met up during the week since he lived outside the city. As a result, going out at the weekends to a disco was even more exciting. I couldn't wait to see him. He loved my dancing, and I loved his kissing. We hadn't slept with each other, though. I was hesitant, and he said it was okay.

Sonja knew about Florian but hadn't met him. I never brought him back to the house; I was kind of keeping him and Sonja in separate worlds. Sonja also had two worlds – the good, clean world and the bad, dirty one. I loved diving into my Florian-world without her, and the 11pm no-more-boys rule came in handy.

In early December, as Christmas was beckoning, Sonja wanted to know my plans. For her, Christmas wasn't beckoning, it was *threatening*: I might want to go up to northern Germany!

"Are you going to celebrate Christmas with Florian?" she asked.

I didn't know. We hadn't been together for very long, nor talked about it, but the idea made me feel extremely light. Like a feather carried by the wind. Daydreams flashed through my mind about Florian's parents feeling sorry for a nice Prussian girl like me, all alone at Christmas in Munich. Sonja could go by herself to Mrs Lange & Co. this year – I definitely wanted to be with Florian's parents and sister.

"Yeah, I'd say so. Will it be okay for you?" I answered.

I knew it was, because otherwise I'd have told her I didn't want to repeat last year's Christmas.

"Sure!" she said. "But just to be clear: I'm not preparing anything for going to Gadburg, then?"

She meant mentally preparing, as well as putting together a plastic bag with clothes and shower gel for her door handle. I got the underlying warning between her words: I mustn't change my mind once she'd rested hers on staying in Munich. I wouldn't; I just wanted to keep flying like a feather in the wind.

It was only Tuesday. I couldn't wait until the weekend when I'd see Florian again. I'd carefully ask him about Christmas. Put the feelers out. However, there was no asking. Because I didn't even see him. He dumped me.

He didn't call any more. When I tried all Saturday to reach him, nobody picked up for a very long time until, eventually, his father did. As soon as I heard Florian's voice, I knew something was wrong. He didn't say much, only that he wasn't ready for a relationship. A brief apology followed, with a hint of bad conscience. Apologising and bad conscience didn't help me, though. I was devastated. No word was suitable to describe my sudden sorrow.

Still holding my phone to my ear, listening to the stillness at the other end, hoping and waiting for a turnaround, I watched my heart shatter as one million little pieces burst out of my chest, cascading down onto the edge of my bed and splashing over the beige floor. I couldn't believe, nor understand, what was happening. I just didn't get what had changed my Florian's mind. Why did he not feel ready for a relationship with me? Why did he mention a former girlfriend being in the way? Why had he taken me out, kissed and danced with me? Was it maybe my ordinary face after all? Or me not having slept with him yet?

I didn't get it. All I got was that I was in love with him. I couldn't see the problem that had, allegedly, hidden something from him.

Once he'd hung up, I dropped the phone handset back onto its cradle and threw myself onto my bed. I stayed there until my head felt swollen from crying.

* * *

I WOULDN'T HAVE believed before then, had anyone told me, that it was possible to be thinking of a boyfriend – well, *ex*-boyfriend – for literally every single minute of a day. When I didn't answer her knocks on my door, Marina had to come into my room. I hadn't heard her; my wailing was too loud. Everybody on the corridor could probably hear it, and Marina had decided to try and calm me somehow. Her attempts – "He doesn't deserve you" and "You'll find another man who's even nicer than him" – didn't work. I guess she was copying what her parents had told her when she and Markus had broken up. Surely she knew she was talking nonsense now. I only wanted Florian. Him or nobody. But I got that Marina was simply trying to help, and I appreciated it.

Only time would heal my wounds. But the days were bumpy. It was hard to pull myself together and not think non-stop of Florian. Particularly at work, I struggled to complete my tasks. I became fed up with the silliest ones that required me to haul court-file pile after court-file pile from the conference room to a lawyer's office. Each time the lawyers had only just got up from their seats after a meeting had finished; they were too important and snobby to carry their files themselves. I quit the law firm; it wasn't the right thing for me anyway.

And there I was, shattered. It was December 1997 – a year and a half since my Abitur – and Dad was once again unhappy with me, heartbroken and with no idea of what I should become. Sonja held me to my word of not going to Gadburg for Christmas. I tried harder not to burst into tears at Mrs Lange & Co.'s this time.

RICH

I'D BEEN OUT all day, not long after Florian had dumped me, browsing through endless information on fields of study and apprenticeships. Now back in my room, I was unpacking my food shopping and listening to music when somebody knocked on my door. Then Jessica stood in my doorway.

"Your mum called earlier," she said.

I arched an eyebrow; it was strange that Mum had called the house phone, given I had my own line. True, I'd been out. So was there something urgent? Indeed there was, only I didn't know it yet: I had inherited half a house. Overnight. Out of the blue!

"Aha? And what did she want?" I asked.

"She tried calling your line but you were out," Jessica said.

"Yes. And?"

"She called the floor's phone because she isn't at home herself tonight. So she can't call you again until tomorrow."

So? I was waiting for the point. Why call the floor?

"Right. And?" I asked.

"Well," Jessica said, noticeably hesitating, "there's some news for you. It's actually pretty bad. But your mum said you won't be too affected. And she wanted you to learn it today rather than tomorrow, so she's asked me to tell you."

"So what is it then?" I almost stamped my foot.

"Um, your step-grandmother has died during the night."

"*What?* Bertha is dead?"

"Yes. Sorry. But I didn't think you'd be shocked, 'cause your mum insisted you wouldn't be."

I was speechless. Because, yes, I was shocked!

"She said you'd be fine, because you didn't really love your step-grandmother."

I could see Jessica needed an explanation about my reaction. I had no true explanation myself, because I had *not* loved Bertha. But, still, I was shocked to hear of her death. I couldn't deny it.

Step-Grandmother had died from a sudden heart attack. There'd been no warning; she'd just collapsed in the middle of the night, having gone to the bathroom. She died instantly. Maybe that was why I was more startled than Mum had expected. Bertha had only been in her mid sixties.

Her death made me a rich girl. Just like that. Not within the next few days, but within some months: the house she'd lived in had already been mine and my brother's while she was still alive. I hadn't known that until she died. Nor had my brother. Dad had made a deal with Bertha, many years before, that she could stay and live in the house until she died without paying any rent to him, after she and he had jointly inherited it from Grandad Ernst. In return for her paying no rent, the ownership of the house had been transferred to my brother and me when we were toddlers.

Mum explained all these details to me the next day. Quite a lot of things to learn. And then, I couldn't stop thinking about how Jessica had introduced the whole story: *There's some news for you. It's actually pretty bad.* Wasn't it *good* news? Wasn't it excellent, brilliant, fantastic news that I owned half a house? That I was bloody rich?

God, I tried to stop it. That thought. That awful thought! How did I dare to think so materialistically?! I should have been sad. Sad for Step-Grandmother, and for poor Bernd, her long-term boyfriend she'd recently got back together with. I forced myself to imagine the dramatic scenes of the previous night, when Bertha gave her last gasp and Bernd bent over her, crying. I even managed to feel sorry for him. But as hard as I tried, I couldn't feel sorry for myself, now the owner of half a house. I rather considered myself lucky, as if I'd won the lottery. Was that allowed? Was I allowed not to be sad that Step-Grandmother had gone? And how did my brother feel about everything? I couldn't imagine him grieving at all. But, surely, we weren't the first to be happy about getting some money rather than mourning the person who'd died?

Had anybody claimed I was *happy* that Step-Grandmother was dead, they would have been wrong. I wasn't happy about her death. But I wasn't sad either.

* * *

As SOON AS I had told Sonja about Bertha's death and my inheritance, she only had one question on her mind.

"Isn't it possible to manage it remotely?"

She didn't want me to travel up north to receive my half of the house, and asked me to see a notary in Munich who could help with providing my signature. The process would take weeks anyway; months. A buyer for the house had to be found first, and it took long enough for me to put it all to one side. Part of this *all* was something I didn't realise was even there: the possible duty of showing thankfulness. Thanking someone for my half didn't occur to me. Why?

Perhaps because it didn't appear that there was one particular person to say thank you to.

Whom should I have thanked? Dad, for arranging, when I was very young, for half the house to be mine and missing out on it himself? Maybe. Probably. Or his dad and his real mum for working hard and building the house in the first place? Maybe. Probably. Or Bertha for dying so suddenly and relatively young? Maybe? Probably?

At no point did I realise I should have been particularly grateful or to whom. I simply took the inheritance, regarding it as something that was just happening to me. I failed to make any gesture of appreciation that Dad might have liked to see. I didn't have a clue that this would come back to haunt me years later.

Absurdly Contaminated Sweets and Volkswagens

By February 1998, I wanted to start training as a lab technician in chemistry. I would have preferred biology, but there was no such school in the Munich area. And I was bound to it.

When I spoke to Dad about my plans I could tell he was happy. The chemistry school was a private one with an excellent reputation. Its reins were tight. Anybody coming from it, with average results on their certificate, didn't need to search long for a job.

The monthly fee amounted to six hundred Deutschmarks. The Bavarian state paid a grant of DM 110, but DM 490 was still a lot of money. Dad surprised me when he agreed to pay it. He really must have been desperate to see me in training.

Of course, Sonja joined me. She too left the law firm. I suppressed the unsettling doubt that I wanted to be with her day in, day out. It was good that we could help each other with our studies; they wouldn't be easy!

School was never out before 5pm and, sometimes, there were three exams per week. We cycled for forty minutes across Munich every morning, from the north to the south. We'd each bought a bike for 199 Deutschmarks, and perhaps these were partly at fault for making the daily journey so hard. Only on very soggy days did we take the Underground. Public transport wasn't cheap, and maybe I'd learned from Dad how to be tight. I mean, he even used to return his strip of dental floss to its dispenser and reuse it over the next couple of days.

Most evenings, we popped into a supermarket after school. Sonja avoided all jars of honey, and all other products made near the Gadburg area. Further, she now attempted to avoid *anything* that came from outside the south. Things from Berlin weren't okay any more. She'd overheard, one day in the distant past, that Goran had a cousin there. The same was true for Bonn, a city on the other side of the country. Sonja had never paid attention to such details about other people; only Goran. Haribo, a trademark product from Bonn (the name being an acronym of Hans Riegel Bonn), was now regarded as highly contaminated. In nearly every supermarket in Germany, Haribo's Gold-Bears, Happy Cola bottles and liquorice wheels flood the shelves.

Sonja also didn't want me to buy the non-Haribo chocolates next to the Bonn products. No matter how much I fancied them. Even if they had been made in southern Germany, or outside the country! Instead, she showed me other sweets. Told me how nice and yummy they were. Told me how much *safer* they were, until I forgot she had a mental illness. Her mouthing 'safety' worked like a silencer. A dummy. An Imaginary Comfort Bubble that I'd long grown out of. And, of course, I liked safety. Everybody does. It had even been a theme in my dreams, like the one in which Sonja told me to remove my AIDS-infected green jacket to create safety, as I was attempting to save Dad from the prostitutes ensnaring him.

Choosing a till at the supermarket was the most difficult part of shopping. Sonja needed to glance into the trolley of the last person in each queue, to make sure they had no Haribos, jars of honey or other forbidden products amongst their items. We sometimes waited fifteen minutes until she was able to approach a till. And if the customer behind us then put a Haribo bag on the conveyer belt that threatened to touch one of our items, she'd gather all our stuff back up again, pull me away and push past the queuing people: "Excuse us, we have forgotten something!" We would do another round of the supermarket, pretend to get the forgotten thing so as to avoid looking stupid, and then try again to find a queue with no contaminated products. And still we ended up, often enough, with a forbidden product closing in towards our clean items in the packing area. Sonja would race against time, stuffing our shopping bags.

At the house, I regularly lied when someone offered me Haribos in the common living room. Yeah, the girls *loved* them. So did I. It was hard to refuse, and even harder to offer a plausible explanation as to why I never wanted any. *No thanks, I'm full. Thank you, but I just had a big chocolate bar in my room. Oh, that's very kind, but these very sweet Haribos really hurt my teeth, I can't eat them.* One day, the girls wouldn't offer me anything any more.

Sonja said these lies were white lies, and totally necessary. Necessary for our image and reputation; for our place in society. She didn't want to be disliked, and admitting to a mental illness could be risky.

One of the most energy-sapping efforts I had to make for Sonja was avoiding Volkswagen cars. Either the northern German VW headquarters itself or one of its suppliers – spread over nearby places – must have employed at least one of Goran's relatives. That was Sonja's logic. The likelihood was obvious: VW is huge, and there was a person in *her* family who worked for the auto group. And that one Goran-relative had contaminated *all* Volkswagen cars in the entire world, even if he or she did not actually exist.

Despite Bavaria being the home of BMW and Audi, there were thousands and thousands of Volkswagens being driven around Munich. Of course, a moving car was easily avoided. But what about all those parked by the sides of the roads? It felt an impossible task to permanently watch out for the make of each car while walking on a pavement or crossing a road.

We were both twenty-one years old. Sonja had started avoiding Goran at fourteen. We'd left our first high school to leave him behind, then the Gadburg area with Fessdorf and Dabendorf. We were now living very far away and she hadn't seen him for ages, and yet he was omnipresent. I didn't even know for sure any more what her real problem was with him. Was she seriously still worried he could give her AIDS over a distance of hundreds of kilometres? That was hard to believe. There were people in Munich who were much more likely to have AIDS than Goran. But they didn't matter. Sonja stuck to her irrational rules and passed them on to me. My world became smaller and smaller. I too was wearing a corset. And Sonja laced it tighter and tighter, taking my freedom away. She constructed a prison for herself and drew me into it along with her.

WHEN SONJA
SURPRISED ME

Three Weeks Later

IT WAS FRIDAY, and I was happy the week was over. My two exams had gone well, but I'd had to work hard for them. My arms were overloaded with food shopping that needed to be put into the fridge in the common kitchen. I stood outside my door and pulled its handle with my elbow. Closed. I glanced across the corridor at Sonja's door and spotted a stuffed plastic bag right in front of it. It seemed rather like a big rubbish bag. Was she sorting out some old clothes? I wasn't convinced, because she didn't have anything old.

In the next moment, I heard the door to our wing open. "Lucas?" I said.

Lucas in Munich? My God, I'd 'seen' my arrogant brother walk into my room when I was on the phone with Florian; I knew I'd hallucinated before. But this was real, no need to pinch myself!

Lucas came closer, grinning all over his face. He said nothing. But was he aware he was walking down the corridor of the girls' house? The bloody girls' house in the bloody clean Munich-world, when he was Sonja's former flatmate and belonged to the bloody dirty northern-Germany-world?! Did he realise what he was doing? That he was about to contaminate everything?

Where was Sonja? She hadn't seen him marching down our corridor, getting closer and closer to her room.

"Lucas, please stop!" I said, trying to prevent what was left to prevent.

He did stop. But he was still grinning. He appeared so happy. And I was so nervous about Sonja coming out of her room and bumping into him.

"Shhh, don't panic, don't worry." He put a finger to his lips. "But—"

"All is fine, I know what I have to do," he said.

What? He knew what to do? From Sonja? What did she know that I didn't? And then I watched Lucas as he walked all the way to her door, picked up that big rubbish bag, and headed back down the other end. He disappeared in the bathroom. I heard the door lock being turned.

My arms were still wrapped around my food shopping as I listened to what was happening. I moved closer to the bathroom door, wanted to be sure that not only had my eyes not deceived me about Lucas, but neither were my ears now: I heard the shower running. Yes, I was hearing correctly – he was taking a shower before doing anything else. He was going through a transformation!

I rushed into the kitchen, shoved my shopping into my compartment of the fridge and dashed back to knock on Sonja's door.

"Lucas is here! And he's in the bathroom having a shower right now! Sonja!" I was shaking.

"Oh, already?" She was sat at her desk, grinning at me in the same way Lucas had. Like a Cheshire cat.

"What? You knew about this?" I asked.

She nodded. "I just expected him in maybe an hour or so."

She had *expected* him!

"So come on then, explain this to me. Isn't he making everything here dirty now?" I said.

"Um, no, he isn't." Her voice was calm. It was confirmation that there was no drama.

She told me Lucas would wash himself from top to toe and then put on some Munich clothes she'd bought for him. They were in that plastic rubbish bag she'd placed in front of her door; along with shower gel, a towel and brand-new shoes. He was supposed to strip off his contaminated northern-Germany clothes and 'seal' them in the plastic bag, and not get them out or touch them until he returned home.

My eyes checked out what Sonja pointed at in her room. She'd bought more stuff for Lucas: a jacket, pyjamas, more clothes and a kit to store and clean his contact lenses.

"So much preparation – you've got him a whole wardrobe," I said.

My blood was rushing through my body. I was undecided whether to be outraged that she hadn't told me earlier or relieved that she had established a new tie with northern Germany – even our home town – that might lift some rules and loosen my corset.

Before Sonja could say something, I already spoke again. "And why is he here at all?"

"Um, well… "

Suddenly, it dawned on me. "No shit – you guys are together?"

Sonja nodded, still with that happy grin on her face, and finally I realised it was an I-am-in-love grin.

Boom! I was shocked. Surprised. Stunned. Astonished. All sorts of things. Oh, and outraged: she was my friend, even claimed to be my only *true* one, but she hadn't told me about this.

"Yes, I think we're really together now," she said.

I'd have expected a lot of surprises from Sonja, but not that she and Lucas would be a couple. The two had been friends for a while, but I had always thought that was it. Nothing more. Particularly because of the OCD. I'd thought it would have been impossible for her to find a boyfriend – somebody who'd love her despite her condition. But now there was somebody who didn't mind; who wanted to take it on. Wasn't that true love? And wasn't that also a sign that Sonja, despite the OCD, was a lovable person – something her father had denied? I remembered him saying that she would need to change herself if she wanted to find a man – that sheet of paper; the arrows on it; the glow-worm in the centre; Sonja's flaws; *just* flaws! But now he was proven wrong: Lucas was there.

I was happy for her. I really was. I hoped their love would relax her corset, and mine. It did seem odd, though, that she'd chosen a man from Goran-contaminated Gadburg. She didn't make her life easy, did she? A guy from Munich would have. She could have gone out with me and the girls, maybe found one then. However, wasn't that a sign that this was true love for her as well?

"So is he washing himself like we did? What does he have to do with his eyes? And his mouth and nose?" I was still in her doorway.

"He doesn't need to wash them like we did. I explained everything else, and he's happy to soap and rinse himself three times."

212

No soapy froth sucked up his nose? No horrible gargling? No retching? No slimy threads in Lucas's eyes tomorrow? So, yeah, she truly loved him. But why had I had to suffer it all? She also loved *me*! I was still shaking. And confused.

"And why haven't you told me? How did you get together? When?" I asked.

"Kind of on the phone over the past few weeks. He told me he'd fallen in love with me at the silver wedding party. But I hadn't declared us a couple. I wasn't sure myself. I even told him I couldn't have him as a boyfriend because he's from Gadburg. But he kept phoning. And wanted to see me again. He said he'd keep trying; wooing me. Until he'd have me."

The evidence: it *was* true love for him.

"But why did you not tell me about that, then, at least?" I asked.

She didn't answer; seemed not to know. I was astonished that she'd managed to keep their affair secret from me, whether it was deliberate or not. I thought I knew *everything* about her. Did I really?

"So have you already slept with him? Up in Gadburg?"

Sonja didn't get time to respond; Lucas emerged from the bathroom. He was wearing different clothes, and his hair was wet. He carried the plastic rubbish bag in one hand. I saw the matching smiles on their faces and understood: it was time for me to go. Their embrace would be passionate.

My question remained unanswered. I could only go back into my room and close the door. If they hadn't slept with each other yet, they surely would now. The two lovebirds weren't likely to play Ludo on Sonja's bed, first thing. They'd play a different game.

WHEN DAD
BECAME REALLY
UNREASONABLE

March 2000

HONESTLY, HE'D ALWAYS been unreasonable. But only now did I start disliking him for it. Before then, it had always been the same thing: no matter what Dad did, I loved him.

Previously, in September 1998, he had surprised me with the news that I had to pay the monthly 490-Deutschmark fee for the remaining one and a half years of my chemistry school myself. The house that Bertha used to live in had been sold, and 149,000 Deutschmarks had hit my bank account. I was actually rich.

I'd accepted that Dad made me use my inheritance without complaint. I frankly don't remember complaining to him, or about him, at *any* time before March 2000. I always assumed that Dad was right, even when he was wrong. It's hard to say why – his aura, his intelligence, his life experience, maybe. I didn't discuss or doubt him. Never!

I had received my certificate from the chemistry school in February, with the fabulous score of 1.9, and was proud of being able to call myself a *Lab Technician in Biochemistry*. Now that it was March, Dad felt I was able to start working straight away – just a couple of weeks after graduating from the school. He stopped paying me the monthly DM 972.34. However, I wasn't ready to start a job straight away. I wanted a break. A nice and unique break which I could only take at that point: between finishing training and starting a full-time job.

Back in January, I'd done some research. And recently, I'd put together a backpacker's itinerary. I'd bought a so-called Junior Round-the-World flight ticket for three thousand Deutschmarks, and booked seats from Frankfurt to Sydney, Sydney to Auckland, Auckland to Los Angeles, Phoenix to London, and London to Frankfurt. Mum and Dad knew about my plan. Sonja and Lucas did, too. Apart from a few cheap motels, I was going to stay in hostels or camp out. I'd asked my parents if they could help me out with a little issue: I hadn't foreseen my desire to go on a world trip before freezing the biggest share of my house money until the end of 2000 at my bank; they'd offered me a special deal with higher interest if I didn't touch it all. My parents had agreed to lend me three thousand Deutschmarks. In fact, Mum was very relaxed about it; it was Dad who needed to be convinced. I was almost certain I wouldn't need to use any of it – it was meant as an additional emergency fund – given how modestly I had learned to live. I planned on giving it back to them at the end of the year, as soon as my frozen money became available.

Sonja and Lucas had been in my room, witnessing everything as I'd talked to Dad on the phone about the three thousand Deutschmarks. Now that my flight from Frankfurt to Sydney was just days away, I'd phoned him.

"I'd need the three thousand Marks in my bank account now, Dad."

"But I haven't agreed!"

I briefly thought I had some odd interference on the line. I couldn't believe what I had heard. "What?"

"I haven't agreed to loan you the three thousand." Dad's voice told me his mind was made up. Irreversibly. He was not going to help me out and lend me a single pfennig. What Mum was okay with, even *wanted* to happen, he blocked.

"What does that mean?" I still asked, although I knew.

"It means I'm not lending you any money."

"But you *did* agree!" All of a sudden, I wanted to use very impolite words.

"No, I didn't." His voice was so very calm and composed, it made the whole situation even worse. It drove me to distraction.

I was on my own in my room this time, and didn't think of rushing over to Sonja's to get her and prove I was right. Yes, it *was* me who was right this time. Dad said *yes* when I had asked him for the money, two months before. Didn't he remember that? I was convinced he did. He wasn't senile.

I was paralysed. Couldn't speak. I only listened to his relaxed breathing at the other end of the line. Then I came round. "So you're telling me you won't lend me the three thousand?"

"Correct." Same cool and unmoved voice. He said nothing more.

I was going mad! I felt like… like what?

I couldn't understand his reasoning. I couldn't see his point or problem. Why did he say he hadn't agreed when he had? Or did he really not remember? But it didn't matter which of the two things was true, because if I was really wrong, why not throw away the argument about whether or not he had agreed to the loan? Why did he not just do it regardless?

My parents definitely had enough money to be able to help me out. Easily. But Dad didn't want to, and I didn't know why – what he wanted to achieve. And then I knew how I felt: let down.

Dad was truly letting me down. I couldn't get it. All I could do was say goodbye and hang up the phone. An unprecedented fear crawled all over me: I'd always believed that Dad, as one of my parents, would help me out. Would *like* to help me out. Sure, he wasn't obliged to lend me money, but the shocking thing was that he easily could have done but didn't want to. He had lent other people money: my brother, when he wanted to buy computer stuff; my uncle (Mum's brother!), when his wife divorced him. Dad lent my uncle fifteen thousand Deutschmarks! But he didn't want to lend *me* anything. Why not? *Why bloody not?* What kind of dad was he, knowing that his twenty-three-year-old daughter would travel around the world on her own, while he wasn't happy to help make sure she was fine and had enough money for emergencies? Was he a good dad? Did he love me? Did he excuse his refusal to himself? *It's not my fault she wants to go travelling and hasn't got the money for it!*

No, it wasn't his fault. It was simply my wish to travel. And I did have the money for it. I just hadn't foreseen that I would want to travel when I accepted my bank's deal. And I would have booked a shorter trip if Dad hadn't said yes, thus providing myself with that damn three thousand Deutschmarks of emergency money.

I had no doubt that Dad was fully aware of what he was doing to me: making things difficult. He loved me *not*, he loved me *not*. Proved!

I thought of Sonja. She'd never really loved her father, and believed he didn't love her either. He'd given her too much of that hard-line treatment. Now I had received some from my dad. Without good reason. I would have even paid him interest on the three thousand, if he'd insisted on that condition. But he hadn't mentioned anything. He had just said no.

I was convinced. Finally. I was rock-solid sure now: the two were brothers. No doubt about it. I jumped up from my bed, my feet thrust into my house slippers like two javelins into the lawn. I had to tell Sonja! She needed to know the truth, and how I sympathised with her for not loving her father. She and I were sitting in the same boat. I wanted to tell her how very sorry I felt that she had such a tough father, and that he was actually my uncle. Well, half-uncle at least. She had to learn we were related. My dad's dad hadn't only been my grandfather, but also hers. And Bertha – my step-grandmother – had been her real grandmother, because Grandad Ernst cheated on his wife – Grandma Gerda – and got Bertha pregnant. The family secret!

I rushed to Sonja's room. During the seconds I was dashing down the corridor, thoughts were racing through my head. How surprised she would be to learn she'd had a granny but never really known her. A granny who'd fled the GDR and used to be a hooker!

My knuckles were ready to rap on Sonja's door, when my racing thoughts collided. *Bang! Pow! Crash!* I slammed on the anchors, could almost smell smoke from the heels of my house slippers on the plastic floor. I held my breath, grabbed my own arm to hold back my hand from knocking against Sonja's door. *Jesus!*

CLICKS

July 2014

IT'S 11.32PM. I'M still lying on my bed. Stretched out, arms folded under the back of my head. The DJ of the radio station I'm listening to has good taste. He just played a couple of my favourite songs. I play them on my phone sometimes. Wearing headphones. Music has always had the power to lift my mood.

I also listen to Sonja – if any noise comes from her room. It doesn't seem she's getting ready for bed just yet; it's a little too early. I'll hear *click, click, click*, and *click, click, click* – on, off, on, off… That's the starting gun. One of her light switches sits on the other side of my wall. Her wall. I'll be counting twenty-five, twenty-six, twenty-seven, twenty-eight clicks. Somewhere around then, she'll be convinced the light is off. She struggles with recognising the difference between bright and pitch dark. Once she knows the light is off, she only uses the one from her bathroom to see, leaving the door open to let it shine into the room.

Sometimes I'm unlucky and Sonja repeats the whole clicking routine two minutes later. To make sure the light switch won't jump back into the on position, she'll press it hard towards the off position. Too hard, maybe. She might

219

have broken it. As well as the cables in the wall and the entire electricity system. A short circuit will set this building on fire; the attached building too. And – good grief, worst-case scenario – all the unattached houses along the road will burn down to the ground. Sonja will be responsible for the damage and the casualties. She doesn't want that, so she makes sure.

How can it be so difficult to tell the difference between bright and dark?

THE POWER OF
MONEY

I WAS STILL in the corridor, right in front of Sonja's door, holding my wrist to prevent my hand from knocking.

God, don't, I told myself. *Don't tell her about the secret.*

If I told Sonja our fathers were half-brothers, and that she was Bertha's *real* grandchild, weren't my 149,000 Deutschmarks supposed to be *hers*?

I panicked. Engaged my reverse gear. Raced back into my room. Closed the door. Turned my key. Twice!

Phew... I leant with my back against the door, took a deep breath and closed my eyes. I had to think this over; to be sure about the consequences. Sonja might claim all my money, or maybe just half of it. I didn't have all 149,000 Deutschmarks any more. I'd spent over 8,500 on chemistry school. But still, what if she now wanted 74,500 Deutschmarks from me? Or half of what I had left?

Maybe she couldn't claim anything legally, because the house Bertha had lived in had been signed over to my brother and me. But even if Sonja wasn't able in legal terms, wasn't she entitled morally?

I reopened my eyes. My back slid down the door, legs folding against my chest, just before my bottom hit the floor. I felt bad – very bad – about not wanting to share my money with my best friend. My cousin. Was I like Dad? Was I tight with money and *loving* it? I didn't know. I only knew I felt bad.

Fear that I could take after Dad washed over me. It was oppressive. I definitely didn't want to be like him. At least not very much. I didn't want to be too tight with money or have his attitude about always being right. I threw myself onto my bed, thinking about money, sharing and not sharing, going travelling, and whether I should ask Sonja to join me on the trip. I remembered the times when my brother, as a boy, regularly went to Grandma's for a sleep over and cashed in a tenner for it. I also remembered how I told Grandma off when she offered me the same reward for staying with her; I wouldn't do it for money. Didn't that confirm I did *not* love money? Wasn't that right? I wasn't sure. Because I didn't always think what I thought was right. Not at all. My self-confidence was far too low.

I could have asked Lucas and Sonja to back me up about Dad agreeing to lend me the three thousand, but I discarded that idea. Instead, I felt pride. I couldn't allow Dad to control whether I came through any emergency situation that might occur on my trip. I couldn't give him whatever he got from doing this. And I wouldn't beg, kneel down to him, for the money.

I picked up my phone again. Dialled. My heart was bashing against the inside of my chest. Two rings and Dad picked up.

"I don't give a shit about it!" I blurted out.

"*Pardon?*" Dad almost yelled. I knew he'd understood me.

"I don't need your money anyway!" I was convinced I'd be fine on the trip. I just needed to be more careful.

"You know what, Finja? Let me tell you something: The money you got from Bertha's house is actually *my* inheritance! *Mine!* Do you damned well understand that?" he thundered.

I did. I got the message. Dad wanted me to feel I had something that was, in his eyes, not supposed to be mine, and that I hadn't realised that. He let me know he had missed out on 149,000 Deutschmarks, and I could tell he regretted it. I suppose he also told me – somewhere between these revelations – how ungrateful I was for what I had, and for him having arranged the deal when I was a toddler. *Guilt for me!*

I was rigid, only breathing into the phone, then managed to sit the handset back on its cradle. One inevitable question wouldn't leave me alone: why had he signed the house over at all?

I had no answer. All I knew was that Dad was a big boggly-eyed green monster. And it wasn't as if he didn't have a house himself. He lived in the other one that had been built and passed on to him by his parents – mortgage-free. He'd never had to pay rent for it. Nothing.

* * *

A FEW DAYS later, I was sat on a jumbo Jet bound for Sydney, with three thousand Deutschmarks for emergencies in my bank account. Mum had put it there, using her personal savings. I'd not asked Sonja to come with me. Lucas would have missed her too much anyway.

FASCINATED – AGAIN!

I STOOD IN the lift going up to the sixth floor. It filled up quickly with the scent of sun lotion that was still nestled into my skin. I had visited lots of American deserts and canyons, making my skin one or two shades darker. In Australia and New Zealand, it had been winter. I'd even walked through some snow on the Southern Island of beautiful Kiwi Land.

My backpack was next to me on the floor, leaning against my right leg. The other girl in the lift was lucky it was sealed – my clothes really needed to be washed. I had dumped old clothes and bought new ones twice during my trip: when going from the tropical north-east of Australia to the cold of southern New Zealand, and then flying from Auckland to the scorching heat of Southern California. My backpack didn't have space for all seasons at the same time.

I was resting against the wall, my back aching. My shoulders, too. I was tired. Tired from my trip around the world, but more so in anticipation of what would come towards me once I hit the sixth floor and exited the lift: Sonja and her rules.

True, she was my best friend, *cousin*, even, but I hadn't really missed her during those weeks away. Honestly, not one bit, which I only realised just now. *How odd!* So did I want to come back to my old life? Was I actually capable of doing so? I had experienced a ton of things while travelling; things that might prompt changes; advance me in life.

The lift came to a standstill. Fifth floor. The other girl got off. *Shall I, too? Shall I carry on up the stairs? Or maybe not up, but back down again? I could just disappear and live somewhere else in Munich. Away from Sonja.*

I stepped out of the lift, dragged my backpack after me. I stood next to the stairs. Which way? Up or down? I took a step down. And another one. I hauled my backpack onto my shoulders and took another couple of steps down. Then out of nowhere, she appeared, mounting the stairs: Sonja.

"Oh, here already?! Welcome back! Wow, you look so brown," she warbled, her smile stretching across her face like the Colorado River through the Grand Canyon. But my breath wasn't anywhere near to being taken away. I just said nothing as she came closer.

"Why are you on the fifth floor?" she asked.

I had a few seconds, milliseconds, to explain. *Excuse.* "I was going back downstairs to reception. There must be some mail in my box."

Sonja widened her arms. She was ready to embrace me and my backpack, overwhelming me. I placed my hands on her sides, feeling her ribs through her clothes. The energy-consuming OCD never let her grow much fat. I didn't care to ask what *she* had been doing on floor four. I knew she used other bathrooms in the house when she felt those on floor six were too Goran-contaminated from the transformations.

"I am *so* glad you're back, Finja! I missed you, you know that?" she said.

Her cheek was resting against mine. "You know that I love you, right?"

And her warmth streamed through my cheek, then flooding my entire body until I felt dizzy and dazed like on a drug.

Inside my room, I felt like a stranger. One, because my long trip had definitely changed me. I was so rich. Rich with experiences. And two, because most of 'my' girls had moved out during recent weeks – moved out and on, just as Sonja had once warned me they would. My girls – like me – had finished training. I hardly knew anybody here now. I'd lived in the girls' house for almost four years.

The majority of the girls on the sixth floor were now younger than me. It was sad to return and find no Jessica, Rebecca, Lydia or Marina any more. Jessica and Rebecca were living somewhere else in Munich, but Lydia and Marina had moved back to their home towns for work. Sonja was, obviously, still around, and so was Lucas on the day I arrived back from my trip. The two were still together. It had usually been him who came to Munich over the last two years. Sonja rarely went up north because of the transformations that required.

Getting used to being back in Munich took me some time. I needed fresh enthusiasm for a new start. It was time for me to move out from the girls' house, too!

* * *

WITHIN ONE MONTH, I'd found myself a job and a flat. I had three interviews and three job offers. I took the most interesting one in a research group, rather than those in analytic laboratories that mainly required me to put blood samples into fully automatic machines, press buttons and wait for all-ready results printed on pieces of paper.

Finding a flat was more difficult. I had to view and apply for *millions* to eventually snatch one. Available and affordable places in Munich were rare. It was no coincidence that Sonja and I rented a one-room apartment each in the same building. I rejected the idea of disappearing from her life forever, after it had struck me in the lift on the day of my return from my trip. She was, after all, my friend. My soulmate. *Family*. I felt obliged to her. I had the house money and had just spent quite a bit of it! I ignored the penetrating thought that I could be trapped; my own hostage, because I didn't want to share the money with her. It would be wasted; drained by a fictitious Goran contamination. Sonja would endlessly throw clothes away and buy new ones, in addition to whenever she went through a transformation. And who knew what other rules a lot of money would have enabled her to invent...

Sonja also found a job. In the same place as mine. Cousins do that – sticking together where they can. The only thing I made sure of was that we didn't live in the same flat. I did want us to be separated from each other. Just far enough.

My flat was on the first floor, Sonja's on the ground floor. The ninety-degree angle of the two-storey house allowed me to look down onto her cute little garden from my tiny balcony. The flats were exactly the same shape, just mirrored.

I bought furniture: a wood-look-alike table, two fine chairs, a good-quality double mattress, a slatted frame, a silvered wardrobe and a chest with three drawers. I missed out on a bed base to fit the slatted frame and mattress in, sticking to the basics. The mattress went directly onto the carpet. A sofa or armchair could come later. My washing machine was delivered and installed in my bathroom. I managed to assemble the chest of drawers, as well as my table. For the wardrobe I was fortunate to receive some help from a neighbour.

Sonja and I lived three kilometres away from our new work place. Cycling was the easiest way to get there. From September 2000 onwards, we rode every morning to our labs together.

For Lucas, seeing Sonja became complicated, because he couldn't use her new bathroom for the transformation. It would have become irreversibly contaminated. Unusable. In the girls' house, Sonja could always use a bathroom on a different floor. Not so in her own flat. Now Lucas's sister's home had to serve. Gabriele had lived in Munich for a while. She belonged to the contaminated people in and around the city, like the tourists from northern Germany. Sonja had felt uncomfortable when Gabriele and her fiancé moved to the clean world, but now they turned out to be the only solution to decontaminate Lucas before he came to stay with Sonja. He needed to pick up the prepared plastic bag that Sonja dropped outside our house, drive to his sister's, wash himself from top to toe and immediately leave wearing Munich clothes. He'd take the Underground to Sonja's and only get his car back from Gabriele's when he went to drive back home. Sonja was very fortunate that Gabriele had some knowledge of OCD and was able to understand this fuss.

* * *

RIGHT FROM THE start, I liked my new job. I settled quickly and got on well with my colleagues. Of all my briefs, I favoured cell culture. I was good at it and easily understood the technique of sterile procedures. Being entangled with Sonja had taught me well how to think in the don't-contaminate-anything way! She herself worked – and this was bizarre – with certain viruses and bacteria in her lab. Bizarre because it was counter to the problem she'd had with one particular virus: human immunodeficiency virus, which could lead to AIDS. How was she now able to *work* with a virus without trouble? To me, it highlighted how much her fears – related to AIDS and linked with Goran – were of her own devising.

After the first three weeks, I started going to the lab even on Saturdays or Sundays. Not for whole days, but for a couple of hours. I voluntarily offered my service to take care of my research group's cell cultures which needed to be dealt with at least every second day. Since Sonja and I had moved out from the girls' house, my new social environment seemed to be exclusively based around my job. I was happy to put in extra hours. One Saturday afternoon, one of my colleagues invited me to play pool. I accepted. The very first time I'd seen him, I couldn't help but stare at the big, lonely curl that sat on his forehead. Then I scanned the rest of him – I guessed about six feet and well over a hundred kilos. Before Chubby Curl had even introduced himself to me, he told me, "When I saw your picture on your application, I said to the boss, 'Do not take this blonde!'" *What?!*

Chubby Curl was a postdoc. As a lab technician, I sometimes worked for him if not for Ursula or the boss himself. His real name was Sven. He loved to make jokes, such as spotting his face with little round stickers and telling everyone in the lab, "Look at me! I've been infected with lab pox. Boss, you've got to let me go on sick leave." He acted like the group's clown. When he threw his head back, laughing, his yellow teeth resembled those of a wild animal. He had wide gaps between them, and I imagined him tearing the flesh off some bones whenever he ate.

It was disturbing, to be honest, how happy I was when he asked me out for a game of pool. I didn't know what it was that fascinated me about him, despite his silly jokes and stupid hairstyle. Maybe I knew, deep down, he hadn't wanted me to get the job because he liked my picture so much. Maybe I sensed a challenge. Whatever it was, my fascination with him got stronger and stronger.

I talked to Sonja. Given she had a boyfriend, she would be less naive than me.

"How old is he?" she asked.

"Um, quite a bit older than us."

"That means…?"

I hesitated. "Err, he's thirty-eight."

"*Thirty-eight?* And you are twenty-three?!"

"I'll be twenty-four in a few months."

I knew I was pathetic. It felt wrong. I even sensed there was something odd about Sven, which wasn't reassuring. I thought I should try to deny my feelings, but it didn't work. Instead, I accepted that I liked him a lot, without really understanding why. And that seemed crazy. Even scary. But it didn't seem scary enough.

STILL VIRGIN

ONE NOVEMBER NIGHT, Sven came round to my flat for the first time. Inside, no less, and not just to drop me by the door after playing pool. I'd even cooked a meal. He helped me with the dishes before we faced the *and-what-now?* situation. Sven had the option to go home, or stay and then... yeah, what then?

I had a bigger TV now than the tiny box at the girls' house. I pretended I was searching for the remote control, even though I knew it was between the flowerpot and the wall on top of my chest of drawers. The problem was, the only really comfortable place to watch TV from was my bed. Well, mattress. Was that okay?

Sven decided to lie down on the carpet. He used the edge of the mattress as a pillow. I zapped through all the channels available two or three times. Then I turned the TV off and put some music on. We were now both lying on our sides on the carpet, heads on the mattress, facing each other. Sven had his arms crossed in front of his chest, and I wondered if I should twiddle my thumbs. His eyes met mine only briefly. I was staring at him, hoping he'd give me a sign to indicate when we should start kissing. Actually, I wanted *him* to do it. He was the man, a lot older than me, and surely had an awful lot of experience. Gosh, this was so unlike with Florian.

"What's the time?" Sven asked.

What an idiot.

"Don't know," I said.

I knew time could be a problem soon, though, because I had deliberately taken off my jumper, and now, clad only in a tank top was beginning to get cold on the floor. And then, *finally*, he looked down at my low neckline. With one finger, he carefully stroked my cleavage.

"I like how your breasts spill out slightly," he said.

Sven had changed from one extreme to the other. I wasn't sure if he wasn't trampling on something sensitive, but I didn't care. It had been ages, and eventually we started kissing.

I knew I was good at it. Because Florian had taught me. I held Sven's lips tenderly in my teeth, then stuck the tip of my tongue into his mouth. Not too far – I was wary of his fangs.

Sven was a smoker. His mouth tasted foul, just like in some of my dreams when I kissed a person that I didn't actually like. I was honestly shocked by how I was able to kiss Sven with such passion.

I'd known he was a smoker, but surely I would be able to make him stop. When our mouths were separated again, the foul taste lingered inside my mouth, on my tongue, around my teeth. I pulled my lips inward to lick them clean. And swallowed. Getting up and rinsing my mouth would have been offensive.

Nothing apart from kissing had happened as Sven and I were lying in my bed. It was midnight. I was still in my tank top and underwear. He'd taken off his jeans. I lay on my right side, head on my folded arm as I gazed at him in the soft darkness. Dim light came in through my balcony door. He was watching the ceiling.

"Do you have any diseases I should know about?" he asked.

What? What did he say? Okay, it was sensible to mention diseases before having sex. HIV and other sexually transmitted illnesses were too serious to remain unspoken. But still, I didn't really like his question. It was upsetting. The *way* it was happening – too straightforward, too cold. We were sharing my king-size duvet, rain streamed romantically down my window. No arm in arm, no cuddling, let alone any sign of foreplay. We made no contact whatsoever, not even with our eyes as his were still looking up at the ceiling!

"I'm a scientist, you know. We always have it on our minds," he said.

Sheesh, yeah, I knew he was. Why not pass me a form to fill out and let me tick yes-or-no boxes for HIV, hepatitis A, B, C, etc.?

"I'm clean. One hundred per cent," I said.

"How do you know?"

"I'm still a virgin. Yes, at twenty-three!"

I didn't have the guts to ask him about his health, and fell asleep, facing the wall, away from him.

*   *   *

WHEN I WOKE, I made breakfast, went to the bathroom and dressed. While Sven took a shower, I nipped down to Sonja's to let her know I wouldn't ride to work with her.

"I'm together with Sven now, so I'm going with him by car."

She wasn't surprised about my news. She'd followed the developments.

"All right, I'll ride alone then." I was glad she didn't ask if she could join us. "I've got news, too, by the way."

"Oh. Really? What is it?" I said.

She rubbed her chin, wiggled her shoulders slightly.

"Anything bad?" I asked.

She took a deep breath. "I split up with Lucas last night. On the phone."

"What? You have? I mean, seriously? No, that can't be true!"

"It is."

My jaw dropped. "But he loves you so much! Didn't you say, in summer, that he wanted to marry you?"

Sonja stayed silent, guilt in her eyes. She sighed. But she didn't seem unhappy. There was no devastation.

"So why? What happened?" I asked.

"I just don't have any feelings for him any more."

And I had thought the two belonged together.

"And that's it?" I asked.

"What do you mean, 'that's it'?"

"I mean that's all that's happened?" But I realised: nothing else was required for breaking up a relationship. No arguments or fights, no cheating or falling in love with somebody else.

"Yes, that's all. But it's the point, isn't it?" she said.

I could only agree. Still, it felt so abrupt, so absolute and rough to me.

I needed to get used to the news. And I needed to go back upstairs to my own flat, because Sven was probably ready to leave for work.

"We need to talk more about this. I'll come down again tonight, okay?" I said.

"All right."

Even though I was with Sven in his car, going to work, I couldn't stop thinking of Lucas. I was sure he was absolutely devastated. He loved Sonja. He had known everything she wanted from her eyes. I was sorry for him, even sad, because I liked him. We'd known each other for several years, and now I would most likely never see him again.

*   *   *

I WAS SITTING in one of Sonja's armchairs, and she was sitting in the other. She had prepared some supper. The guilt in her eyes had vanished.

"When you told him, what did he say? How did he react?" I asked.

"He wasn't happy. Obviously. He said he didn't want to give things up like that and we should just see if I'm 'going through a phase'," she said.

"And are you?"

"No, I don't think so. I'm pretty sure it's over."

I cut a slice of bread from the loaf that Sonja had taken out for us, put some butter and cheese on it and had a few bites. I was hungry.

"Well, is it because him showering at his sister's is so complicated? Is the OCD too strong for this relationship?" I asked.

"No, definitely not. It's not that. Really! I just haven't got the same feelings as I used to, any more."

There was nothing else to it. She simply had no more feelings left for him. I accepted that and stopped prodding her to give me a different reason. I didn't want to try and convince her to stick with Lucas. After all, a relationship couldn't be forced. And I didn't want to blame her for the break-up.

"And you and Sven? Are you properly in love?" she asked.

Did I *not* look like I was in love? Did I *not* have a Cheshire-cat smile?

"Yeah!"

"Are you sure he's the right guy for you?"

She certainly put me on the spot. Because I wasn't. There was that fascination with Sven inside me, but there was also the awareness of him possibly being odd. It felt like something difficult.

I ignored a possible dark side to him. "Oh well, what does 'right' mean anyway?"

"So is he staying overnight again?"

"I hope so."

Sonja held a plate of pickles towards me. I grabbed a couple and crunched them. When my mouth was empty enough, I dared to ask her a very personal question – I could do with a girl's advice.

"Um, sorry if this is a little direct but— Err, I mean, I wanted to know how it was the first time? I mean, you and Lucas? Did it hurt? And later, was it great?" I was so curious and couldn't wait for her answer.

But Sonja coughed. Some of her bread had gone down the wrong way. She turned red like a tomato.

"You all right?" I said.

She coughed a few more times, waving at me to indicate I didn't need to pat her on the back.

"Yes, yes. I'm okay." She coughed again.

I waited a few seconds. She didn't answer my question, though. I had to ask her again. "So, please, how was it when you first slept with Lucas?"

Her look was unreadable. Was she amused by my question or something else?

"Sorry, but I can't tell you. I've never slept with him," she said.

"Aaaaah, ha ha ha. Good one!"

"Why are you laughing, Finja?" She frowned.

"I laughed at your joke. But I understand if it's too private and you don't want to tell me. As long as you know that you actually could."

"I am *not* joking!" she insisted.

And then it was me who swallowed down the wrong hole.

"What? You are *serious*? You've never slept with Lucas? In two and a half years?" I coughed.

"Correct. I've never slept with him."

I stopped coughing, but my throat was hot. Sonja blushed.

"I'm totally puzzled. Why not? Did you not want to? Or did *he* not want to?" I said.

"I did want to. Or, maybe, who knows…" she said. "Maybe I was wrong and never really—"

"Loved him?"

Her words from when Lucas first arrived at the girls' house flashed up: *He kept phoning. And wanted to see me again. He said he'd keep trying; wooing me. Until he'd have me.* Sonja hadn't chosen Lucas; he hadn't been a challenge. He had chosen *her*.

"Who knows why it didn't work. We tried. But I just couldn't manage."

"Dear me, is it that painful the first time?"

She shrugged, her face less red now. "Lucas had never done it with any other girl before. So we both didn't know too much. But it was more difficult for me."

"Oh dear, I'm sorry," I said.

"It's okay. We still had fun. There are other things you can do."

I could imagine which other things she meant. I wasn't *that* naive. But, certainly, I was shocked that Sonja was also still a virgin.

DARK CLOUDS

SVEN CAME REGULARLY to my place. Each night I was excited to hear the sound of my bell, even though I saw him all day at work. Only during those two hours after I left work before him did I not see him.

We'd had some intimate contact but not 'proper' sex. Now that we'd been together for a few weeks, I pointed out that I hadn't seen *his* place yet. He had only told me where he lived.

"My tiny place isn't as nice as yours. It's not worth going there," he said.

I was disappointed but accepted it. We were eating dessert after the dinner I had cooked, and he was in an odd mood. He was different to how he had been earlier at work. Quiet. His expression was grim. I would have explained it as hormonal, if he'd been a woman. But he was a man!

Sven dropped his spoon into his emptied dessert bowl and plopped it on the table. "I'm too old for you!" he said.

His tone cut through me. It left me unable to speak.

He added, "And I've got to focus on finding a new job."

I knew that his contract was due to expire, but I couldn't see the link between that and me. My ribcage closed tight, as if he was squeezing it. His mood was directed at me, a dark cloud hovering above my head. I took a breath, then dared to speak.

"I'll try and help you find one."

"I can't do this! It's not going to work out." His eyebrows met and deep lines were etched on his forehead. He got up from the table, searched for his shoes and put them on. He took his jacket, collected a few clothes that he had worn during the recent days, and went through my door. Gone!

I threw myself from my chair straight onto my bed, rolled over, and stared at the ceiling. A few tears trickled from the corners of my eyes, crawling into my ears. The dark cloud was now raining on me. What had happened to him so suddenly? How did age play a part in all that? It seemed like he'd talked nonsense.

I sat up, grabbed a tissue from the box next to my mattress and wiped my face. I couldn't get my head around Sven's behaviour but, somehow, I didn't want to believe he'd truly broken up with me. The whole thing was very different to when Florian dumped me. Sven was probably just a little unsettled about his future; about facing unemployment. He'd overreacted, nothing more. He didn't know exactly what he wanted. But I knew what *I* wanted: to get him back. It felt like a challenge. Again! It was almost like the more he didn't know – and didn't show – that he wanted me, the more I wanted *him*.

I seemed to be drawn by his odd behaviour and negative mood. I was convinced I could handle them; even change them. I had never heard that, sometimes, girls are attracted to men because of problems – *their* problems. Nobody had ever warned me how hard it could be to try and solve them. Particularly if those problems were more than just a contract at work…

* * *

TWO DAYS LATER, on a Friday after work, Sven's mood had passed. He invited me to play pool. I didn't actually like pool that much but accepted, totally thrilled. I went to the toilets and locked myself in a cubicle, dancing and fist-pumping.

Around the pool table, his words were sweet, making my heart purr like a pussycat. I wiped the incident of the other day from my mind, being more than happy to forget, and we drove back to mine after three rounds of pool.

Christmas Eve 2000

I HAD BOUGHT my very first Christmas tree. Not very big, but cute. I put lights on it, baubles and plenty of other decorations. Now I stood there, viewing it with my arms crossed, smiling and slightly wiggling my hip. I *loved* it.

The cardboard box I had kept from my new TV was superb as a tree stand. I'd turned it upside down and covered it with a cloth. There were candles as well as my Christmassy handicraft things around my flat. I was proud of how beautiful I had made the place. It was cosy and looked like a proper home.

Sonja had convinced me to stay in Munich and not travel to dirty northern Germany. It was impossible since we had nowhere to go through the transformation, really, unless we found a way to sneak back into the girls' house. It wasn't difficult for me to stay down in Munich, because this time I did have a boyfriend. For real! And Sonja had let me travel and celebrate Christmas with my family the previous year.

Sven knew about Sonja and her OCD. Of course he did – not only was he my boyfriend but also a scientist; he had an idea about such things, didn't he? He was trusted with the problems of dirty northern Germany and the

Goran contamination that existed in Munich. I'd told him why I didn't go to touristy places within the city, which products at the supermarket I couldn't get, and why I had to say no when he wanted a bag of Haribo wine gums. He also knew how very handy it was that he drove a Ford. I was genuinely grateful for the way he handled those restrictions. He didn't appear annoyed at all and had been okay about it when I asked him to choose a different brand of wine gums. Regarding avoiding tourist places, he was so nonchalant I almost thought it suited him. He had zero interest in any of them. It was then that I realised we only moved between my flat, work, a couple of supermarkets and the pool hall. Now, on Christmas Eve, Sven had gone into the lab for a few hours, even though everybody else was on holiday. Ever since I'd met him, he'd gone into work at the weekend; mostly for about two hours on Saturday morning and then again on Sunday in the late afternoon.

Sonja came upstairs to mine. We were going to celebrate as a threesome, and she and I prepared for the afternoon when Christmas would begin properly. She put her presents under my super-cute tree. I added mine. We went out to do the last bits of shopping before the shops closed. When we returned, we put cakes on my table, ready for Sven's arrival. When he turned up, he brought a couple of presents for me and Sonja, placing them under my tree.

In the evening, we ate our home-cooked dinner and opened the gifts. Festive music chimed throughout the room. Everything was perfect. Mum called at some point to wish us a merry Christmas, and I was able to tell her how nice everything was – there was no reason for her to worry about anything.

By 11.30pm, the three of us had cleared up and made

our way to bed. I was stuffed with food, including dessert, and nicely tired. Sonja went downstairs to her place, and Sven and I lay down in my bed. I was very pleased to have successfully hosted Christmas for the first time. I was happy.

Christmas Day

I GOT UP to make the day as perfect as Christmas Eve had finished. Sven was still dozing in my bed. I took a shower and made coffee in the kitchen. I laid the table with toast, the remaining Christmas cakes, butter, jam, cheese, juice and yogurt. I also got out the bacon Sven liked so much. Back in the kitchen, I saw him get up and disappear towards the bathroom. Huh – he didn't come in to say good morning. Was he in a bad mood? At Christmas?

I wasn't convinced he was, but it felt like something could be wrong. Maybe he just needed the toilet first thing; nothing serious. And, it was *Christmas*, when people weren't in bad moods. *Nobody? Really? No exceptions? Not on purpose, just in time, like Dad?*

I rushed to the window in my living room and glanced down to see if I could spot Sonja in hers. I could – she looked up from her window to see if I was awake. That's what we did most mornings. For Christmas Day, we had agreed to have breakfast together at nine o'clock, if we were all up. It was 9am now. As she looked up to me, I saw her lips moving. Maybe she was only letting me know she would come upstairs. But maybe she was saying something else? *Don't be daft!* Sonja and I both knew very well that it was possible for people to be in a bad mood at Christmas. At Christmas and on birthdays in *particular*!

A moment later, my doorbell rang and Sonja was there.

242

KATJA SCHULZ

She had her folding chair under her arm, like the day before, since I only had two chairs myself. She came in and noticed my nervousness straight away. Her eyebrows went up.

"I'm not sure but, somehow, I have the feeling Sven didn't have a good night. Oh well, maybe I'm going on about something that isn't actually there," I whispered, and switched on some Christmas jingles. Mum flashed up in my mind – she used to turn music on to distract from Dad's comments or moods. And then the two weather dolls from the little plastic house on my parents' terrace followed. Suddenly I was sure: Sven looked pretty blue this morning!

When he came out from the bathroom, he hardly glanced at me and Sonja. We were sat at my table, waiting for him. I'd hoped he would give me a kiss or a hug to say good morning.

"Morning," he said. Nothing else.

I could see from the corner of my eye how Sonja was observing me as I stared at Sven. He sat down at the table. Despite the jolly music, a chill ran down my back. I had to be brave to keep looking at him. He hadn't shaved. His stubble was two days old. I didn't like it. Chubby Curl resembled a thug.

I lifted the coffee pot and filled up his cup. He grabbed a slice of toast and went with his knife into the butter. I heard him puff his cheeks out and dared to ask, "Did you not sleep—"

Sven slammed his knife onto the edge of his plate. Sonja and I twitched. He jumped up from his chair and his fist hit the table next to his plate. Dishes vibrated. "No human being would be able to stand this, would they?!" he shouted.

I was unable to answer. I was frozen. I didn't even know what he was talking about. His question sounded rhetorical anyway.

"I'm going to the lab now. To my office. I'll make some

more job applications. I'll be back about three o'clock," he said.

He put shoes and jacket on, took his briefcase and banged the door of my flat. Gone!

I hadn't moved an inch. Neither had Sonja. My eyes were glued to Sven's plate, his toast and knife. The majority of the butter he'd taken was still sticking to the blade. Another dark cloud hovered above my head. It felt like ice-cold rain. A storm. An earthquake.

"What was *that*?" Sonja asked.

"I think another of his weird moods."

"Like when he broke up with you recently?"

"Yes, something like that. But today it was harsher. He was much angrier."

Sonja looked at me, waiting for me to say more.

"But he hasn't broken up with me this time, has he?" I said.

"I didn't hear him say those words, but…"

"But what?"

"But, honestly, I don't know, really."

"Yes, you do know. Come on, what do you mean?" I actually didn't want to hear. I could guess what she was thinking.

"Well, maybe it would…"

"Would be what? *Good*, if he did?"

Sonja stayed silent.

"How can you say that?" I asked.

"Sorry, I'm sorry. But it's no good. I mean, his behaviour. I don't want to sound as if I'm preaching or anything. I just have experience of these kinds of sudden moods. My father, you know."

And yes, I did know. But I didn't know if I wanted to hear it – that comparison.

"Do you love him?" Sonja asked.

That question was sort of logical. I could see why she wanted to know after Sven's performance.

"Yes, I do love him. Definitely. He attracts me. I'm fascinated by him."

But, of course, I was thoroughly devastated about Sonja and me sitting by ourselves with all that breakfast on the table. I was rather angry with Sven, and it didn't matter any more whether he came back at 3pm or not. The day was spoiled. The result: another sad Christmas.

*　　*　　*

WHY HAD I done this? Why had I fallen in love with such a difficult man?

Although I knew I should question myself, I didn't do it properly. I ignored my own concerns about Sven and stuck with the belief that I could help and even change him. Without really knowing how. I believed in God and regarded my relationship with Sven as something possibly given by him. I trusted I was meant, *chosen*, to help this strange character – a great excuse...

Was it time I slept with Sven properly? We *still* hadn't done it. He'd made sexual comments, and I understood he was keen on the idea. But he hadn't really pushed for it, and I thought he was being considerate. At the same time, his 'boys' talk' about my looks made me uncomfortable. I didn't know whether it was a compliment or simply crude when he said I had a hot ass and then threw his head back, laughing, his fangs looking so wild they'd mangle my delicate hot bottom into pieces. And each time he commented on Heidi Klum in TV beauty ads, I felt forced to change channels.

Such a Weirdo

End of January 2001

IT WASN'T LONG since I had turned twenty-four. Sven hadn't come to my place for a couple of days. He told me he was too busy at his new job – one he'd found with a different research group but still in the same building. All he needed to do was go to a lab on the first floor instead of the third. I was pleased.

I had understanding for him being busy with his new job and wanting to get settled. But I was unable to see why he had no time for me at all. I decided to go around to his place – without letting him know or getting permission.

I went down into the garage to get my bike and pushed it up to the gate and over the path to get to the road. My breath condensed in the air. The tyres made a grinding noise as they moved over the frozen snow. It wasn't going to be a pleasant ride. It was dark and bitterly cold.

Once on the road, which had been cleared of ice and snow, I cycled towards the place Sven had told me was his. I arrived after about half an hour and stood in front of the huge block of apartments, unable to tell which window was his. Light came from some; others were black. I locked my bike against a street light, making sure it wasn't too close to a Volkswagen. I went to the main entrance and through the front door of the building. My eyes searched a board of doorbells for Sven's last name. Loads and loads of names were displayed. It took me a while to find his.

Just before pressing the bell, I hesitated.

Come on, don't be silly. Relax, I told myself.

But I was tense. Objectively, I couldn't see anything wrong with going to my boyfriend's. However, I wasn't objective in this. I felt my heart beat inside my thick jacket, expecting something strange. A surprise?

With two fingers I pressed the bell labelled with Sven's last name. Seconds later, the little loudspeaker on the board crackled.

"Yes?"

Was he sleepy? It was only eight o'clock.

"Hi, it's me," I said into the holes on the metal board.

"You? What are you doing here?" the holes asked.

"I wanted to see you. Visit you. And see where you live."

"You shouldn't have come here," the holes said. "I've told you there's nothing worth seeing at my place!"

"Well, now I'm here. I've cycled all the way. Are you going to let me in?"

A pause. I pictured an eye-roll.

Then he said, "Second floor."

The buzzer of the second door went and I slid through. I walked up the stairs. My nervousness didn't dissipate at all. But I was also excited to see him.

On the second floor, he popped his head out of a door. I smiled. But when I stood right in front of him, I refrained from giving him a greeting kiss. A strong smell stung my nostrils.

Sven gave way to let me into his studio.

"I told you my place isn't as nice as yours. And there's nothing to do here," he said.

He was right. I stood with my back to the wall at one end of the studio – an estimated size of eighteen to twenty square metres. On the left side was a kitchenette. At the far end, a window and a balcony door. My eyes were wide, scanning the place. I tried hard not to let my jaw drop, and even harder not to throw my hands up in horror. I. Was. Dumbfounded.

Sven lived like a bum. There was not a single piece of furniture in his studio. Only a tiny black TV, if that counted. Newspapers and magazines were strewn over the floor. Some were black and white, some illustrated. I saw full magazines as well as loose sheets. Clothes were spread around. Dishes and cutlery on the floor. On one side, against the wall, I spotted his briefcase. Gnawed bones sat on a double sheet of newspaper – the remains of a chicken. I could perfectly imagine how it had been mauled by Sven's fangs. Next to the bones stood a ravioli tin on top of a small piece of wood with four little wheels. The tin was open, a spoon sticking out. The rolling board underneath was a tool to transport heavy furniture. But there was no furniture!

"I used it to transport my washing machine up here," Sven said. "And now it serves as my meals on wheels."

He laughed. But I didn't feel like laughing. I was put off; completely disgusted. I realised I had interrupted my boyfriend's wildlife-esque dinner: he'd been sitting or lying on the carpet, dressed in a shabby old T-shirt and undies, shovelling cold ravioli into his mouth, and munching the fried chicken with his fingers. He was standing next to me, rubbing his tummy. And as if I hadn't already seen enough, he let out a loud belch from the depth of his stomach and sour fumes wafted over. Jesus Christ!

My eyes moved to a bottle next to the 'table' on the floor: wine. Almost empty. I had thought that his pungent breath had a whiff of alcohol.

"Did you have all of that? Tonight?" I asked.

"Yeah. You want some? The rest, I mean?"

No, I didn't. There was no way I wanted a single sip from that bottle. It was coated in greasy fingerprints.

"Do you drink that much every evening? I mean, where do all those come from?" I pointed at another eight to ten glass bottles next to the balcony door. The last time I had seen that many empty bottles on a floor was at Sonja's, years ago.

"Yeah. But it's weak like water."

I didn't like his answer. I didn't like anything I was seeing and learning here. And I didn't know what to do. Go home? It was a long way to ride. And cold.

I stood still, thinking, remembering that maybe God had picked me to help Sven. Thinking that I had declared myself a 'missionary' sent to change him.

Sven started to crumple up the papers he had used as a place mat; the chicken bones inside. He also tidied up the other magazines.

"Where do you sleep?" I asked.

He stopped moving and pointed at a bedraggled blanket on the carpet by the window. "There."

"On the floor? You've got no mattress anywhere?"

"Nope. I don't need one. The carpet is good."

Although Sven hadn't wanted me to come to his place, he now seemed okay with it. He smiled and was in a good mood. He appeared relaxed. I hadn't seen him like that too often. He'd rather been uptight, sometimes even with a slightly aggressive attitude towards other people. Was alcohol maybe the reason for him being so relaxed? One litre per night seemed quite a lot. Even though he claimed it was weak, but I had my doubts.

"We could go together and buy some furniture for you? Wouldn't that be nicer?" I said.

"Thanks, but I really don't need any."

He sat down on the carpet with his back against the radiator, below the window. He covered himself with that bedraggled, filthy blanket. I stepped over and around his papers, clothes and dishes, and stood next to him. I briefly glanced through the window onto the balcony and noticed an ashtray overloaded with cigarette ends. Some were scattered around it, stuck in the snow. I got down on the floor and also sat with my back against the radiator.

Then Sven's hands reached out and pulled me towards him. He cosied up to me, almost cuddling. I loved that the wild animal made a purring sound like a tamed cat all of a sudden. He slithered down onto his back and kept his hold on me until we lay in his 'bed', covered by his 'duvet'. Me on top of him.

"Wouldn't it be nice if you let me inside you now?" His hands moved under my clothes until they reached my skin. I was still wearing my jacket, not having been prompted to hang it up anywhere! It was awkward. Surreal. I didn't like the way he'd invited me to have full sex for the first time, but I did like how his hands ran over my skin. I'd have preferred a nicer environment, different circumstances, for my very first time; without the smell of alcohol and cigarettes on his mouth. But my instinct told me this was a rare opportunity – he was being sweet! I shouldn't miss out, and his touch under my clothes was enough for my hungry body to get excited.

Before long, Sven managed to take off my trousers and panties. Thoughts rushed through my mind: Sonja had never slept with Lucas; the first time would hurt a lot; Florian, who had been very attractive, had a soft, warm bed in his room – gosh, how I would have loved to be loved, for the first time, in the missionary position. But here I was, after all, in Sven's off-putting place, on top of him. The floor was hard, the blanket filthy, and the studio as a whole frankly resembled a rubbish dump. Still dressed in my jacket, I was riding him while he was doing nothing except for resting his hands on my thighs. His eyes closed. His head tilted backward slightly. An inebriated, tired and chicken-gorged man couldn't do more than lie on his back, make zero effort and let *me* do the job.

He moaned and mumbled some words. I knew I had to go for it; enjoy the moment for my own benefit. I took the act as an experiment. Nothing hurt. Everything was fine. Everything felt good. But it didn't seem like making love. It was more like making shag. Nothing a girl would truly want for her first time.

"Is this what it's really like when a man and a woman sleep together?" I needed to know if there was more.

Sven opened his eyes slightly but then closed them again. He kept moaning. "Yeah, it's great, isn't it?" he said.

Was it great? I had to admit I did like the actual physical feeling very much. I even regretted having waited for it until the late age of twenty-four. But, despite enjoying the sex, I found it hard to answer Sven with *yes*. Because of the circumstances.

I concentrated. On myself. One hundred per cent. Like Sven did on himself. His body seemed to stiffen a bit. Maybe shake. I felt his nails cutting into the flesh of my thighs. I didn't close my eyes but tried to reach my climax, too. He got louder and louder. If I wasn't ready myself, I was going to miss out. I didn't want that.

I heard a last loud groan and then the one hundred-kilogram-meatloaf underneath me slackened. The hands on my thighs dropped to the carpet. Sven's eyes stayed closed, a smile of satisfaction on his face.

"That was so good, so hot," he said.

I was unable to respond, suddenly overwhelmed by a bad feeling. Unknown. Unexperienced. I moved off Sven's belly and sat on the carpet, leaning against the radiator again. He stayed on his back, a narrow slit now opening up beneath his eyelids. I didn't know what to think of what had happened. I didn't know how to feel about it, how to judge it. Did he now want me more than before? Would we have sex regularly? Including cuddling, at least as foreplay? Were the empty wine bottles next to me on the carpet a condition for this – for him being gentle with me?

I felt lonely. It was odd. I wasn't on my own, but felt so. A good old Imaginary Comfort Bubble would have been great.

I reached for my panties and trousers, stood up, slipped them on, and went to the bathroom. I needed a pee. When I came out, Sven was still lying on his back on the floor. Maybe he would snore soon. Going to sleep in his dump was a no-go for me. And now I was rather angry at that drunken, self-satisfied, lazy meatloaf anyway.

"I'm going home," I said.

He finally sat up. "Okay, let's go to your place then. I'll put your bike into the boot. You drive."

My anger was chased away instantly. Well, it's okay when God tells you that you should go home with such a weirdo.

252

ON AND OFF

I WENT DOWN from my lab to Sven's to find out if he would come to my place later. Without me even asking, he held his car key toward me. I loved that gesture. I pressed a kiss onto his cheek, before leaving the lab again.

"Oh, can you please get a bottle of wine? I'd like to have some at yours as well," he called after me.

I hesitated, but said, "Which one? I don't know anything about wine."

"Any is fine. Just make sure it's a one-litre bottle."

Were there different sizes?

I bought a bottle of wine for Sven every single evening that he stayed at mine. And he emptied them all until the last drop was gone. I started to hate it. Sometimes, I poured myself a small glass. I sipped and then, when he wasn't watching, poured it into the kitchen sink. The more relaxed and good his mood, the easier I could fill myself another glass. But what a risk if he surprised me in the kitchen as the wine went down the drain...

When I'd bought 0.75-litre bottles a couple of times, I was forced to come up with an explanation. I said I'd been in a hurry, unable to search the shelves properly. But my efforts were useless. He started to drink somewhere else, on his way to mine. I noticed a strong, sharp smell of alcohol from his mouth, and asking him where it had come from only got him annoyed and very loud. If I wasn't happy with it, he would go home to his own place. I ended up buying one-litre bottles again, because I wanted him to stay with me. The risk he would dump me was real. He'd done it three times already since we'd got together, six months ago. And each time I had to work harder and longer to get him back. I had to write letters and stick them under his door. He never opened when I rang the bell. I wrote longer and longer letters, more and more apologetically. I had to be very patient. Weeks went by until he would come back to me. Maybe months.

*   *   *

"Why do you do this, Finja?" Sonja asked.

Of course I knew what she meant.

"Because I want to be with him," I said, even though I knew it was absurd.

"He's no good for you, you know that?"

"But I love him."

"I don't understand you. What is it that you *love* about him?" she asked.

I didn't know how to answer. Because I knew I couldn't say, *That he dumps me all the time.*

"You know who you remind me of?" Sonja asked.

"Who?"

"My mum!"

My eyes flew to her and met hers.

She said, "Yes, indeed – just like my mum and my father!"

I had nothing to say. I knew what was coming next.

"You run after Sven, begging him to be good to you

again. Exactly like my mum used to do when my father didn't speak to her for several weeks."

I still had nothing to say.

"You ask him to be good to you and love you while he is so mean. You beg for his affection, and he enjoys it!" she said.

And she was right. That was exactly what was happening. The more Sven rejected me, the bigger my efforts to get him back. The longer I was made of air to him whenever we bumped into each other in the corridors of the institute, the more I dropped to my knees, clasping my hands as if in prayer – in the form of writing letters to him. He wallowed in this particular sort of affection that he extracted from me while I was suffering. And he knew the juice would keep coming as I dropped even lower.

The first time a man had rejected me that way was Dad when he moved me off his lap at his desk. Sometimes he had tolerated me sitting there, but sometimes he had not. He had also told me I was annoying, that day when I desperately tried to have a conversation with him while he was gardening. I didn't want to believe I was repeating an old pattern with Sven. I couldn't admit to myself that I was reliving an old story. I didn't want it to be true that I was looking for compensation for the lack of fatherly affection, hoping to get it from Sven in the same way I'd craved it from Dad when I was a child.

But Sonja rubbed it in: "You remember my parents' silver wedding, right? You were pretty disgusted by the event and felt it was a show based on a lie! You were boiling about my mum having consciously wiped out all those terrible years with my father and his nasty treatment. And now you behave just like her! What is *wrong* with you?"

And *still*, I had nothing to say. I had no answer because I didn't want anything to be wrong with me. I wanted to believe in my missionary zeal, although I realised I was suffering in my relationship with Sven. Was I supposed to? God *had* chosen me to help Sven, hadn't he? Or was I simply making excuses for him? Was I paralysed like Sonja's mum? Did I take after her? How could that be possible?

It just couldn't.

BANG!

It was Saturday, early afternoon. Sven had been at the lab for two hours and now came to mine. Sonja was there when he arrived. She had received her first water bill and brought it to show me. The bill was a shock to both of us, but only because we were looking at the figure: DM 1,035.45. The numbers appeared huge. I wasn't truly surprised. Because I knew how much water she used daily. Nine minutes for washing her hands, for a start... The bad thing was that Sonja actually had to pay, unlike at the girls' house where her excessive water consumption was covered by the rent and couldn't even be pinned on her directly. Her name wasn't written anywhere. But now this bill spelled it out in black and white!

As Sven walked into my living room, he was curious to see what the sheet of paper on my table was. He realised quickly that the bill covered only six months. "You have used that much water since you moved into your flat? *That much?* Are you crazy?" His voice was raised, and he clutched the bill in both hands. He shook the paper like he knew he mustn't shake Sonja.

"Hey, calm yourself. Would you please use a different tone?" I was baffled as to how I stood my ground against him. I'd always bowed, not risking any break-ups. We had argued about his drinking and smoking, but apart from that I never dared to tell him my opinion when it differed from his.

It was, admittedly, crazy how much water Sonja had used within half a year. But it wasn't a crime. She hadn't even *chosen* to spend over a thousand Deutschmarks of her modest salary on water. A mental illness was at fault, for goodness' sake!

Sven stared into my eyes. I could tell he didn't like that I had stood up to him. Sonja got up from the chair she'd been sitting in.

"I'll go down to mine," she said, and aimed for the door.

I tore my eyes away from Sven's scary stare and went after her. "We'll talk later about this!" I wanted to help with the bill, using my house money. We were cousins!

"Okay," she said, and left.

I returned to the living room and stood in front of Sven, and twitched as he slammed the bill onto my table. Sonja hadn't even taken it with her.

"You're nuts!" he said.

"Pardon?" I had actually understood, but felt so strong all of a sudden.

"You're defending?" He seemed to feel I had been cheeky towards him because I actually defended Sonja. Against *him*.

"What's your problem? It's not *your* bill. *You* won't have to pay it, will you?" I couldn't believe I was speaking so loudly. "It's not even your business."

"You know what? I'm done!" he shouted.

I knew the rest: he pulled his bunch of keys from his pocket, searched it, and turned the ring. A couple of seconds later, he held my spare key out to me.

"This is it. This time, it's really the end!" he said.

I snatched the key and tossed it onto my table. I was

furious about his same old method. "Wait, then! This time, you'll take *all* your things with you. I don't want anything left here – none of your clothes, none of your wine bottles, not even a single teabag. Don't leave anything for me to hang on to you; no reason for you to come back!" I said.

Sven didn't say a thing. He just stared at me, his face pale as if in a cold sweat. I rushed around, collecting his belongings. I put his clothes next to him on the floor. Then I hurried into the kitchen, opened the cupboards and grabbed the four cardboard boxes of teabags that were his. I didn't know why he'd brought them anyway – he never drank tea. Then I went back into the living room. He hadn't moved at all.

"Here, take everything with you!" I was seething. Maybe I appeared cool and collected. I wasn't. But I didn't want to show him. I acted as hard as I could, playing confident. Then I saw the flush climbing up Sven's neck and cheeks toward his forehead. He didn't take the teabag boxes I held in my hands. My eyes shifted and glanced at them, when I suddenly heard a very loud bang.

I didn't understand where it came from – where it *had* come from. I felt strange, as if I wasn't fully conscious. As if I knew something had happened but didn't know what it was. Like viewing the scene as an out-of-body experience. Was I dreaming?

I saw the teabag boxes falling from my hands and onto the floor. My left hand grabbed my forehead in an automatic move. I only saw it happening, I didn't do it. Then my legs collapsed underneath me, and I fell onto the floor myself. Half lying, half sitting on the carpet, my right elbow supported me as I slowly came to understand what had happened: Sven had given me a powerful smack on the head.

I was frozen. Didn't speak. No screaming, no whining either. I made no noise whatsoever. There was not a single tear in my eyes. I only noticed how fast my chest was moving. It was pumping air. And pain was spreading through my head.

Sven remained standing. He didn't bend down to me. I couldn't tell what he was looking at – if anything. I was unable to lift or turn my head. All I saw of him were his feet.

It was dead quiet in my flat. I couldn't judge whether it had been seconds or minutes since Sven had hit me, when his feet finally made a move. They walked away from me. The further they went, the more of his body I could see, until he disappeared from my living room. I heard the door open, and then close. Gone!

My mind was shaken and I was filled with consternation. My body felt wobbly and stiff at the same time, and wouldn't move easily. I tried to search the flat with my eyes, as if I needed to make sure Sven was really gone. Unable to walk, I crawled to the table and pulled myself up: my spare key was still on it. I crawled to the door and pressed my shoulder as hard as I could against it, making sure it was shut. A long, vertical mirror hung in the corridor next to the door. I brushed my hair to one side and saw a big bluish-red bruise developing on my forehead. Still moving on all fours, I crawled back in the main room and rolled onto my mattress. From there I saw that Sven had taken his clothes with him, but not the teabag boxes.

*　　*　　*

SONJA TOLD ME to get my head checked out by a doctor, and to report to my boss what Sven had done to me. I took her first piece of advice but didn't speak to my boss, even though Sonja claimed I must also tell *Sven's* boss. I knew she hated him, but I wasn't convinced I wanted to test my power over Sven and get him into trouble at work. Instead, I would wait for some time and see what happened – *if* something happened. Would Sven apologise to me? Didn't he feel bad about hitting me? Very bad? Surely he had a conscience and would ask me to forgive him. I hoped he'd be full of remorse and regret, only to be let down. Sven didn't approach me. He didn't search me out at the institute. He didn't come upstairs to my lab. Didn't care how I was. I couldn't stop thinking about how he could have seriously hurt me, had he struck a slightly different and more sensitive spot on my head. Now *that* brought tears to my eyes. It hurt so much more than the punch itself.

I wouldn't have been myself – the missionary – if I hadn't searched for an explanation for Sven's indifference. I *needed* something to console myself; to keep going. I thought that maybe he couldn't approach me because he felt *too* guilty? Or his mother hadn't taught him how to say sorry? Perhaps she had failed at bringing him up properly; teaching him how to behave, how to feel. How to love. I didn't know much of his family background. He had two brothers, and his dad was already dead. And when his mum had died, I had to watch the burial from behind a tree until his brothers and their wives and children had left. Some months later, when Sven and I stood by his mother's grave, he told me he wished he could jump on it to make sure she wouldn't come out again. Poor Sven!

I shoved the truth out of my way and instead managed to think of *him* as the victim in our case. I was being so stupid. But God would always want to see me be a good person anyway. I should be considerate, helpful, forgiving. If I weren't soft, maybe he'd get angry with me. As a kid, Sonja had shown me what her parents had: rules and punishments – the brown family meeting folder. Ever since I'd flipped through the pages, I'd been even more wary of God. Maybe he didn't just have ten commandments; maybe he had a folder, too…

* * *

I EVENTUALLY SOUGHT out Sven at the institute. All he needed to do was breathe out a gentle "I'm sorry." I forgot it was me who'd been smacked, because *he* was the sad one who didn't know how to love and hadn't been loved properly by his mother. Now I was able to handle the bruise on my forehead.

Sven invited me for a game of pool. I was over the moon. I knew it was the most affection I would get from him, and I was so thirsty for it. Dying. Desperate. I'd always longed for affection from a man I loved. My problem was that I didn't understand how dangerous desperation could be.

SUSPICION

SONJA WASN'T HAPPY that I was back together with Sven yet again. She had grown up with that approach: carrots and sticks. Her father had never been physically violent with her mother, but had certainly been mentally abusive. In that way, he'd been very violent.

"So you're forgiving *and* forgetting the fact he hit you?" Sonja had said.

I'd only shrugged.

"I mean, *you* forgive, and *he* forgets." She'd poked at the point, and didn't refrain from ripping open my wounds. "Have you even talked about *why* he smacked you? I mean, like you said, my water bill wasn't even his business!"

I'd just closed my eyes, taking a deep breath so I could bear her words – the truth. I still didn't feel I had been cheeky when I defended Sonja about her bill. I'd given her DM 750 to help with it and not told Sven. Because it was fact: it wasn't his business.

* * *

I NOW HOPED the carrots would last. But they didn't. I knew Sven was bad for me, but I kept dismissing it. I carried on lying to myself despite seeing how my life had changed since moving out from the girls' house: I didn't go out, I didn't dance, and didn't even know anybody any more with whom I could have gone to a disco. Sven and I spent every evening at home. We ate and watched television. He followed the snooker. That was it. No excitement whatsoever. Not even in bed. There'd been the one evening when he deflowered me on his carpet and a few occasions in my flat afterwards. Not making love, only making shag.

But now it was spring 2002, and Sven and I hadn't had sex for over three months. At mine, in bed, he flinched each time my hand reached out for him in the mornings. Even when I didn't look for sex, but only contact. He would leap up and flee the bed, asking, "You want a coffee?"

I made an attempt to ask what the problem was.

"I don't know what you're talking about, there's no problem," he said.

"Hmm." I was scared to contradict him, but I just had to. "There is. You're almost terrified of me touching you."

"I'm impotent, okay! It's not my fault that I can't have sex with you!" His tone was aggressive. "And I don't like physical exertion anyway."

I actually believed the last bit. He was lazy regarding exercise and had gained quite a bit of weight since I'd met him. He was almost fat. I couldn't afford to ask another question. Sven's tone indicated that, and he'd once joked that I wouldn't be allowed to ask more than one question per day. I see some truth in most jokey things…

Was it enough, what I had with Sven? Playing pool, watching TV and eating; without cuddling and sex? I didn't even get a platonic hug. I knew the saying 'Nobody is perfect', but our relationship was nowhere near. So why could I be in this unsatisfying relationship?

Sonja kept challenging me about the same thing. She

asked the same question again and again, as if she was using a drill on my skull to get into my head. She hated Sven! And I wondered if he despised her too. Was she maybe the reason why our relationship had foundered? I failed to kick that thought out of my mind. Sonja had always been there, since she'd walked into my life and sat next to me at primary school. At first, she almost made me puke, but then I liked her; loved her! She came to my rescue, being the only one to understand why I needed Imaginary Comfort Bubbles. Her father was nastier than mine, she so knew what it was like to miss out on love and get the hard-line treatment instead. But I hadn't really *chosen* her. She just came along – whether I was okay with that or not. I had chosen Sven, though. And he competed against her, getting angry and even hitting me when I defended her for using too much water. He was my own choice – someone who would love me, since Dad didn't. Someone I would try and *make* love me.

* * *

I HAD STAYED at Sven's overnight for the first time. He had recently moved into another building, much closer to the institute. His new studio was fully furnished, but he still slept on the carpet so I could use the single bed.

He was up very early that morning and took a shower – safely out of my reach. I was sitting up in bed, my head spinning from tiredness and awkwardness. I didn't like his new place much either. I got up and went into the tiny kitchenette, searching for his instant coffee. Sven came out from the bathroom as I was about to open the cupboard beside the cooker. He sprang between me and the cupboard, holding the doors closed.

"No, don't look inside. Please. I'm sorry, but you wouldn't like it. I have a bag of Haribo Gold-Bears in there!" he said.

He waved his hands around in either concern or panic, I wasn't sure. I didn't know what to do – I understood his warning, but it wasn't me who didn't like Haribos. That was Sonja! But Sven knew there were no Haribos allowed at my place, in order to cater for my best friend's needs. He respected that. I acknowledged he was very considerate to warn me about the wine gums inside his cupboard. Or was it rather inconsiderate that he'd put them there in the first place? Had I expected him to miss out on Haribos in his own home, I would have forced another person's OCD onto him. Would that have been okay?

I didn't try to open the cupboard or make him to do it. He reached into the other cupboard for the instant coffee and heated up some water. I went to the toilet, and when I came back, he handed me a cup as he sipped from another.

"Well, I need to go to the lab now. I have work to do," he said.

"Right. I need a shower, too. So I'll walk, later," I replied. "Are we meeting for lunch?"

"Okay, 12.30. All right?"

I nodded, sipping my coffee. I was sat in his chair as he gave me a quick kiss on the head. No cuddle, no hug.

"See you later," he said and left.

"See you," I mumbled, bored and lonely, not caring if he heard.

The door clicked, and I found myself on my own. The place was silent. No radio to switch on music. The stale smell of cigarillos lingered. I thought it fitted our rotten relationship.

I let my eyes wander, bouncing everywhere. I saw glass bottles under the sink. All wine bottles, all empty. His shelf had barely anything on it. It wasn't particularly tidy, but rather empty. Only his remote control sat on it. Then my eyes fell upon that cupboard again; the one with the Haribo bag inside. Sven must have trusted I wouldn't open it. He knew how faithful I was to Sonja's rules. This time, however, I just had to take the risk of breaking one. Because I suddenly doubted that a single Haribo bag had made Sven that nervous.

Silently I promised Sonja that I would pay attention and make sure I didn't touch the actual bag as I carefully opened the cupboard door. My heart bashed inside my chest.

ME: THE NOBODY AND CUSTODIAN OF PROBLEMS

July 2014

THESE DAYS, I'M able to laugh about what I found inside Sven's cupboard, because he doesn't mean a thing to me any more. Sounds harsh, I know, but it's honest. But when it happened, back then, it was one of the worst things on earth.

Sven certainly had a mental problem. One with no real name – unlike Sonja's OCD, for example. Still, he was sort of disordered. It was actually pretty sad for him. I'd even believe he struggled within himself. And it was that struggle that he – consciously or subconsciously – was looking to get rid of; maybe by trying to share it with somebody, maybe by passing it on completely to a different person: me. It's the same thing my father does! My father also has a mental problem with no name. He's a sad man and he struggles within himself. And he's always been looking to free himself. One person he passes his problems on to is my mother. The other is me. All my life I have carried a problem my father dumped on me, which is the origin of his own. Part of it I would name *jealousy*. But I don't know the rest. All I know is that this is the truth, no matter how much he would defy and deny it. I have served as a tool: a custodian for his struggles. He can't use me that way any more, because I'm gone – my mother will have to bear it all. But I am still left with his problem.

My father doesn't care about me. All the signs – meaning *no* signs – speak for that. If I were more to him than a custodian, he would at least call me now and again; ask how I am. When I used to call and had my mother on the phone, I asked about him. Sometimes she advised me not to speak to him as he wasn't in the best mood.

To my father, I'm not a proper person. Not at his level. Whereas he is high, I am lower. I don't remember him asking me any question except for once, when he wanted to know if it was correct that water shouldn't be poured into an acid but only the other way around. As a lab technician, I knew there was only one method of mixing acid and water to avoid a dangerous reaction. I was flattered he wanted to know anything from *me*. Apart from that one occasion, he wouldn't even consider my opinion about anything, at any time. The same is true for my brother: when his long-term girlfriend split up with him, I offered support. I cared about how he was feeling. But he told me he had other people to talk to. Gosh, how that made me feel like a low person. A non-person. A useless thing. A nobody! High-Level Brother would *never* ask for Low-Level Sister's opinion. And if I offered it, he'd belittle me, like he had on the day I dared to say what I thought for once. He told me he didn't have the slightest need for it. And why would he – nobody needs anything from a stupid cow with an ordinary face!

Both my parents have let me down; my father even

before my mother. He's made my life really difficult. I guess I wouldn't be so angry with him if he took responsibility for that. I'd love to think he didn't make things hard for me on purpose, but there is the fact that he didn't lend me the three thousand Deutschmarks for my trip around the world at twenty-three.

I agree that most parents try their best to raise their children and believe in what they do. Even if they're mistaken. That's not a problem yet. But it's bad when a mistake – *that could be forgiven* – is not admitted! My father would never, ever admit he did something wrong. *Dad was right*, remember? He'd also never regret what he did to me or how he treated my mother. If asked about it, he would deny any wrongdoing and stand by everything. Self-criticism is impossible for him. And if time was to be turned back, he would do the same things again. *That* is why I am so angry with him.

I really used to love my father – despite his jealousy, despite him being so powerful and nasty. Despite his unloving behaviour and not holding or kissing me. Even when he didn't give me Christmas or birthday presents, but let me watch how my brother unwrapped his. Arrrrrrgh – I could scream out loud right now! I carried on loving my father until, eventually, I had to give up. Because I understood there is zero recognition from him of me.

I thought it was ridiculous when my mother once said, in an attempt to defend my father and herself, how much they'd done for me in my childhood: "We drove you to places for tennis and ballet!" Roger says these are normal things that every parent should be happy to do. Yeah, my father could have pulled it out in time, the night they made me. Alternatively, my mother could have got me sucked away later…

My mother seriously started to piss me off when she defended my father regardless. I thought it just couldn't be true that she rushed to defend him having left for a holiday in Yugoslavia, leaving her and me behind, alone, while I was life-threateningly ill in hospital as a three-year-old. She excused him, telling me he had called every day instead – in tears. So? What the fuck? All my father did back then was excuse himself to himself, and to my mother. He needed her 'there, there' for what he had done. And it was sickening when she had nothing to say in reply when I reminded her: "You've always told me how horrible it was when he left you behind with a small, ill child."

*   *   *

IT's 11.45PM. I'VE just counted twenty-eight clicks next to my head, through the wall. Sonja's made sure the light in her bedroom is off now, and will be using only the one from her bathroom. But she may start over with the clicking in a minute or two.

I'm a little tired. I took a nap today, but suddenly my bed just feels really cosy.

...And Proof

2002

I spotted one Haribo bag. Only one. It was just like Sven had said: Gold-Bears. I pulled the other door of the cupboard towards me. There was nothing in there except for a pile of papers. Some seemed like newspapers, others like magazines. Did Sven still use them to put under his meals now that he had furniture and didn't actually need to eat off the floor any more? I was curious, reached up for the papers, and took them down to lay out on the table. I only needed a second to realise what I was looking at: porn. Hard-core porn.

I opened the first magazine and turned page after page. I started to shake. Naked women in different, close-up positions were facing me. Long, milky streaks over them. Some of the pages stuck together when I tried to turn them. Of course Sven wasn't impotent – I hadn't believed that anyway.

I opened another magazine: more 'used' women. They were trembling on the pages now, as I was shaking all the way into my fingertips. I scoured the paper that was more newsprint than magazine and found a picture of Heidi Klum I had last seen in my recycling bin. I'd thrown it away along with other ads from my letter box.

Then I abandoned Sven's porn, an earth-quake within me. I didn't know if it was caused by rage, disgust, disappointment, sadness, or the feeling of being cheated on. I staggered into the shower, and the warm water calmed my body. But not my thoughts. I remembered how Sven had once said I had micro-tits. It was devastating to realise that the women in his magazines had such big boobs. The worst was the presence of Heidi Klum. I felt like I knew her personally – from Sven's comments whenever she'd flaunted her beauty on TV. And he had pulled her out from the rubbish; taken her home. She was dressed in the photo, but also had streaks all over her. Sven hadn't even needed her in close-up, but he couldn't have sex with *me*.

Was I that unattractive? Ugly even? I found myself attractive enough, at least. More than Sven, to be honest. Didn't he see that? I was slim and sporty. He had a belly and admitted to being too fat.

I stepped out of his shower and wrapped a towel around me. Chin on my chest, I rocked myself by moving my body from one hip to the other. Someone just *had* to feel sorry for me! I peeked into the mirror, and the damned dull, ordinary face peeked back. It was pale and sad. It was true: I was ugly.

I slipped on my pants and a T-shirt, then stood in front of the mirror. I was able to recognise the beautiful blue eyes and cute nose that good-looking Florian had once pointed out to me. But I couldn't make my mind up whether I was pretty or dull.

I left Sven's studio and walked to work. At 12.30pm, I met him for lunch in the canteen. My heart was beating as frantically as when I'd opened his cupboard doors.

"You're so quiet today. What's up?" he asked. He knew

it wasn't normal for me to neither talk nor eat, but just tap the back of my fork on the table.

Of course, I'd been waiting for him to ask. "I've seen your porn magazines!"

I expected him to get angry, because I had invaded his cupboard – his personal stuff. But, nevertheless, it was *him* who was the guilty one, simply because of what I had discovered. He spluttered, his face turning bright red. The next moment a pause. Then he grinned. "Well, every guy does that. Men are like animals. They see things, they react. I'm just a man."

I hated it. I hated him. "But you never react when you see *me*." I said.

Another pause. Sven didn't come up with any further excuse or explanation.

"I don't like this. Your filthy porn. What you do. Especially because you avoid me!" I said.

He seemed to accept, without arguing, that what he did wasn't right. At least not the way it happened. He had voluntarily taken a seat in the dock. But he also knew how to defend himself. "It's just pictures. Paper. Not real women!"

I hated it. I hated him. "Just pictures? No! You can't play it down like that."

"It's something very easy; takes the energy of a single spaghetti; no real effort required. It's quick and then over. No meaning," he said.

"You don't seem to understand!" I raised my voice and slammed my fist onto the table. Dishes vibrated.

"Shhh, not so loud. My colleagues might be around," he implored.

He leaned in towards me and moved a hand to his mouth as if he was covering it up.

I got even angrier. His colleagues and reputation – in short, his job -- always came first. "I don't give a shit!" I said.

"Okay, okay, calm down. I'll throw the magazines away."

I was instantly happier. He'd understood and would do the right thing. He would finally make an effort with me. I wanted sex, and dared to picture us making love instead of shagging – even perfectly: him on top of me, in the missionary position.

*   *   *

BACK IN THE lab, I struggled with my pipetting. I had an awful lot to do. Dozens of test tubes stood on my bench, all for just one experiment. My lab journal needed to be updated, cells cultivated under the sterile hood, and I hadn't autoclaved any pipette tips for several days. But how could I focus when Sven had told me that every guy looks at porn? I pictured my boss kneeling on a carpet with a clipping of Heidi Klum and…

The lab door flew open. Somebody walked in.

"Stop, but focus on your pipetting."

"Dad? You do that too?"

"Stop thinking. You'd better not fail at your job!"

Dad in my lab, in Munich? That was *impossible*. I frowned. He turned around and left, banging the door so hard it hurt my head. My hallucination passed.

*   *   *

AFTER WORK, SVEN and I went by his place together. I watched him dump the stack of porn into a big recycling container outside the building. Problem solved, we drove to mine.

Sven let my hand get a bit closer the next morning when I reached out under the duvet. I touched his shoulder, drew closer and almost cuddled his back. He lay on his side, facing away from me, one leg pulled up to protect what he didn't want to be sought out by my greedy fingers.

And so it was every night and morning he was at mine. Nothing changed. We only worked, and ate together in the evenings. Saturdays and Sundays, I spent some hours alone or with Sonja while he went to the lab. And when he could finally afford some leisure time, we either drove south of Munich for a quick walk in the woods, or played a couple of games at the pool hall. No sex!

I knew the problem was not solved. It couldn't be thrown away along with his magazines. It stayed with him. Or did I have the problem and he didn't tell me?

*   *   *

I MADE ANOTHER attempt one night in my flat, just after we'd gone to bed: "You *need* to tell me the real reason why you reject me all the time, please! Don't you agree there is a problem?"

"I'm just not able to have sex with you."

"And why is that? Tell me more," I said and sat up. "Please tell me, no matter what it is. I need to know."

"'Cause you're always so uptight. Those rules 'n' stuff. I can't get excited," he said.

"'Those rules 'n' stuff'?" My God, he meant Sonja. Sonja's rules!

"Yes, you're fussy and uptight. It's in my head; makes it impossible to get a hard-on."

What? How could Sonja and her OCD be at fault? I

276

only followed her rules to avoid hurting her. She was my soulmate. "Seriously?"

"Yes!" Sven had turned the tables. I was sat in the dock now. Guilty. Silent. "I'm your boyfriend. It should be you and me. But it's like a threesome. Those rules always have to be considered. All the time, the most important thing," he said.

"Are you kind of jealous?"

"No, I'm not."

I wasn't convinced he was jealous. But I could sense he felt neglected. It wasn't justified, though. Not really. Because despite following Sonja's rules, I was just as considerate toward him. I had racked my brain over and over. Whenever I thought I recognised a problem of his, I tried to help. I had played the missionary a million times, forgiven him for hitting me, put myself second. I had changed parts of my personality, such as stopping socialising with other people. I'd copied his grouchy behaviour, being a grump myself when talking to colleagues, in order to please him. I'd worked my fingers off by endlessly articulating my apologies on paper when he'd broken up with me and not opened his door. I had bent myself and adapted to him as much as Sonja's mother had done to suit her father. I wasn't me any more! But still, I was unable to defend myself, because I couldn't dismiss the impact of Sonja and her OCD.

"There you go, now you know why there's no sex," he said and suddenly sat up too.

I was still stuck in the dock. My blood rushed around as if lava was flowing inside my body. I got so annoyed. With Sonja.

I moved closer to Sven, who was now sitting on my mattress with his back against the wall, and kneeled in front of him. I lifted my arms to put them around him, saying, "We need to try and talk more about this problem in future. We have to solve it somehow, don't you agree?"

He puffed his cheeks, pushed my arms away and jumped up. "Typical! You always want to talk, talk, talk! I'm fed up! It's too much; I'm going now."

He dressed, pulled his bunch of keys from his pocket, turned the ring, handed me my spare key, and marched out. Gone!

Still on my knees, I fell flat onto my mattress. Tears streamed along with the lava. This time, I thought, was serious. Sven had properly broken up with me. He meant it. Because this time, he gave a real reason; a name: Sonja. And I was linked to her.

ONE OF US HAS TO GO

I HAD WAILED for hours but eventually fallen asleep. It was quarter past eleven on Sunday morning when I woke. The sun was frazzling the screen of my balcony door. I peeked out. Not a single cloud in the sky – unlike in my mind. The darkness in there was unbearable. And Sonja was the reason for Sven breaking up with me again.

I had a mobile phone now, purchased a little while ago. I'd texted Sven twelve times the night before, starting right after he'd walked out of my flat. I told him I would cut Sonja out of my life, so that he and I could stay together. But I'd received no reply. He probably didn't believe me. And that caused the volcano to erupt: I became furious, and I wanted Sonja to pay for destroying my relationship.

She didn't know I was single yet again. I picked up the handset of my wireless landline and dialled her number. I heard it ringing, got up to stand by my window and glanced down through hers. It was still ringing as my eyes wandered around her little garden. And there she was – flaked out on a towel by the edge of the lawn, sunbathing. Right below my balcony. Plugs in her ears, probably listening to music. I hung up the phone and sidled over to my balcony, opening its door without a creak, and stepped out on tiptoes. I stood right above her. Her face shiny, eyes closed. I sensed my chance. I just *had* to prove to Sven that I would cut her out; I had to get him back. I couldn't stand the world without him.

"Sonja, it's not working any more, both of us together. One of us has to go!" I told her, knowing she didn't hear me. She didn't even know I was there.

I checked out my balcony. I had grown lots of tomato plants on it, despite it being tiny. It resembled a jungle. Only a few gaps were left around the metal bars of the railing, since the leaves covered almost everything. I saw the knife I used to cut off the ripe tomatoes, kneeled down, picked it up, and turned it a couple of times in my hands.

I'm going to flick it through this gap onto your body now, Sonja. But I only carried on turning the knife. *It's not good enough. I might miss her. And it would only hurt her a little bit.*

I sawed with the knife through the stems of the two plants in the biggest pot, then dumped them on the floor. I lifted the heavy pot with all the soil in, supported it on my knee, and heaved it up onto the top of the railing. *That should do, it'll crush her skull.* I slid the pot slightly to the right, getting it into position. I only had to give it a little push to topple it directly onto Sonja's head; the position was perfect.

Just push it!

Suddenly the pot started to wobble between my hands, as if a drum roll was building up to a crescendo. I couldn't control the volcano inside me. My heart almost burst through my chest and the wobbling became stronger and stronger. So did the drum roll. The whole balcony was vibrating. My head boarded a roller coaster. I saw the dead body of my best friend circling around me. Dozens of bright flashes pierced my vision. Everything was turning – I was so dizzy.

Do it, do it, do it, said a little devil's voice in my mind.

No, she's your best friend, replied a little angel.

Come on, go for it! Be selfish and free *yourself!* said the devil.

But she's your cousin – a family member!

Don't care!

But you've got her house money! the angel said.

Yeah, just keep it! Take it and blow it all, you deserve it!

You'll go to prison! the angel countered.

No you won't! Pretend it was an accident!

Too strange an accident – planting tomatoes on top of a railing? Nobody will believe you!

Never mind, never mind, 'cause nobody is watching anyway! The devil almost blasted it.

And suddenly, the angel's voice turned soft and calm. He admonished, *Are you* sure *nobody is watching? What if God is?*

The roller coaster wound round the loop of its circuit, as I watched my two hands holding the big, wobbling clay pot. Just as I reached the peak of the loop – my head upside down – I lifted the very heavy thing down from the railing, slid it onto my knee and further to the floor, next to my feet. The angel had won.

Hell, what had I done? I almost killed her – my very best and longest standing friend! My cousin!

I leaped inside, rushed to the bathroom, and stared into the mirror. I saw a monster. With both hands I supported myself on the sink. I stayed there for seconds; maybe minutes. I didn't really know.

My insides didn't feel right. I waited for something to happen, retched a little. All of a sudden, my stomach churned and I threw up into the sink. My body was being rattled. It was awful. I hadn't even eaten anything. Seconds later, I was finished. As abruptly as my insides had started troubling me, they stopped. I remembered how Sonja had nearly made me puke the day she became my neighbour in class at primary school. I looked back in the mirror and saw the pale face of a ten-year-old.

Who are you? the face in the mirror said. *A monster!*

I couldn't respond. Then my doorbell rang.

I rinsed my mouth, splashed some water onto my face, and went to answer it. Was it Sven? Had he changed his mind? Was he coming back to me?

"Hey, you – morning! Are we going to the park later, when Sven is at the institute?" Sonja knew he would go to work in the late afternoon – it was Sunday.

Jesus Christ – she stood there, with not the slightest clue about what had been going on inside my flat; on my balcony; above her head. Suddenly she was covered in black, and bright stars flashed before my eyes again, as I had to hold on to the wall before my legs collapsed.

"Oh dear, your face is totally white! What's wrong? Shall I call a doctor?" Sonja said.

I couldn't believe what was happening. My best friend was caring for me and asking if I needed a doctor when she just might have needed one herself, had I dropped that pot on her head.

"No thanks, I'm okay." I stumbled through the living room and lay on my bed.

"Have you caught too much sun working with your tomatoes?" She looked through the open balcony door at the cut-off plants and soil spilled on the floor.

"No, I haven't. Stop asking me questions, I can't stand it!" I said.

"What's wrong?"

"Sven has broken up with me. Seriously, this time!"

She said nothing; I didn't give her the chance to speak. "Sonja, you will have to do something about your OCD. I'm demanding it. *Commanding*, if you'd like! You *must* travel up north, go and meet Goran, and put this nightmare to an end. You need therapy!"

I lifted myself up. She was sat on my mattress, next to me. Frowning at me. Speechless.

"Yes, indeed, that is what you must do. Otherwise I'll leave you and never return, and you will be alone," I said.

THERAPY, OR
TRYING TO PLEASE
OTHER PEOPLE?

SONJA AND I were on a high-speed train to Gadburg. We'd taken two weeks off work. Our last visit up had been ages ago. Sonja knew that, this time, returning to Munich would be different – there would be no transformation.

Her parents knew about the plan to meet Goran. Her father surprised me when he offered help – he would talk to Goran's father the next time he saw him – they were still attending the same sports club. I was sure the whole thing would appear like an error. I mean, why would Sonja urgently need to meet Goran after nine years, when she'd never had anything to do with him? At least, *he* must have thought that.

Sonja had to stay in her parents' house in Fessdorf. She couldn't escape to Lucas's any more. But the Goran contamination at her parents' didn't really matter – she was going to *meet* him! It felt strange, even for me, to be sitting in their guest room that used to be Sonja's bedroom; more because of remembering all the tears shed over empty glass bottles, rubbish bags, and crumbs in her bed, rather than the Goran contamination. This room held very dark memories.

* * *

TWO DAYS AFTER we arrived, Sonja met Goran in a café in Gadburg. He'd moved from Dabendorf to the city. Her parents had enlightened his, and they in turn had ensured Goran understood the effect he had on Sonja. It was incredibly fortunate, and a surprise, from Sonja's point of view that Lasse, Goran's brother, had been lightly touched by OCD himself. Not a huge surprise, really, given that two per cent of the world's population suffer from this mental illness!

I escorted Sonja to the city centre, but then I let her go through with the meeting on her own. She had to. But no doubt my heart was racing as fast as hers when I watched her walk into the café.

One and a half hours later, she returned. I could barely believe my eyes when I saw the smile on her face, and Goran walking right next to her. He had changed so much from the long-haired, greasy layabout. He was a young man of twenty-five with short, clean hair, lovely blue eyes, and a charming smile. *Handsome.* I shook his hand and thanked him. I was overjoyed that Sonja's long-term problem was solved and trusted that her mind would finally be free of OCD, now that she had spoken into the face of her fears.

* * *

I KNEELED ON the carpet, my elbows balancing on either side of Grandma's lap as I held her hands, and brought them to my lips to kiss them. She was sitting in her armchair, the smell of old skin and anti-ageing moisturiser crawling into my nose.

"I love you, Grandma!" I looked up into her eyes, slightly milky now with age. A nasty sting pierced all the way through my heart, ripping it apart. Like the long, fierce zigzag lightning I had seen in Munich's humid summer skies, it was seemingly never-ending.

"I love you too, my poppet."

More lightning struck, as if the first hadn't caused enough damage. Grandma still called me 'poppet'. I had lost some years of putting my head into her lap, hugging and playing Rummy with her – all down to Sonja. Grandma was an eighty-one-year-old woman now, and it felt like torture that I hadn't attended her eightieth birthday. An aunt had criticised me for it, maybe not understanding how shitty I felt anyway, and how frustrating it was that my best friend's OCD hadn't allowed me to take a trip to northern Germany.

*   *   *

THE TRAIN WAS travelling fast; 330 kilometres an hour at times. It was taking Sonja and me back down to Munich.

"What's wrong?" I asked. She hadn't talked for a while, and her face was pale as chalk.

Her eyes met mine, and she burst into tears. Her hands flew up to her head, fingers pressed against her skull as if she was suffering a sudden attack to her brain.

"What's up?" I said.

She couldn't speak. Other passengers turned around, glancing over.

I reached out to put a hand on her shoulder as she sat opposite me. "Please, try to calm down. And tell me!"

Her words stumbled out. "I'm scared to tell you."

My jaw dropped. I was flabbergasted at the fact that

somebody — my best friend — was afraid of telling me something. Afraid of *me*? *My* reaction? I had only known this the other way around. *I* had been scared of Sven, and of my father. Now, I seemed to have that very effect on somebody else. How terrible! I didn't want that. Particularly if it was unreasonable.

"It's okay, you can tell me. Whatever it is, you can tell me." I tried to speak with my softest voice.

"My problem isn't solved. I feel so much fear right now. It's overwhelming, all coming back over me."

"Your problem? Goran? The OCD?" I could clearly hear the shock in my voice, and realised why Sonja was afraid to tell me.

She was still sobbing as she slid forward to the edge of her seat and clasped her hands. "Please don't leave me. Please, I don't want to be all alone!"

My jaw dropped once more. I was disgusted by Sonja begging me, like her mother had done when she kneeled down in front of her father.

"Stop it!" I said. "Calm down. Sit back and we'll talk about this."

She slid back in her seat, and we talked.

"I need to wash myself as soon as we arrive in Munich. I'm dirty. Very dirty. I have to throw all these clothes away." She pulled at the material of her pants; a sleeve of her top. "I'm contaminated!"

I sighed. "And I thought it was all good, when I saw your smile as you and Goran came out of the café."

She shook her head, waving her hands in denial. "Goran isn't my problem any more."

"What is it, then? Who?"

She hesitated. Stared out the window. Her eyeballs were

racing from left to right, taking in the countryside that flew past. Then she looked back at me. "My parents!"

"*What?* Your parents?"

"Yes, my parents. I now have exactly the same feeling about them that I had all those years about Goran. *My parents* are dirty."

Her parents? Dirty?

"And does this mean the OCD isn't gone? Not at all? Not improved? Nothing?" I asked.

Sonja stared out the window again, eyeballs racing. I knew that was her 'yes'. And she knew that I knew. Going up to Gadburg to meet Goran hadn't removed the OCD. It had only uncovered that the people Sonja really had a problem with were her parents. She looked back at me. I felt pressure behind my eyes. She moved to the edge of her seat once more, but I didn't let her beg me again.

"It's okay. You tried. That's the main thing," I said, the lump in my throat growing bigger. It wouldn't have been fair to punish her. She *had* tried. Hard! I pretended I needed a pee and disappeared to the toilets, where I burst into tears myself.

* * *

IN MUNICH, WE both underwent a new type of transformation in our respective bathrooms. I took a very thorough shower after throwing away my clothes from the trip. I was glad Sonja hadn't mentioned any eye, mouth, or nose-washing. After the shower, I cleaned my tub wearing rubber gloves, then disposed of them and washed my hands again. I made my best effort possible.

For Sonja, the north of Germany remained dirty. All

products from the northern half of the country were taboo. All her OCD symptoms remained – only their cause changed. Things weren't associated with Goran, but her parents. Haribo suddenly became an okay product, because Sonja's parents had nothing to do with the city of Bonn. But places that she knew they had been to were dirty now. It was tough, because Sonja's parents liked travelling Germany as well as the rest of the world. My corset was tightened further as hers changed colour once again. 'Colour'... or the meaning of what she thought; what she felt.

DAD'S ULTIMATE
WITHDRAWAL OF
LOVE

IT HADN'T MATTERED to Sven that I'd made Sonja fight her fears and meet Goran. He'd had no interest in whether or not it would be just him and me in our relationship now anyway. No, it wouldn't, but Sven didn't know that. He kept letting me work to get him back. Five months had gone by since Sonja and I had travelled up north; five months since he'd broken up with me. Whenever he saw me at work, he could probably tell I was still attracted to him. He enjoyed me running after him.

Now, in summer 2003, I was troubled. My three main issues:

1)   Sonja and her OCD.
2)   Sven's aggression – he had only just been able to hold himself back from bashing me with a pillow.
3)   My contract couldn't be extended after winter 2003/2004 due to further research money not being sanctioned. I was facing unemployment.

Mum's birthday had just been and, for the very first time

ever, I hadn't given her a present. I was unhappy about it but believed she had been truthful when we spoke before the day and she had told me it was no problem. She understood I struggled with work, Sonja and Sven; that I was too stressed out to make her a present. However, *Dad* did not!

I called my parents' landline to wish Mum a happy birthday.

"Hi, Dad, can I speak to Mum, please?"

"No, not yet. Let me tell you something: if you ever again don't give your mother something for either her birthday or Christmas, then you will get *nothing* from me any more!" His loud teacher's voice blew my ear away. I had to hold the handset away from it.

This clap of thunder was more violent than Sven's aggression, striking deeper than any smack on my head. Because this was *Dad*. Not just a boyfriend. This was my father, who confirmed, once again, that he didn't love his daughter. His voice was so sharp it could have cut through me, like he was stabbing me. Had I committed a crime by not giving Mum a present?

Dad – the powerful head of the family, who was always right – now wanted me to say something; to respond to him when I knew already that whatever I could say would be wrong. I was scared.

"But I wasn't able to make her a present this time. I just wasn't able. I have quite few problems at the moment. And I didn't forget Mum. I'm calling to speak to her right now!" I tried.

"You should have bought her something instead!" Dad said.

As expected, my point was meaningless to him. Going to a shop and buying a present hadn't occurred to me. I had never *bought* presents for my parents; neither for Christmas nor their birthdays. I had always put more thought into things, involving at least some sort of handicraft. Buying a book or a CD hadn't been the way I'd done things for over two decades.

Dad launched into a speech about what was proper and improper in life. He talked about the idea of family and respecting parents. He went on and on about peoples and races in which parents are honoured and given presents as a sign of thankfulness. As if he was reading commandments; *his* commandments. As if he was God. I was blown away. Seriously. He made it sound like I had failed completely, not respected my parents, sinned, and needed to be thumped: *You will get* nothing *from me any more!*

My body trembled with fear. But Dad couldn't see that. The lump in my throat made my voice shake, but maybe he didn't hear it. I pulled all my reserves together and attempted to withstand his threats. "Well, do what you want, then! I can miss out on your presents if you put me under so much pressure!"

Dad was conditional towards me. He only wanted to give presents under certain conditions. I didn't like that. I couldn't accept it. How regrettable that I didn't continue quickly enough and tell him how little his idea of a family fitted with the fact that he had left his wife and sick three-year-old behind in hospital, pissing off to Yugoslavia on a holiday.

I hated Dad. And I hated him again and again, each Christmas and birthday that he put no money into my bank account. He made it happen: I got nothing from him any more. Ever again.

SAVED

Spring 2004

I STILL CALLED Dad 'Dad' – unlike Sonja who, ever since I had known her, had only spoken about her 'father'.

Dad seriously hurt me in not giving me anything for Christmas and birthdays. I was disappointed with Mum, too, because she never mentioned that she had tried to defend me. Since I didn't live with my parents, I had no chance of overhearing any discussions they might have had about my failure to give Mum a birthday present. I wondered about her reaction when Dad told her she would now have to make her own money transfer if she still wanted to give me something. Had she challenged him? Had she forgotten how she'd told me it would be fine for me to not give her anything for once? Hadn't she tried to stop Dad from telling me off; threatening me with his consequence? What was her role in all this?

I couldn't help thinking that something about it had impressed Mum. Because not only had Dad never been the most protective father or treated me like his little princess – he also never treated Mum like one! He was no charming husband, never brought her flowers; no pralines in a nice box. So did she interpret his reaction to my present-neglect as standing up for her and a proof of his love? Did she even like, maybe *love*, that Dad had 'thumped' me? Did she enjoy his action at my cost? Did I now have to pay the price for a problem or a lack of love in my parents' relationship, each Christmas and each birthday? I didn't know. Nor did I appreciate just how scared of Dad I was. I didn't realise it: I was scared he would punish me further; withdraw it all – the little bit of love that I was hoping was left for me. I needed to cling on to that.

* * *

SVEN HANDED ME my spare key, for the umpteenth time. We'd been on a trip to Cologne in the west of Germany. He too was unemployed and had a job interview there. We were surprised when we discovered that the hotel we stayed in had no television; too bad it was *me* who had booked the room. He didn't say one single word to me while we drove the six hours back to Munich the next morning.

"Right, this time you've got to be stronger. You must not run after him any more. This time, you and I together are stronger. Do *not* try to get him back!" Sonja was sitting next to me on my mattress, her arm around me. She rocked me slightly. I was so glad she was there. She was a real friend; my only one. Not even my parents were able to give me comfort. Sonja was. She felt for me. God, but was I glad. Glad I hadn't dropped that heavy clay pot on her, the previous summer. Glad that little angel had appealed so well to my conscience.

I turned my head and stared at my balcony. Nothing was left of the tomato plants. I had removed them without leaving a single trace. A neighbour had gratefully taken all my clay pots. I saw a shadow on the railing and stood up from my bed to stand by the balcony door. What the devil…? Err, no – what the angel was he doing there? The little angel from last summer was sat on the railing, dangling his feet, his head inclined.

Do you have a bad conscience? His eyes were on me.

The angel was alone, no devil this time. His question tightened my chest.

Suddenly Sonja's mobile rang. I turned around as she pulled it from her pocket. She looked at the display. "My mother," she said, and picked up.

Then there was silence. She stood up, brushed her hair off her forehead and started pacing up and down.

"No, Mum, you cannot come to Munich. Please. I'm not ready for you to visit me," she said, her face red, eyes wide.

Sonja tried, to no avail, to stop her parents' planned trip. They knew she had replaced Goran with them.

"Mum, please, I have explained this to you. Why are you ignoring it? I've told you that you shouldn't just book a hotel room and come down!"

Silence as Sonja's mother was talking.

Then: "Three nights in a hotel don't cost the world if you can't cancel. Just leave it. But it'll cost me *everything* if you come here. I'm not ready. Mum!"

A catastrophe was approaching. Sonja's world was about to close in so much that it would leave no space for her to live – nor even to exist. Just like when she had been trapped in the wood, in the student flat back at Gadburg.

She hung up the phone. Big pressure was now on her. I could see it pile up on her shoulders, her mind. Her parents would come to Munich the following week!

"I have to leave!" Sonja said.

"Munich?" I asked. "Where to? For how long?"

"Forever!" she said. "As soon as possible. Anywhere that is clean of my parents and northern Germany. And please: you've got to come with me!"

I was unable to respond. Leaving Munich as soon as possible and never returning sounded very hasty. And I *loved* Munich! A while ago, I had thought I would live there forever. Leaving felt like ripping everything apart.

I turned away from Sonja and looked out at my balcony again. The little angel was still on the railing, still dangling his feet.

You do *have a bad conscience!* he told me.

I squeezed the bridge of my nose, wiped both hands over my face, and blew out my cheeks. Thoughts flashed up: my life at the girls' house, which was history; friends in Munich, which I didn't have any more; work, which I could try to find somewhere else; my unemployment money. I was entitled to sixty per cent of my last salary in unemployment money; for twelve months with the condition of proving that I was looking for a new job. But eight hundred Euros a month didn't last long at all in expensive Munich. My rent alone was six hundred! I thought of Sven and what I really felt for him. And I didn't know.

I turned to Sonja again.

"Please, leave Munich with me. I cannot live here any more. And you'll benefit, too. Don't go back to Sven, don't think of him. Once we're gone, it'll be easier for you. You've got to draw a line now," she said.

It was such a good point. I could be saved from Sven. The angel was right, and so was Sonja. Once physically away from Sven, I wouldn't be able to stick my apologetic letters under his door any more. No more rides past his studio to see if the light in his window was on.

*   *   *

WITHIN FOUR DAYS, Sonja and I advertised our furniture and sold it all. On the fifth day we left Munich. It had been over seven years since we arrived, and it hurt when I couldn't see it from the window of the train any more.

We rented a furnished studio in a village in south-western Germany with a population of four thousand, about 250 kilometres away from Munich. It was a clean, tiny spot on the map – not somewhere that I could imagine Sonja's parents had visited. When her mother would ask about our new whereabouts and if she could have the address, Sonja would reply, "Sorry, but I can't tell you, Mum. You know why."

I knew I couldn't live there for long, especially being so crammed in with Sonja. But with eight hundred Euros' unemployment money and a modest life-style, I didn't have to touch my house money.

Sonja's phone rang several times the day after our arrival in south-western Germany. A number from Munich was displayed on the screen. She never picked up but listened to the voicemail her father left: her mother would be crying. Guilt for Sonja! Sure, it must have hurt for her mother not to be able to see Sonja. But she had tried to explain honestly, and apologised for being unable to meet up with them.

My own mobile also rang. A hundred times. It was always the same person: Sven. I never picked up. Sonja held me back. Sven kept calling me for days and days. Each time he let it ring for minutes. I had disabled my voicemail and enjoyed him running after *me*. Tables turned!

When I saw a different number displayed, I picked up. It was the police. Sven had reported me missing. Haaaa ha ha! He'd got what he deserved: he was the fool, and I was saved.

*   *   *

BY THE END of November I had made what was probably my best-ever Christmas present for Dad. I had collected fruit from around the village and made jam with it. Dad liked jam a lot. I mixed different fruits together and filled twelve jars that each had a covered label on them. Dad was supposed to taste and guess which kinds of fruits he ate on his morning toast, before reading the label. I had decorated each jar lid with patterned cloth, before packing them up along with a home-made gift for Mum. Then I carried a well-padded and taped box to the post office. My father, who wasn't going to give me anything for Christmas, would receive his present a little early, but this way I was guaranteed no reproachful speech. And I couldn't send it any later. I was too busy preparing to leave the country.

IMMUNE

I WAS LOOKING through the cute little dormer window of my room on floor four – the converted attic of a big old house. Snowflakes came down in the glow of the street lights. I loved the wintery view just as much as when I was little, only I didn't quite press my nose against the window now. Snow always swallows up every noise and makes even the busiest roads silent.

It was between Christmas and New Year, when the days are short. People say that this time makes people prone to depression, due to the darkness. But I wasn't depressed. Not at all. Instead, I enjoyed the beginning of a new life in Zurich, Switzerland.

I had only worked a few days leading up to Christmas and was now on holiday. My new institute in Zurich was closed until early January. The same was true for Sonja. She too had a new job. We'd each been offered two different jobs and had had the choice.

Sonja lived in her own room, on floor two of this old house. Three nuns ran the place. My new Swiss boss had arranged my room for me, and Sonja managed to get one as well.

I couldn't pull myself away from my dormer window. The view was just too good. The wooden windowsill I had my elbows on, and the playfully folded, short, dark green curtains gave it a perfect frame. A tram wound through the snow as it went up the bendy road. I didn't mind the short days. I loved them.

Beep, beep. I twitched. *Huh?* My phone sat on the sill next to me. Who was that? Sonja, maybe? I grabbed the mobile to see who the text was from. My body clenched when I saw the person's name on the display: Sven.

We hadn't been in touch since I had left Munich. What did he want from me now?

I hesitated. Did I actually want to know? My thumb ran in circles over the key to open his message. Then I pressed it. *PLEASE, HELP ME*, it said. What? Help him? Now? How? And why *me*?

I fired some warning shots across my own bows. I had to think first. Think about whether I really wanted to get involved with Sven again. Think about whether I wanted to help him – with whatever it was. The missionary had resigned!

I walked up and down my room. The wooden floor creaked with each step. *Selfish* – that was what I wanted to be. I didn't want to believe any more that God had given me the job of a missionary, and I didn't fancy any appeal from my little angel. I would only talk to the devil this time. But, because I was still me, I replied to Sven's text.

What's the problem?

Thirty seconds later, another text: *I need your help. Please, can I speak to you?*

I'm not in Germany any more. In Zurich now! I wrote, and then sent it. Then I regretted mentioning Zurich.

Doesn't matter. Can I call? PLEASE!

I recognised it was urgent, because this hadn't ever happened before. I texted him the landline number of my floor, and heard it ringing straight away. Down the corridor, I picked up and listened to Sven speaking in a voice I'd never heard from him before. It sounded like pure desperation. He told me he was unemployed, lonely and depressed. *Lonely?* Heidi Klum and her naked friends sprang to mind. Were their two dimensions insufficient? Oh, but they didn't run after him. *Depressed? Sven?* People said it was the time for depression. But Sven? He had never appeared to be lonely before, let alone depressed.

Although his desperation surprised me, it didn't get under my skin.

"Can I please come and be with you?" he asked.

Ouch! What a horrible question. I wanted to ignore it. Not answer. Not have heard it. Just hang up the phone.

"Err…"

"Please, you've got to help me. Please. I tried to kill myself this morning," he said.

Jesus! I didn't want to hear this. Again I wished to ignore him; just hang up. He couldn't reach me. Not the soft part of my heart. And that was the problem – *his* problem. I was immune to him now.

I didn't reply. I didn't even make a sound.

"Can I please come to you?" he asked again.

I thought of the twosome in my head – the angel and the devil – and suddenly they showed up. Only I didn't even need help. I could make my own decision. And I wanted to be selfish. Healthily selfish. I covered their mouths with my hands and gave Sven my answer. "No, you cannot come here!"

As soon as I had spoken, I worried I'd been too harsh. My hand nearly slipped away from the angel's mouth. Sven didn't speak. I only heard him breathing.

"I'm sorry, but I've started a new life here. And I need to focus on it – my job," I said.

My words must have been familiar to him. He had said something very similar to me. Still he just breathed into the phone. Was he going to cry? I pressed my hand very, very firmly over the angel's mouth. I needed to make sure he didn't plead with me.

"I enrolled at a clinic for psychiatric treatment. But I have to wait *weeks* before I can be admitted. There's no bed available right now. It's so hard having to wait every day," he told me.

Wow, Chubby Curl really seemed to be in trouble. He wasn't the person I used to know. And still, I remained selfish. He couldn't soften me up. He hadn't cared about *me* when I was desperate – because of *him*!

I wondered how he had tried to kill himself, and why he'd failed. But I didn't ask.

"You definitely cannot come here, but I have a suggestion," I said. "I'll call you every day until you're admitted; help you through the waiting period. All right?"

My 'no' was not negotiable, and surely he could tell. He must have realised I had changed, and that it was too late now even if he'd shown remorse for how shitty he used to be with me. All he could do was appreciate my offer.

Once he was admitted, I discarded my German mobile number and bought a Swiss phone.

DIRTY GERMANY
WASHED OVER

I HAD MADE a new friend in Zurich, gone out regularly and built a social network. I hung out in bars and pubs; watched films in the cinemas; went dancing. Zurich was the perfect city – not too small and not too big. The twenty-three-kilometre long lake was enticing, especially in summer, when people would swim in its crystal-clear water, the Alps towering right behind it. Life was good again. And I fancied a new man: Gareth.

Gareth was English. I had met him on a Saturday morning in a launderette, given him my email address, and he wrote to me almost every day. In English! Although I had travelled to Australia, New Zealand, the US and Canada, where I'd had to communicate in English, my foreign language skills were still just as bad as they were at school. And so I found myself consulting an online dictionary a gazillion times – typing, deleting and re-typing – until I had stitched together a paragraph or two that would make sense to Gareth.

He was very persistent. His charming emails had chased me for three weeks until I agreed to meet up. I thought I knew what he wanted. We went out for dinner and then back to his hotel room. Yes, of course, it did happen. His dark hair and eyes, his lips and his hands were even more charming than his emails. A Star of David on a leather cord decorated his masculine, slightly hairy chest. I couldn't resist. It was more like making love than anything I'd had with Sven.

I was disappointed that Gareth didn't want a relationship. He was a football fan, so I tried to track him down in Zurich's English pubs, after he didn't respond to my emails any more. I was sad I couldn't find him, and slept with another Englishman instead. And another one. Each month I changed them. When I sneaked good-looking Steven into my room at the boarding house run by the nuns, I risked getting kicked out by Sister Gertrud. She was the strictest, but also blushed the most when all three nuns stood by the stairs, unable to pull their eyes away from Steven.

I named my Englishmen according to the months in which I saw them: Mr April, Mr May, Mr June. Mr July was non-existent; then came Mr August and Mr September. I knew it was wrong, what I was doing. I knew I was attempting to prove something to myself: that I was popular. Liked. *Loved*. I was desperate for it – the same old pattern. I was unbearably thirsty for a man who would reciprocate my love.

Sonja had no misters. She had no interest. Sometimes she came out with me to a pub to watch football. But that was it, and it was fine with me.

* * *

I WAS SAT at my desk at work when she stormed into my office. She looked like a distraught scientist whose experiment of their life had gone wrong, her arms thrown up to her head, hair messy.

"We've got to leave Zurich!" She almost shouted at me.

My eyebrows shot up. "What? What are you talking about?"

"We've got to leave Zurich! It's all dirty!" She paced up and down, left to right. I didn't understand a thing. Oh yes, I did understand *one* thing: I knew something would suffocate me. Something was coming towards me that I couldn't stand any more. Whatever it was this time, I had gone through too much and given my all for Sonja. She would kill me now with her demands.

My lower arms were leaning on my desk. They suddenly felt like rubber, threatening to let me down. I pictured my torso slumping, face smacking my lab journal in front of me.

"Why, this time?"

"Because my former landlady from dirty Munich has found me. She Googled me. Saw my name on the list of employees on my department's website. Here. And she's sent me a bill. I've just found her letter in my box. Imagine!"

I wondered what the bill was for. But it didn't really matter. The next catastrophe was rolling on anyway. My desk started to tremble, like the water in *Jurassic Park* as the dinosaurs approach.

"The bill is for additional water costs. They were added up and sent out by the water company in Munich after we left. The landlady wrote that she's only just forwarded it to me, because it took her so long to find me," Sonja said.

I had understanding for the landlady. She didn't want to pay for Sonja's excessive washing routines.

"I don't care about the cost. The point is, she sent me a physical letter from Munich, contaminating everything here!" Sonja was really shouting now. She came closer.

Very close. She grabbed my shoulder and shook me. "Do you understand what this means? I'm trapped! I can't do anything here any more. Not work, not live. We have to leave!"

Her shaking made me nauseous. I wanted to resist, stiffen my body, but she shook me again.

"Say something, for God's sake! Answer me!" she commanded.

I wasn't able to stand her any longer. My body wobbled like jelly. My brain span. It was hurting. *She* was hurting. She was going to drive me away again, from a place that I liked. That I *loved*.

"Hey, speak to me! Look at me!" she demanded.

My brain, my organs, my will – everything collapsed. Everything inside me was vomiting. Sonja's shaking was violent.

I did eventually look at her. My eyes filled with tears. One blink and they streamed down my cheeks. I bowed and slipped away from Sonja's grip. As fast as she had come into my office, I ran out of it. Down the corridors, around the institute, past several departments and up some stairs, until I reached the roof terrace.

I was panting as I stood by the edge of it. It had a railing. I climbed over and put my feet down on the other side. My arms bent, hands grabbing hold of the railing. My eyes stared down – a long way down.

I was still panting. I saw how my chest pumped air for me. It seemed a wasted effort now that I was about to let go of the railing. I lifted my head and glanced over at the roofs opposite. Then I closed my eyes.

The railing was vibrating in my hands. Lots of stars danced on the inside of my eyelids. And a white garment, further in the distance. It was flying towards me, coming really close. A wet hand grabbed my neck, then the collar of my lab coat. I was pulled towards the railing. Strongly. Very strongly. The lab coat tightened around my throat, making me cough. I felt my legs and feet pulled back over the railing again, before my back hit the tiles of the terrace on the other side. The angel's robe and wings were flapping. He raised a finger.

Don't do that! Don't you ever do that!

I was unable to answer; just stared at him.

You must not throw your life away like that! You are stronger than this, do you understand? he said.

I could still see the angel through my closed eyelids. But then he faded away, the sun was so bright. Warmth seeped through my lab coat; the terrace's tiles were baking. My body slackened. I moved a hand to shield my eyes from the light as I opened them.

"What the hell were you doing? Don't! Don't!" Sonja's face was close to mine. Eyes wide. Scared. Worried. "Don't jump. Please! I beg you, don't do that. I love you. And I *need* you, Finja!" She was panicking. "Okay, okay, I give in. We stay here in Zurich and I accept that I have to live with it this time."

I closed my eyes again.

BETWEEN THE
BLOOMS

SONJA HAD ACCEPTED that it was far too difficult for us to leave Zurich and go somewhere else. Giving up our jobs would probably have meant losing our residence permits for Switzerland and we'd have to go back to Germany within three months or less. I just couldn't imagine going through all the turmoil of applying for jobs, finding one and moving to a different city in Switzerland fast enough. And where would we go if we did return to Germany? Her parents had almost been everywhere! We stayed in Zurich.

She got by. Somehow. But she declared that the box at work in which she had found the letter from Munich to be too contaminated. The letter itself she discarded, then washed her hands for nine minutes, and showered for an hour back at the boarding house. She moved out of her office, leaving the letter box behind, and adopted a table in her lab as her desk, with the excuse to everybody else that writing her lab journal right next to where she conducted her experiments was better for her. Her abandoned letter box was now overflowing with job-related mail and lab catalogues. The catalogues had the potential to contaminate all the labs in her department, maybe the entire institute, if they were taken out by the postdoc she used to share her office with. Every day, when hopefully nobody was watching, I slid two pairs of disposable latex gloves over my hands, walked over to her department, and emptied her letter box. Then I still had to wash my hands each time, in case the contamination had somehow managed to permeate my protection.

I was tied to forty-two hours per week in my own job. I was under pressure not to mess up my experiments; to deliver results. Some experiments lasted as long as two weeks. I was in terrible trouble the day I returned too late to my lab, after Sonja had made me wash my hands forever after emptying her letter box. The protein pellets in my test tubes had dried out, and the experiment was ruined. My boss exploded. His anger grew when I forgot to clear up a sterile bench, on another day when Sonja kept me in her department for half an hour. She was straining me. Draining me. Strangling me.

At home in the boarding house, I still didn't get enough relief from her. She started locking herself in each night. She made sure she turned the key in her lock twice, counting *one, two*. Always doubting it was properly turned, she turned it back, restarting the sequence and listening to the clicks: *one, two*. Over and over again. If *one, two* didn't work, she tried *A, B*. Then she rattled the door to check it was really closed. She rattled and rattled and bloody rattled.

Sonja was convinced it was possible that she regularly attempted to leave her room in her sleep, and wander around in an uncontrolled way. She would walk down the roads, reach the train station, board a train bound for dirty Germany, make a return trip, come back to her room, lie down in bed, and wake up in the morning without knowing what she'd been up to. Or she would go by foot (trams didn't run during the night) all the way to the institute, unlock the half-dozen doors on her way to her old office, and push her hands inside that damn letter box. Every morning she wanted solid proof of not having sleepwalked, and so she introduced 'controlling the key': once she was sure her door lock had been turned twice, she slid her key into an envelope and sealed it overnight.

A pile of envelopes with dates on them lay on her floor, next to the door. Trusting that the relevant envelope was actually closed and sealed each night soon became as difficult as trusting that the door itself was closed. So, *I* locked her in. She would send me a text in the morning, and I'd rush down to floor two to unlock her.

There were those weekends, though, when I met up with Mr September – Nick. Nick wasn't like my other misters. Because he stuck. For longer than just a month. Or, maybe, I stuck. Whenever I couldn't serve Sonja to her satisfaction, she had to lock herself in. Turned out she threw the key out of her window and down into the flower bed, as she felt unable to determine whether or not an envelope was sealed. Each time I didn't respond to her texts the next morning and pick up the key from the flower bed to free her, she had to find somebody else to do it. I wondered what her explanations were – how she claimed the key had ended up between the blooms. She would say she had shaken out her trousers to get rid of dust and forgotten her key in her pocket. Or maybe she had spotted a spider inside her handbag, screamed, and rushed to get rid of it by shaking the bag out of the window, leading to her key falling out. Sonja's imagination was great but, logically, she would soon run out of explanations. Her stories didn't appear realistic any more after another resident of the boarding house, or a nun, had already unlocked her once. She was forced to wait by her window until a stranger came past on the pavement below.

One day as I came around the corner on my way home from Nick's, I tried to hide behind some bushes. I really didn't want to have to search for the key in public. Sonja was standing by her open window, waving to get the attention of a total stranger down the road.

A little boy holding the stranger's hand pointed up to Sonja. "Dad, look at that woman. Is she a loony?"

I watched the man from behind the branches and leaves as he combed the flower bed for Sonja's key. Then he went inside the house to unlock her.

My Brother: The Better Child

Dad's birthday had been and gone. I hadn't given him anything. I just couldn't do it any more. He had given me nothing for all the recent Christmases and birthdays. At no time had he changed his mind about his principle.

Mum hadn't helped, she'd not defended me; not even when my brother failed to give Dad a present for his birthday!

"What did Dad say to him?" I was talking to Mum on the phone.

"Nothing, I believe."

"What? *Nothing?*" I felt my heart twist.

"No."

"Not even a hint of a moral speech?" I couldn't believe it.

"No, I don't think so," Mum said.

My brother had got away with it, completely unpunished. *Why?* Just why, why, why did Dad make a distinction between his two children?

"This is so unfair!" My tight throat made it hard for me to speak, and tears loomed behind my eyes.

"Maybe Dad's going to say something later," Mum had said.

By now, it was Mum's birthday, almost five months after Dad's. My brother had only now given Dad a present. A belated one. The point was that Dad hadn't been able to foresee that he would get a present sometime later, but he still hadn't said a single word to my brother about receiving no present on his actual birthday. Dad had stayed quiet for *five months*. He hadn't shouted at my brother, he had made no speech about respecting and honouring parents, he hadn't threatened him with anything. My brother was in no trouble. He had faced no withdrawal of love from Dad. My brother was the better person – the better child for him. And Mum watched it all.

My heart was bleeding. It turned out to be the last birthday that I would make Mum a present. I couldn't stand it any more.

I wandered around Zurich. To the lake, along the river, across both parts of the Old Town, and back to the lake. I needed to find something. Something sharp and strong to distract me from this pain. Something to fill in the hole inside me, the lack of love. Dad would never treat me as his princess...

Maybe Nick would. He nicknamed me 'Petal' – a word so sweet and strong it warmed my heart until it felt like it was glowing. But his orgasms seemed unemotional; so fast. They had no depth. They were smooth and cold like the sharp blade of a knife. They cut my glowing heart into pieces right away again. Because I never had an orgasm, and Nick didn't care.

"Shit," he said each time, but did nothing. He'd taken me, my face pressed into his mattress.

I lied and told myself I needed this, accepting getting hurt and abused at all costs, killing the last remnants of my sanity. I wanted Nick to be my boyfriend. I was his petal, and I loved that. I loved *him*. I wanted him to love me back, and pleasured him every night I stayed at his.

I had known exactly what Nick was looking for when he'd sat me on his lap the night we first met. He'd pressed his nose into my neck, told me how special I smelled, and rocked me slightly. He was a master at pulling girls, and knew to the smallest detail how to woo me – like a princess. Like a petal.

I never dared to pluck a daisy, not wanting to see how it finished: *He loves me not.* I knew I was only one of many petals on his flower.

Nick lived by the lake. My pain, caused by Mum and Dad and the better child, was gone immediately when I received his text: *You can come over, I've nothing else planned tonight.* Blinded Petal didn't see that she was his last thought.

* * *

By AUGUST 2006, I had given up all self-respect. I let Nick use me as a sex object and forgot about myself. Even on a public toilet, when he was in the mood, I let him do it to me. Back or forward. It wasn't very pleasant to watch him, as he held both his hands over his mouth so as not to be too noisy while he came. Nobody was there to protect me. I didn't even get to see the little pair – the angel and the devil. A *Flush him down the toilet* from the devil would have been just the thing for me to hear. But I heard nothing. I just ran headlong towards emotional self-destruction, straight for disaster. I could write a book about Nick's selfishness, and include my ideas and female tricks to keep trying to get him to fall in love with me. But no matter what I tried, it didn't work. In my last gasp, my very last try to point out that I was worthy of his feelings, I told him I would leave. He'd never see me again. I wanted him to beg me to stay. Badly.

"I'm considering leaving Zurich and moving to London."

"Wow, that's a *great* plan. London is fantastic. You'll love it," Nick said.

Why did he not take a freshly sharpened knife and ram it all the way into my chest?

* * *

AT WORK, MY concentration was non-existent. Too many private things were torturing me. My father's preference for my brother; Sonja calling me daily into her department to empty her letter box; and Nick who just didn't give a shit about me. My boss reprimanded and criticised me daily. We argued about my mistakes. Pressure on me mounted and mounted. I even had understanding for my boss, because he needed my results. He was under pressure *himself*. But I tried so hard – life just wasn't fair.

Sonja had kept me away from my lab bench for forty-five minutes when my boss asked me to resign. He pushed me into it, since I couldn't be fired. Not easily, at least, since I was in a permanent position with human resources protecting staff who failed to perform due to something other than a lack of skills, laziness or bad timekeeping. Every morning my boss saw me come in as I passed the open door of his office, his eyes darted across to me, saying, *I want to tender your resignation right now, even before you've written it.* Eventually, I did resign.

With no job, a broken heart, and plenty of painful memories of this lovely city, I made it happen and left Zurich for London. Maybe leaving meant forgetting again, just like when Sonja had made me leave Munich to get over Sven.

A CLEAN ISLAND

AT THE BEGINNING of September, I was on a plane to London's Luton Airport. I had made good money during my time in Zurich; enough to spend some weeks in London without having to work. Meanwhile my house money was resting in a German bank account.

Going to England seemed like a new chance. But not just for me. Also for Sonja: England – a dreamland on an island separated from mainland Europe and far away from both her contaminated letter box and dirty Germany.

She wasn't with me on the plane when I went. I'd left too spontaneously. But she vowed to come over later, after she'd finished preparing for her new life. *Again.* She didn't know, though, that I hadn't been honest when I promised to tell her where I'd settle.

* * *

THE PLANE LANDED at Luton. It had stopped raining, and the sun turned the wet runway into a bright mirror.

I didn't have much with me; just money and a few personal things and clothes. I hadn't owned furniture since leaving Munich. My room in the boarding house in Zurich had been furnished.

England felt like being properly abroad. Zurich hadn't

been quite the same, because people there speak German. Even with a strong Swiss accent, it is still German. And everybody understood my High German. London was different. Here, I had chosen a place with a very fast pace of life. Lots of stressed people; very cosmopolitan; cars driving on the wrong side of the road.

I used my newly exchanged and very first British pounds to buy a ticket for a train from the airport to London city centre. The train stood still for a long time, and then an announcement told us they were waiting for a driver to arrive. What? I first thought it was a joke, but turned out it wasn't – after thirty minutes, the train pulled out of the station.

The bed and breakfast I had booked online wasn't easy to find. When I finally got there, I regretted having actually found it. It was nothing more than an upgraded barracks in a slum. My room used to be a garage. Its only window faced another room – the kitchen. The curtains needed to be closed permanently, unless I didn't mind being watched by people cooking their meals. Big grey breeze blocks made up the outer wall. An amateur must have plastered it – wind blew through some of the holes in the blocks. Oh well, at least that way I got some fresh air. A neon tube on the ceiling provided the only light. With no window to the outside, it had to be on all the time. The sterile light and white-tiled floor made the room cold like a prison cell.

"Welcome to a new country. Welcome to a new life!" I murmured to myself, rolling onto a bed which was as hard as a board.

I was shocked at where I had landed – a shitty place somewhere in the London borough of Mile End. I didn't know whether Mile End was a good or bad place to stay, how close it was to the famous sights of the city, or whether

I had been particularly unlucky with my accommodation or if it was standard here. I only knew that it cost thirty-five pounds per night. Seemed like a nightmare to me.

* * *

THE NEXT MORNING, I woke to knocks on my door. I rushed to open it, and my neon-light-dazzled eyes recognised the big fat lady from reception.

"Good morning, sweetheart, here's your breakfast," she warbled and thrust a tray towards me.

"Thanks." I squinted, taking the tray.

My English was okay by then. Since becoming fond of Mr April, Gareth, back in Zurich, I had learned English and spoken it a lot. By the time Mr September – Nick – had turned my heart inside out, I had improved even further; not only by speaking it, but also by exchanging countless text messages. I was able to speak English relatively fluently, but when the big fat reception lady handed me the tray, I didn't feel like saying more than was necessary.

The English breakfast turned out to be a disappointment. The tea was tepid, the beans not even that; the sausages were blackened, and the crusts of the toast were full of mould. Outrageous! Only the fried egg and the two strips of bacon were edible, although I didn't actually fancy any of it.

I left my garage room and went to the bathrooms, walking along a plastic carpet down the corridor. Each step I took was accompanied by a noise from my shoes – the floor was that sticky. Standing by the bathroom window, I glanced into a backyard. *One, two, three, four, five, six,* I thought, counting the disposable razors on the outer window ledge. *And seven, eight, nine, over there. How did people get them on the roof of that shed?*

I counted three rusty washing machines in the yard, and four rotten mattresses; all soaking wet as it was raining.

My goodness! I never saw a place like this in Germany...

I opened the door of the first cubicle. A smell of chlorine wafted towards me. *At least they clean their toilets!* The toilet itself had no seat. And how did people wipe their bottoms? I saw no toilet roll. Not even a holder for it. The only fitting was a long tube with a head. *No shit – do I have to spray my ass with that?* I let the door of that cubicle close and opened the second one, hoping to find something better. But it was the same. The third cubicle was a shower: a windowless box covered in black mould spots. The fourth and last cubicle was a dumping ground, loaded with wooden planks. It may once have been a shower...

I didn't really want to, but I just *had* to take a shower. I hadn't washed myself since leaving Zurich. I stepped into the third cubicle, locked it, hung the towel I had wrapped around myself on the hook on the inside of the door, and held my head and body under a trickle of water. It was ages until I felt clean, mostly because I was trying not to tread in the black stuff around the tub. And then I couldn't get out; the lock wouldn't open. I panicked and shouted for help. I heard Big Fat Reception Lady shouting instructions through the door. I pulled the key out and reinserted it at a different angle into the lock, then rammed my upper arm against the wooden door. It flew open, and I stumbled into Big Fat Lady dressed only in my towel.

Back in my prison cell, I sat on the bed. I heard the rain pattering on the roof, and the wind blowing through the holes in the wall, making my wet body even colder. I was feeling low. Lonely.

I suddenly missed Sonja. Can you believe that I missed her so badly? Never mind all her rules and corsets. Never mind that she'd almost made me jump off the roof of the institute in Zurich. Now she was sorely missed in this strange, horrendous new world. Why? Because she was my friend. My only one. My soulmate. I was used to her more than anybody else. And she cared about me. Nobody else really did. Dad didn't care about me. Mum, maybe, who knows. Nick had probably already forgotten my name. But Sonja, she would *never* forget about me. She had cared about me when Sven had smacked me. She'd wanted me to get away from him, knowing he was bad for me. And she'd saved me. I had been mistaken about who my first priority was when I tried to kill her with that clay pot, for Sven's sake. She had cared about me when I was little, slipped with me into my Imaginary Comfort Bubbles. She got involved with my life! And she was my cousin. I had a moral obligation to her.

* * *

AFTER A FEW days in the shitty B&B, I found a room in a flat in Whitechapel. I haggled the initial 330 pounds per month down to three hundred. Two single beds, a dodgy table, a rickety chair and a wardrobe that almost fell apart when I opened its doors made up the furniture. The mint-green wallpaper was a shocker, and I would need something to cover the big hole in it that exposed the grey concrete beneath. I spent an hour or more removing dust and filth. A Chinese girl had just moved out, and she'd left enough hair on the carpet to make a wig.

The landlord – a snobby guy with a foreign accent

– would collect my rent weekly, calling me on my new English mobile first and then waiting for me in the Sainsbury's car park opposite. He would be sitting in his dark green Jaguar, and only wound down the window of the driver's door as I handed him my cash, before tearing off a scrap of paper from a small notepad, scribbling onto it and claiming it was my receipt.

My new room was big compared to the others I had viewed around London; hopefully big enough for two people. Sonja would sleep in the bed closer to the door – that is, if I decided to tell her my address.

Back in Zurich, she'd resigned from her job and given notice for her room to the nuns. For England – a clean island – she would wipe out everything to do with Germany except for the fillings in her teeth. She knew that no dentist would replace them based on her reasoning.

Volkswagens were rare in London; so were German foods and bathroom products. Just like when we had left Gadburg and moved down to Munich, Sonja would come 'naked', with only the clothes she was wearing, and money from her Zurich job. She'd make sure she came without a molecule on her of that German landlady's letter. She would wash and wash and wash herself. Anything remotely linked with her parents would need to be eliminated. Her roots were putrid. Where she came from was bad. In fact, she admitted she had an identity problem, because she hated her father.

Good heavens, wasn't I in the same boat with Dad? Dad, who had proved not to love me but only my brother, the better child? I hated him, too. Wasn't I vulnerable to becoming disordered?

I realised I was at a point where I could become prone to a mental illness. My God, maybe I could catch OCD?

IMPLEMENTING THE PLAN

July 2014

I HEAR A bang. It's not too loud, but enough for me to open my eyes. The last images of my parents are fading away – long, extended tongues behind a window, drawing huge, juicy sausage skewers into my parents' greedy mouths, while I was locked out of their house, camping on a mattress between two cars and the kerb. Thank goodness, I have only been dreaming.

I hear a clicking sound. Twice. I'm on the bed in my room in Paris, blinking at the ceiling. I'm wet. Sweat covers my back, neck and face. I've had another nightmare.

What was that clicking? A door being locked? Oh, Mr Stumble-Late has come home.

By the way, late: what is the time? I sit up, rub my eyes and nose. Gosh, have I overslept? Have I missed my chance? Frantically I turn around, still sitting in bed. My clock radio shows 3.46. Phew, it's not too late. Sonja should be sleeping tight, her mouth slightly open.

I check my phone. No call, no text messages – confirmation that I'm on my own right now. Am I feeling lonely? Am I worried? Worried I could choke and withdraw from my plan? NO – I am determined. This time, it's got to happen. And this time, I won't go soft again.

Time to grab the knife. I've been thinking for a while about how to do it. Just pressing a pillow down on her face may not be sufficient. Sonja can be strong!

The knife is in my fridge. Inside the freezer compartment, in fact. I climb out of bed, go to the fridge. There's juice in there, and I have a sip. I'm very thirsty. So, yeah, why not have another sip? And another? Am I delaying? Am I nervous? Going soft? Weak? *No*, no way.

I open the freezer compartment, pull out a family-size bag of chocolate balls. The knife is hidden in there. I don't have any other cutlery in my room; no dishes either; nowhere to cook. There's only a fridge in this room; a bit like in a guesthouse. The kitchen is downstairs in the common living area. That's where I took the knife from – well, I've *borrowed* it. I've slipped it into the bag of chocolate balls, so the cleaning lady won't find it. Yummy, these chocolates. So crunchy. I munch. Shall I have more? Shall I delay? No!

I free the knife, turn it in my hand. So sharp, so cold. It's been in the freezer for days. For a moment the blade is covered by a film of moisture. Hot air from my room condenses on the metal. I wipe it with a finger, see my own reflection. Briefly, it seems as if Sonja's father is looking back at me, and then mine. When I was little, people always said I resembled my father a lot. I used to like that; I thought it was good to take after him. It made me proud. These days, it's different.

I place the knife on top of the fridge, then glance through the window. Nobody is out there in the yard. All is calm and quiet. No smokers. I picture WHWM-Dad at home, asleep in his bed. I can see closed curtains behind some of the windows. People in this quartier are sleeping, hopefully having nice dreams. No nightmares.

I step in front of my sink, next to the fridge. I turn on the cold water tap and splash some onto my face. It's very refreshing. I'm properly awake now. I turn the water off and dry my face with a towel. Still fully dressed, I only need to put on my shoes. Then I can go to Sonja's room. No noises are coming from there. It's a good sign – she's all finished with her routine and fast asleep. She must be ready – ready for me. I just mustn't flinch.

My heart suddenly starts to beat faster. I feel it bashing. So distracting! Is it because I realise how close I am, how few excuses I have for following through with my plan? Like, *zero* excuses: I've strapped a bum bag around my waist and put my mobile phone into it. The bag itself sits at my front. My shoes are on. I hold the knife in one hand and take Sonja's key off the shelf with the other. Both go in the bag. I'm ready.

My left hand sits on the handle of my door, and I switch off the light with my right. One last glance at my radio on the bed-side table: 4.03 – perfect, nothing to complain about, although an hour later than originally planned.

My pulse is beating in my neck now as I push down the handle of my door. Slowly, silently. A click, and the door opens a couple of inches. I pull it towards me. The corridor is black, but the movement detector will spot me as soon as I step out of my room and the light will come on. *Click* – there it is.

Nobody else is here in the corridor. Everybody is asleep. I turn to face my door, close it as softly as I opened it, and turn back again. Sonja's door handle is only a few feet away from me. So close. I step forward, stand right in front of it until I'm *really* close. I have practised this – it's a blind spot for the movement detector.

I wait until the light goes off. It won't be long; only a few seconds. Enough time to go soft? Enough time to board a roller coaster? Am I ready to kill her? Am I really ready? Mentally strong enough? Maybe I should withdraw, go back into my room and curl up in bed. Withdraw like I've done before.

I feel dizzy. I need support. Where are my little guys – the angel and the devil? Nowhere. I'm on my own. Well, I must bear the dizziness, then. Fight it. Because one of us has to go. For years I thought I needed her; thought she was my safety, my backbone. I was delusional. She recognised what I was lacking, my desires, my fears – her chances. She used me, abused me. Because I let her. I didn't believe in myself; didn't trust I'd be able to create strong bonds with people other than her. I get it, *I let her*. But she needed me, too. On her own, she wouldn't survive. I've hosted her. We're codependent – as long as we're both alive.

I think of that picture – the captured embrace. Sonja has blackmailed me, and that is *so* bad. So very bad. It's fatal.

I just mustn't flinch.

Click – the light's off. Pitch dark. Black. My heartbeat thuds in my ears now; so loud. Hopefully it won't alert Sonja. I search blindly in my bag for her key. Got it! My fingers feel for the door's lock. Got it! I insert the key very slowly. It's in. I turn it around. No, I don't! Damn, what's happening? It is stuck. How can that be? It can't!

I try again; it's impossible that I'm unable to turn this key. I've done it a million times – locking her in and reopening the door the next morning. It's not long ago that I *personally* closed this door. Only a few hours!

I try again but no, doesn't work. The key won't turn. I have to stop or I may break it. Is it not supposed to work?

Is it not supposed to happen? Has Sonja done something to the lock from inside her room? She never does! And I doubt it anyway.

I also doubt myself. I must have lost control somewhere in my preparation for this. Have I swapped her key with mine? I'm convinced I took Sonja's from the bag. I must focus harder at this crucial moment.

I pull the key out from Sonja's lock and search for the other one in my bag. It's so dark here in the corridor, I can't see a thing. My right hand hits the tip of the knife. Ouch. Well, I knew it was pointy and sharp.

Bzzz, bzzz. My phone vibrates in my bag. The screen lights up as I twitch. *Jesus!*

I've got a message. At this time? Déjà vu. Like last time I tried to press a pillow down on Sonja's face, and my mother's text stopped me. It can't be her this time. So who is it? I guess Roger, he's often awake early in the morning. But I mustn't read his text, his loving words. Not now. They might delay me, distract me from my plan, make me flinch – who knows.

The light from the phone has illuminated the inside of my bag. I have the other key. I switch off the vibration on the phone, close the bag's zip halfway, and insert the key in the lock. Good job – I can turn it this time.

The corridor is still black. I expect it to be less dark in Sonja's room. She doesn't close the shutters or curtains. Light from the yard always shines in. My left hand is ready to press down the door handle. My heart is so loud and fast, it could wake everyone, even drunken Mr Stumble-Late. I hear him snoring through his door.

I've turned the key twice. The door opens slightly. I open it into the room and step in with one foot. Not just light from the yard, but also the moon brightens Sonja's room tonight. I slip my right hand into my bag, take hold of the knife, as I push the door further and squeeze all the way through. Inside. My eyes scan Sonja's bed. She should be sleeping. But no, her bed is empty! The duvet folded, an imprint left on it. I need to see her before she sees me.

My eyes race across the room. *Where is she?*

I must be quick, come on. I'll have to look in the bathroom; perhaps she's got trapped in her washing routine. No time for hesitation, and I sprint to the other end of the room and pull open the bathroom door with my left hand, knife in my right. The bathroom is dark; I hit the light switch. I stick my head into the room, scan: nothing. No Sonja. Damn, what's going on here?

I keep rushing. Back in the main room, bend down to the floor and see if she's hidden herself under the bed. No.

I step in front of the wardrobe, the last possible place in this room she could be. My left hand rests on the handle of one of its doors, my right still holding the knife. I pull open one door, and the other. One glance and… no Sonja.

I'm puzzled. I don't know what is going on. Sonja isn't in this room, the room I locked her inside some hours ago – *as usual*. I turned the key twice!

Has she dissolved? Has she evaporated into some kind of gas, or what? This is a total mystery; a miracle. It's impossible. Absolutely. She cannot have left this room without me unlocking her door. Unless…

Yeah, unless she's got her second key out – the one that is sealed in the golden envelope. But she never does that. She's far too scared she might sleepwalk! Has she really got her second key out and opened her door?

PLAYING IT ALL DOWN

2006

MY ROOM IN Whitechapel was on the first floor of one of several terraced houses. I would have loved to live in a Victorian house but hadn't found an affordable room in one. My window faced the yard, and I could see over to Canary Wharf.

I had four flatmates. At first there'd only been two guys, but then two more moved into the last available room. Downstairs lived an African man. Upstairs it was a Chinese guy in one room, two Italian friends in another, and me. My room shared a wall with the bathroom. I could tell through the wall which of the guys was currently in there. The African always tapped his shaver softly in the sink.

One very rainy Sunday afternoon, I wandered out of my room to see if I could find a flatmate for a chat. The Chinese man's door was wide open. I sat on the railing of the stairs in the corridor and started talking to him. He was lounging on his bed, watching football on TV. He knew I liked football and invited me in. Maybe it was my fault that I believed that living with so many guys wouldn't be a problem. I entered and sat on his chair. Less than three minutes later, he invited me further.

"Why don't you sit here? It's much more comfortable." He patted next to him on the bed.

"I'm okay here, thanks." I suddenly wasn't sure if I shouldn't be suspicious.

"Don't worry, everything will be fine. You don't need to be afraid of me," he said.

"But this is good," I insisted. "I can watch the game very well from here."

Sixty seconds, maximum, went by. He patted again on the mattress to his right. "Come here, you'll be safe, no worries."

The word 'safe' touched me, deep down. I loved it. When Sonja and I were little, she used it many times. She convinced me to follow her directions, which would result in safety. Removing the green cushions from Grandma's sofa and counting to 120 to let the AIDS virus die had been just one of those directions.

I gave in. Maybe I was overcautious; his door was still open anyway. I moved next to the Chinese guy, onto his bed. I'm sure it was only three seconds before he pushed me backwards until I lay flat on my back on his bed. He climbed on top of me and started riding. It was a blessing that he took off neither my clothes nor his own. He was 'just' riding and rubbing himself on me. With real force he pressed me onto his mattress, as I was flailing about to try to shake him off. I called for somebody – some other flatmates – but nobody else seemed to be at home. I watched my assaulter moving in ecstasy, sweating as he turned into an animal. I gave my all so he wouldn't succeed in pulling my hand into his jogging pants. He bit me on my chest and breast, so I screamed louder. He rode faster and faster, making more and more noises. Then he slowed down.

"It's out, it's out," he said.

He let my hand go. I slipped away from underneath him, rushed into my room, closed the door, and shot the little bolt over to the frame. Then I pushed the other bed – Sonja's future bed – in front of the door, before sitting on my own, cowering and with my back against the mint-green wall.

I just sat there, thinking. I didn't cry. Nothing hurt, apart from a slight pain in my breast. Not too bad.

I felt dirty. Contaminated. I had a real idea of what Sonja had so often spoken about. Especially when we were kids; when she scraped her arm along the brick wall inside our classroom, removing dirty Lucie-bits from her sleeve.

I stripped off my clothes, stuffed them into a plastic bag, and slipped some others on. I slumped back on my bed. Used. Abused. Disrespected. Robbed. As if something had been taken away from me without permission. The Chinese guy had stolen my trust. He'd fooled me. There was no safety whatsoever.

I was still not crying, but I was in need of comfort from someone. Who? A strong man, who would have wanted to thrash my Chinese flatmate to within an inch of his life. Who would have protected me and punished the guy for what he'd done. I didn't think of Dad. He was far away in Germany, anyway, and I had no wish that he were closer. Nor my brother. Not even Mum occurred to me as someone to talk to.

I grabbed my mobile phone.

Hi, just had a really bad experience with my flatmate. He forced me onto his bed. Rode me. I wrote.

My fingers searched my contact list. I selected Nick. Pressed send.

I was hoping he would respond this time. I was still in love with him. Very much. There'd been zero days that I didn't think of him. A spark of optimism remained that we'd be together one day. I'd texted him almost daily, confirming what a great place London was, telling him about all the sights. Sometimes he replied, sometimes not. Often enough, he didn't. I was a case of 'Out of sight, out of mind.'

Maybe now I would get some attention from Nick, some real care. Some 'there, there'. I wanted it badly.

Nick replied five minutes later.

Are you telling me you've been raped? his text said.

I got excited as I read his message. Yes, *excited*! I sensed some concern from Nick. Some worry. Proper worry. That was how I interpreted his message; maybe my favourite one I'd ever received from him. I held the screen to my lips, kissed his words, then pressed them against my chest. I was suddenly glad about what the Chinese guy had done to me. That he had assaulted me, devoured me, abused me. I was grateful I could use the incident to attract Nick's care.

Hmm, had I been raped, though? Not really, I suppose. Because there had been no penetration. What's the definition of rape? Although to me the word fitted, I knew I hadn't been raped. It wasn't fair for me to use the term to describe this incident -- though my soul surely had been raped!

I typed a reply to Nick, but didn't send it just yet. What if I didn't respond straight away -- would he call? Would he worry even more?

I waited. And didn't realise -- not with a single brain cell -- how desperate, damaged, worn out, screwed-up and crazy my mind had become. How *sick* I was. How low had I sunk that I needed to try and benefit from having been sexually assaulted, to satisfy my thirst for attention from a man? How huge was my lack of comfort and 'there, there'?

Nick didn't call.

Yes, I think that's the word to use, I texted back.

Don't wash yourself, but go to the police, he replied.

Nick's advice was bone dry. As if it was an unemotional thing, going to a police station and reporting how your flatmate had smeared his dirt on you.

I didn't go. Instead, I would deal with it by myself. It was just another scar, much smaller than when Dad had withdrawn his love for me. Because the Chinese guy didn't mean anything. And that is how my life had screwed me up – a sexual assault didn't really seem to matter. But I did start crying at last. Nick, too, had raped my soul.

Through my tears, I glanced at the screen of my mobile as I typed the address of where I now lived. My fingers pressed the arrow key until Sonja's name showed up. *Send*. I needed her here in England. For comfort. For care. For safety.

TRAPPED ON THE ISLAND

IT WAS LATE November when Sonja arrived. She was pleased with the room I had found for us. My Chinese flatmate had moved out only a few days after the assault. I was more than grateful. Another Italian now lived in his room.

Sonja had disconnected herself from Germany physically, and still she strived for more. In Germany and Switzerland, she had avoided all honey. In England, she additionally avoided everything that had honey as an ingredient. Not only cakes, sweets and muesli bars but also certain shampoos, shower gels and hand soaps. If a product's colour resembled that of honey, she was unable to buy it. She had tried to use a bar of soap to wash her hair, but it didn't work. Then she used a cheap, harsh white shampoo. For washing her body, a pink dishwashing liquid was the only product she felt had nothing to do with honey. Four days later, hundreds of white flakes were strewn over the carpet in our room, some as big as the size of my little finger nail. Sonja was shedding her entire scalp.

* * *

I TRIED TO find work in London. Plenty of opportunities

were around during the weeks leading up to Christmas. At least for part-time jobs – lots of places wanted temporary help for the busy season. But all of those cafés and shops were in Oxford Street, Tottenham Court Road or Covent Garden – all tourist areas with too many German visitors; too many parts potentially afflicted with molecules from Sonja's parents.

She knew I still had money from my Zurich job, but that I couldn't carry on forever without finding work. There was also my house money, resting in a German bank account. Would I be allowed to access it, or was it far too dirty. The pressure was on: either a job in London soon, or a transfer from my German bank to my brand-new one in England.

Sonja tied us down on the island – the clean world. I wasn't able to cut Mum off though, not emotionally. Neither was Sonja, despite having declared her mother dirty. She also needed to speak to her now and again, but only by mobile phone. This meant no physical contact between the two. If she'd used a landline, like a public phone, she would have been touched by her mum. A telephone cable under the sea connects England with mainland Europe. Only a mobile system could break that physical contact and let Sonja speak with her mother. Radio waves transporting voices were okay. But she didn't trust her own senses enough about not going to a public phone. She was never sure whether or not she stood in our room or in a public phone box. Seeing our ugly mint-green wallpaper or her bed didn't convince her. She asked for reassurance from her mum who had to listen and tell Sonja that she was able to hear it when Sonja flushed the toilet in our flat. In a public phone box, there would have been no flush.

When Sonja's mother called while her mobile was

plugged into a socket for charging, she threw the phone away afterwards and bought a new one. The call, and hence the dirt, from Germany might have come through the cable of the charger. It happened twice that she washed herself after speaking to her mother and then threw her phone away. The first time, she dumped it in a public bin outside in the road. She waited nearby until the bin lorry made its round to empty all the bins. She wanted to be sure the contaminated mobile was gone before she went to bed. The threat of sleepwalking and getting the phone back was too great. There was no point sealing her house key up in an envelope; all our flatmates were able to open the flat's door at any time. Sonja got soaking wet from the rain and came back home with blue lips and a frozen body. She'd waited two hours for the bin lorry – it was late on that day.

The second time she needed to discard her phone, she put it in a bin inside Sainsbury's below a self-checkout machine. The supermarket closed at night, so she was unable to get inside, while asleep, and reach the phone.

Sonja couldn't do much about her fear of sleepwalking. The door of our room had no lock. We could only use a padlock attached to a metal bar, linking door and frame on the outside. There was no such thing on the inside of the door, only that little bolt to stop someone from opening it. There was nowhere for a key to be inserted. But thank goodness England didn't border Germany, unlike Switzerland. Being on an island wouldn't allow us take an unconscious return trip by ferry or plane to dirty Germany during the hours we were asleep. Even Sonja trusted it was impossible. But when I told her I wanted to go to the coast for a day, she still didn't allow me to travel south or south-east. Both coasts were too close to France and

Belgium; I might fall asleep on a bench somewhere and set off to mainland Europe by mistake. I chose to go north-east instead, and found a nice walking trail along the coast. Sonja came to guard me.

"It's so lovely here!" My eyes were spoiled; the view stunned me. I thought it was unjustified that people thought it only rained in England. True, deep clouds hung in the sky quite a bit, but the English also didn't just eat fish and chips.

We hiked down the trail that led to fenced-off farmland. Loads of sheep dotted the green like woolly bushes. I wondered if people there knew more than 'green', like Eskimos have countless different words for snow. My hand reached out to lift the little bar at a gate within the fence.

Then Sonja freaked out: "No, don't open it!"

I rolled my eyes, tired of what would come after my question: "Why not?"

"I won't be able to close it again."

"Eh?"

"The gate! I can't be sure whenever I close doors 'n' things that they're really shut."

"Well, *I'll* close it then," I said, wanting to open the bloody gate.

"No, no. *Please!*" Sonja dropped to her knees, clasping her hands. "I would still be responsible if a sheep escaped, ran into the village, went mad and got violent. It might kill a child – imagine! It's *not safe* to open the gate."

'Safe' again.

I couldn't stand her begging me. "Stop it!"

Ten minutes later, we boarded a train back to London. I didn't fancy hiking somewhere else instead, like Sonja had suggested.

*   *   *

CHRISTMAS IN LONDON was yet another sad one. We knew nobody and spent it by ourselves. I was grateful to find an open kebab place that cared as little about Christmas as I pretended I did by now. Not a single Santa was stuck to the walls or windows, no *Jingle Bells* came from their radio. Chris Rea's *Driving Home for Christmas* inside Sainsbury's had simply stung too much.

I'd lost count of all those sad Christmases in my life. I only knew it had been over four years since I'd last been to Germany to see my family. My heart ached as if held between pliers, poised to shut tight, as I pressed my phone against my ear, trying to hear the words on the other side of the mobile line.

"Hello? Hello?" Grandma was only breathing those words. She seemed too ill to say more. She'd been in a care home for half a year.

"Grandma, how are you?" I knew she wasn't well, but still asked – out of habit.

Grandma was still just breathing. She struggled to understand it was me on the phone. Mum had said she'd asked to speak to me. But Grandma was confused. She'd become senile lately and had instructed Mum to thaw the five geese in her freezer so she could host the family at Christmas. There was no freezer in the care home.

I heard Mum in the background, talking to her. "It's Finja, it's Finja!"

"I'm tired. I'll hand the phone back to your mum. Goodbye, my poppet," Grandma said.

A lump in my throat was suffocating me. I was worried. Worried that Grandma would pass away and I'd never see her again. But I pulled myself together as Mum talked to me, and said nothing about it.

* * *

"Sonja, are we ever going to leave this island?" I asked her late on Christmas Day. "Am I ever, at least?"

We were sitting on our respective beds. She didn't respond, just chewed her lip. I knew she had no real answer. And she knew that I knew.

THE GOLDEN
ENVELOPE

2014

I STRETCH HIGH. My left arm at full length, I reach up to that second shelf on the left-hand side of Sonja's wardrobe. *Got it.* I hold the golden envelope in my left hand. It is ripped open, the key gone.

I sit on Sonja's bed in the imprint her bottom has left on the duvet. It fits perfectly. No surprise – we are the same size. It's made for me. Has she prepared anything else? Clearly, this has been done on purpose. She has pre-empted me, smelled a rat. She is so clever.

I wonder what she's doing; where she is. What's her plan? Something like mine? Does *she* maybe want to kill *me*?

My gaze drops, and so does everything about me: I flop forward, my elbows balance on my thighs, my chin plops into my hands, the golden envelope between my fingers and my cheek. I sigh. Sonja has been better than me; stronger. As usual. So, have I failed?

Suddenly, her door flies open. I watch as two bare feet are walking towards me. Big feet, the toes perfectly shaped. I know them well; no need to lift my head to see who's planted themselves in front of me. I've always been astonished by my father's pretty feet – the same ones I've got from him.

"Yes, you have!" His voice is just as cool and harsh as ever.

"I have what?"

"Failed!"

My blood reaches boiling point within a second. I lift my head and stand to meet his eyes. "What do *you* know about *failure*? And what do *you* know about *me*?"

"I know that you—"

"Stop! Because you don't. And if I have failed, then you have, *too*!"

My father in Sonja's room, in Paris? That's *impossible*.

I feel my pulse hammering in my neck, my temples. It hurts. I see my arm move; fully stretched out, my index finger pointing to the door, and my father leaves the room again. My hallucination passes.

Now I notice music. Not very loud. I hadn't noticed it before. Sonja has the same little clock radio as me. It too stands on her bedside table. I peek over my right shoulder. The radio shows 4.09. Above the radio is the window. Closed. Sonja has definitely not gone through it. It would be far too tricky anyway.

I listen to the music. A choir is singing. I love it. The first time I was deeply touched by a choir singing was when my mother once took me to church as a young girl. It felt like the moment when God was closest to me. God? Does he know that I want to break free tonight? Free of Sonja, free of our relationship that is based on lies; on Sonja being self-satisfied; on delusion; manipulation. How does God feel about her? Do I need her? Still?

I used to believe in God. Prayed every night, by myself. These days, I don't, and my belief is kind of gone. I'm agnostic now, not convinced that God exists. But I'd love it if he did. And if so, I hope he'll forgive me for not really believing. But in any case, I'm not okay with 'using God' and what he might have 'given' to people as an easy excuse – as if he'd given me Sven and I must stick with him; as if he'd given me Sonja and disallows that I remove her; as if my mother can excuse her actions and claim *Well, God knows I have done my best for you and so it's okay* and so she doesn't have to say sorry.

I'm staring at the empty golden envelope, while listening to the music. Sonja isn't coming back soon, I don't think. I guess it was her door that banged and woke me from my nightmare. And it was her lock that clicked, not Mr Stumble-Late's, as she turned the key from the golden envelope twice. Then she left.

My fingers run over the envelope. I flip it over. A picture is stuck to it. Oh my God, *the* picture – the embrace she's blackmailed me with. She's printed it out. But, hang on: it's not what I thought. I didn't see it close enough when she held it up to me on her phone earlier tonight. It's the picture of the embrace between the two lovers I saw recently in the park; the couple that had inspired and encouraged me to be in a real romantic relationship with Roger, without staying in this guesthouse each night locking Sonja in. I'm not even *in* this picture – I have *taken* it!

Ha, there is no blackmail. Sonja doesn't have a picture of me and that upset guy I comforted with a hug. Bitch.

Well, is it okay to flinch, then? To withdraw from my plan of eliminating Sonja? Or do I still have reason enough to free myself of her? To loosen my own corset, break my chains?

I tear the picture off and turn it over. A note! For me?

I recognise Sonja's handwriting: *You have changed how you feel about me. I knew you were going to do it.*

Huh, she knows that I wanted to kill her? Does she know about my other two attempts, when I failed? A shiver runs across my back. Sonja has planned all this. She didn't just know *that* I was going to do it, she's also been spot on in guessing *when*. I challenged her, argued with her usual text, demanding to lock her in at 11pm!

Thinking of text messages, I drop the knife into my bum bag and get out my phone. I press a key to open the inbox: *Sonja*. I was convinced it was from Roger. My hands are shaking. My thumb manages to open her message.

Our fathers are half-brothers. I know. You're my cousin. I know. We are family. Meet me at the primary school on the way to our favourite café by the Seine!

The family secret – she knew! Another shiver prickles, even on my scalp.

Meet her at that primary school? What for? I slip the phone back into my bag and turn to the radio. It's 4.13am, and I switch it off.

I leave the room and descend the stairs quickly to the ground floor and exit the house. I catch sight of WHWM-Dad's spot, where he smokes and I chat with him. I won't be able to any more if I move in with Roger. Maybe he'll miss me. Maybe not.

I look up to the sky. Still dark, but it'll be dawn soon. I rush around to the front of the house and onto the pavement, then along the street. I start to run, cross the road at a red light for pedestrians. But there's no car. I turn right into the next road and keep running. Just running, further and further. Around corners, down little roads and alleyways – some made of cobbles, some of flat asphalt.

I take a break; am out of breath. I walk. Quickly, though. And then I carry on running. I don't know what awaits me. What should I expect when I meet her at that primary school? Am I actually meeting her? What am I doing? A few hours ago, as I was waiting for the evening to pass, I had a proper plan. Now this has all changed. But the knife is in my bag. Maybe I still have a chance.

I stop running again and walk. I'm out of breath. Panting. I've run down several roads, turned quite a lot of corners. About fifty yards separate me from that primary school. Good grief, I am so close to her.

I'm listening to my heart: *Boom-boom, boom-boom, I am nervous. Boom-boom, boom-boom, but keep going. Keep approaching that school!*

I stand close to an old building at the last corner before turning into the school's road. With both my hands against the wall, I incline my head slightly to the left and glance down towards the school. The road seems quiet; I don't see anybody. I move around the building and onto the final path, start walking slowly. Fifty yards to change my mind, turn around and run away. I keep walking for the moment, passing two slim trees on the pavement.

Now the pavement becomes narrow. So very narrow that I step in the road. I carry on walking. I don't expect any cars to drive past. I know this road. Even during the day there is little traffic. My path meets another narrow alley. I cross the small junction. To the right, a hairdresser's shop with its shutters down. Nothing unusual except that I've never seen that ugly graffiti on it before. On the left side of the road, a tiny nostalgic place also has its shutters down. A metal sign next to it, reading *Bar*, swings in the breeze. It's actually very warm right now, and the air smells of summer.

I have about another thirty yards left to reach the school. Or to run away. Shall I? Shall I be a coward and fail? For the third time?

But does it actually matter how many times I have already failed? Do I have to prove anything to anybody? My father comes to mind again, and how he told me I had to change. His damaging email, how it listed everything I hadn't achieved. Perhaps not achieving isn't necessarily the same as failure. Because I try; very hard.

Maybe I haven't failed. Maybe I'm not to blame. Maybe I'm not weak, but sick. Maybe *he* is to blame. Maybe that is the truth.

Angel? Devil? Where are you?

I carry on walking. It must be 4.30am by now. My feet are heavy. Suddenly I stop and look down to the ground. I've trodden on something. A piece of cloth? A homeless guy hangs out here during the day; it could be his. I bend down, pick up the cloth. Huh – who would have thought that: an old oven cloth. The loop to hang it up is broken. Faded colours – purple with a red trim. It is crocheted and relatively small, as if for a child. Hang on – a *child*? Is it? It can't be – the one that Grandma crocheted for me; that I handed in as my homework on the day I first met Sonja? At primary school?

What? Did I just say *primary school*?

I'm turning the oven cloth in my hands. It's old but still so neat. I keep hold of it and start walking again, closer to the school. It's on the right-hand side. I see the gate now. It is open. I might only be fifteen yards from it. I take a deep breath.

At the gate I face the entrance of the school. No sign of Sonja. Adrenaline rises, setting my heart on fire. *Boom-boom,*

boom-boom. I've never had trouble finding Sonja, she's been like my shadow. But here I am *looking* for her. Is she playing a game? Hide-and-seek? Or is she going to shoot me now, as I'm walking under the arch and down the passageway at the entrance?

One step, two steps. I stop. Again, I have trodden on something. I bend down, pick it up. A pen. A red pen with a silver cap. I take the cap off. It's a fountain pen. An old one. Small and just big enough for a child's hand. *My* hand when I was little and at primary school? Yeah, I remember it. And Sonja's fountain pen was blue. Twenty-eight years ago.

FIVE MISSED CALLS

2007

IT WAS JANUARY. I returned to the flat, walked upstairs to our room. I had popped over to the Whitechapel Sainsbury's for some shopping and then handed some cash through the window in the driver's door of my landlord's Jaguar. I told him our toilet was broken, flooding the bathroom floor with each flush. He shrugged and said he'd have a look tomorrow or the day after, and that we should use the other toilet, downstairs. When I'd asked for a receipt for my rent, he had no paper on him or in the compartments of his shiny car. I handed him the receipt from my shopping, and he scribbled on the back of it.

Up in the room, I sat on my bed. Sonja wasn't in. I grabbed my mobile, which I had forgotten to take with me and still lay on the duvet. The screen indicated five missed calls. My eyebrows shot up. Never before had I had five missed calls within one hour. I pressed a key. The screen showed *Mum*, and my neurons started buzzing.

I tried calling her back, but nobody picked up. Not even Dad. And then I thought I knew. I just had the feeling.

Waiting to get confirmation was torture, so I called again. And again. But nobody answered the phone. I could only leave message after message. I went back outside and wandered around in the streets. It was a dark day, drizzling and cold. I kept hold of my mobile so I would feel it vibrating. And then it did. I cried out loud as Mum broke the news to me: Grandma had died.

Mum sounded strong. She had anticipated her mother's death; been prepared as much as possible. She told me how Grandma had passed away peacefully. I was overwhelmed by bad feelings. Sadness. Guilt. Since Christmas I'd known from a cousin that Grandma had expressed the wish to see me once again. *Once again* – as if she was sure she wouldn't recover. The idea that this had been Grandma's last wish crawled up my spine. I shivered, my shoulder blades clenched and my mind turned darker than the clouds in the London sky. Grandma's wish had been so simple, so uncomplicated. And yet it was so difficult to fulfil! It had competed against the mental illness of my best friend that didn't allow me to leave clean England. It had lost against the beast of OCD. *I* had lost! I was torn, my heart crushed.

* * *

I WALKED MILES across London, from Whitechapel to Tower Bridge, along the other side of the Thames. I sat by a dock, waiting for the ferry that would take me back across the river. My hair was plastered against my skull, cheeks and neck. All soaked with rain, just like the rest of me. I didn't care. I rather wanted it to be like that. I deserved it.

Late in the evening, I lay on my bed, staring at the ceiling. I told Sonja, "My grandma has died."

More tears ran down the sides of my face. Sonja didn't say a thing, but I knew she'd heard my news. She had known

Grandma. She had stayed overnight at hers with me.

"Remember the day when we played Rummy, Memory and Ludo at my grandma's? When we ate cake and watched TV until we fell asleep in her *Stube*? You probably got to watch as many things in one day as your parents' brown family meeting folder allowed in a month."

I'd hoped that Sonja would engage with my memories. She didn't. She still said nothing. I turned my head, but she didn't look at me. Her face in profile was pale and difficult to read. She was picking at her duvet. Did she feel guilty?

I turned back to the ceiling, tired, and closed my eyes.

* * *

WHEN I WOKE it was the next morning. I was still fully dressed, and so was Sonja in her bed.

"Sonja," I called. "I must go back. I've got to go to my grandma's funeral!"

She sat up, a tired and confused expression on her face. Then her eyes started darting. Left, right, up and down. Action in her mind!

We both knew what it meant for me to go to Germany: a total breakdown of the clean world. On my return I would contaminate London, England, Great Britain – heck, the entire UK. Irreversibly. Sonja would need to look for another clean place to live, although she had already driven us to the edge of Europe. Not many places were left; her parents had travelled the continent widely. But she knew I had to go. I just *had* to. For my grandma. I hadn't seen her alive in so long, and Sonja knew why.

"And imagine what my relatives will say about me if I don't go."

Sonja still sat on her bed, her eyes flitting around. She looked at so many things in the room, but never at me.

* * *

IN THE EVENING, I told her I had booked a flight for four days' time. She was going through hell, I knew that. She would have loved to stop me, but I didn't want to have to suffer for the rest of my life because I hadn't gone to Grandma's funeral – mainly out of love for Grandma, but also concern for my reputation. I didn't want to be the cold and uncaring black sheep.

I promised Sonja I would help as much as I was able to, and find a way that she could live with. Some sort of transformation for my return, maybe. I hoped she would cope, despite her getting quieter with each day that drew closer to my departure.

The only time, really, that Sonja spoke to me was when I said I would nip to the shop to top up our electricity pre-pay key system. It was my turn, and I had collected the money from the other flatmates. We had already used up more than half of the five-pound emergency credit, which was granted after fully depleting the key. We were in debt.

"Well, I'll go to the shop for you. Maybe you want to pack," Sonja said, as I buzzed about in our room. My flight to Germany was scheduled for the next day.

I was grateful that she'd offered to help. The key really needed to be topped up; the power might run out any time soon. It had happened before when I listened to the radio and suddenly got cut off.

"Oh, thank you, Sonja!" I opened the drawer under our desk and took out the money. Ten pounds per flatmate.

* * *

WHILE I LAY in bed that evening, Sonja cleaned the house like a dervish. Her timing left me puzzled but I didn't complain. I was just glad that she seemed to be coping, and it wasn't late yet. I was happy enough to rest, knowing that I had to get up at 6.30am to get to the airport. The noise of the vacuum cleaner faded once Sonja went to clean downstairs. I felt nicely tired and dropped off.

When I woke, it was bright outside. I pulled open the curtain on my side of the room.

Hang on, why is it already so bright? It's not supposed to be like that at this time of the day. Not in winter!

I sat up in bed and glanced at our alarm clock. It was a digital clock radio, and the very thing that had been cut off, that one time when I was listening to music. Now it was off again. No time was shown on it, not even a blinking *00.00*.

"My God, what's going on here? Are we having a blackout?" I suddenly panicked.

I stared out the window. It was bright but cloudy. People in houses around the courtyard had lights on. Yes, *lights!*

No blackout, then! I jumped out of my bed. Sonja finally turned and woke. I thought she might know what was happening.

"What's going on here?" I asked.

She didn't respond, just squinted. I tried the light switch by the door, but our light didn't come on. I left the room and went to the bathroom. I stood by the sink. Only cold water came out of the tap, although I had turned the wheel for the hot. The boiler was also off. I stormed downstairs, went to the electricity meter and checked the credit: £0.

"*What the fuck?*" I stormed back upstairs to our room.

Sonja was now sitting up in her bed. "Did you not top up the electricity yesterday?"

"Um, yes I did," she said meekly.

"So how come nothing's working? The power is off!" My blood was boiling, nerves shaking.

"Well..." she said.

I didn't really listen; I was frantically searching for my phone. "What's the time? What's the time?"

"I could only get a top-up for five pounds. The machine at the shop wasn't working properly; it wouldn't give me a bigger one," Sonja said.

"What?" I'd only half heard. "Oh my God! I've overslept!"

My mobile showed 8.25am – there was no chance now that I'd still catch my flight.

Restlessly, I marched up and down. I kicked my bed and hurt my foot. I hit the windowsill with my fist and hurt my hand. Then I looked at Sonja and didn't know whether to blame her for not getting a proper top-up, or myself for not setting a backup alarm on my phone. It was hard to believe she hadn't managed to get a bigger top-up. She could have gone to another shop, or bought two five-pound top-ups.

"I'm sorry. I thought it was enough money to get through today; even longer. I didn't think we would run out of power overnight," she said.

"If you got a top-up of five pounds when we had already been using the emergency credit, then there was only a couple of pounds' worth left on the key, maximum. And you used the vacuum cleaner like a madwoman!" I snapped.

I didn't know what to do. Tear Sonja apart? I couldn't dismiss having failed myself by not setting the backup alarm. I went downstairs again to the electricity meter and hit the button: five pounds' emergency credit. The light came on and the boiler started humming.

Minutes later, I called Mum and burst into tears as if Grandma had died again. I couldn't fix the situation; my plane had left without me. The funeral was going to be held the next morning. I wouldn't be able to go and would have to stay in England instead. *How lucky for Sonja!*

Mum had to console me, and she did so well. She promised to explain the unfortunate situation to our relatives and let them know that I wasn't to blame for not being there. But still, from now on I would have to live with not being at the funeral to pay tribute to Grandma – on top of the fact that I hadn't fulfilled her wish of seeing me one more time, before she died.

Second Attempt

In March, I'd had to back Sonja into a corner. "Either I take this job at the airport, or some of my house money from the Wrong Country has to be transferred to my English account. There's barely anything left of what I made in Zurich, and I still have to pay for the rest of my language course." I'd been taking professional English lessons since January.

Sonja soon decided to let me take the job at the airport. She had to stand the possibility of dirty Germans passing by me.

"You also have to let me buy a comb now. I have to look decent in my uniform."

She hadn't wanted me to buy a brush or a comb. All the ones we could find resembled ones we'd had before. She couldn't trust that they hadn't sneaked over from Germany or Switzerland, hidden somewhere between my clothes, if she saw a brush or comb in our room. She'd made me detangle my hair with a fork from our kitchen.

Now it was June and my turn again to top up the key for our electricity pre-pay system. I went to the shop, the collected money from our flatmates in my pocket. I smiled when the owner greeted me: "Hey, Finja, how's it going?"

"Hi, Shawn. Pretty well. How're you?"

We talked about football. He teased me a little about Germany's latest games. Then we talked 'business'.

"Can I get a key top-up for sixty pounds this time?" I winked, teasing him back. I was going to tell him the story of how I missed my flight to Germany after Sonja had only been able to get a five-pound top-up.

"Course you can. You can get any amount you want. This machine is like a woman; gives me anything I ask for, never broken." He smirked and patted the casing of the machine like the cheek of a person.

Never broken? Something inside me stung, made me flinch. My head started spinning. Maybe I'd boarded a roller coaster. All I saw was black.

"Hey, you all right?" Shawn asked.

Stars and circles danced in front of my eyes. My little devil and angel fluttered by. I felt Shawn's arms wrapped around my shoulders. He'd come from behind the counter, and held me as I staggered.

A few seconds later, the squall passed. I was clear and stable.

"Sure, I'm fine, thanks," I pretended, handing him sixty pounds.

Now I was in a hurry to leave. I was burning to get home; could hardly wait for 'his woman' to load the sixty pounds onto the key.

Outside on the pavement, I ran back to the flat. No stars, no circles, no devil and no angel distracted me. I knew that Sonja would get to see me in a state she hadn't seen me in before.

* * *

I FLUNG THE door open and raced up the stairs to get to our room. It was still padlocked from the outside, just as I had left it. Sonja wasn't in there. I searched for her throughout the house, dashed into the bathroom, knocked on the doors of the other two bedrooms upstairs, went back down to check the kitchen and guest toilet. Last chance – I knocked on the African's door. Sonja was nowhere. In fact, nobody was in the house. The only 'people' I could see were two little guys when I unlocked our room. They were jumping on my bed, elbows up, hands down and clenched into fists, faces bright pink: *two* devils. Hell's teeth, they were *fuming*.

You've got to do it, you've got to do it! they called unanimously.

Not even the devilish angel in disguise had complaints about my intention this time. No appeals, no excuses were made for Sonja. Because she had *lied* to me.

Where was she? I dropped onto my bed. The two little guys bounced unremittingly on top of my tummy. I watched them.

Then I called Mum. I talked at her for over half an hour, unloading my fury. I hardly took a breath, drowning myself in my home-made sorrow. I had been so bad at realising Sonja's trick. I mean, we were *so* close. I knew her! It wasn't that I didn't *want* to get it, was it?

I stayed on my bed until the evening. I heard my flatmates come home. One of the Italians ran his bath – he never took a shower.

Sonja was still not home. I drafted a few texts, asking about her whereabouts, but never sent any. I grew impatient, got up, and paced up and down the room. Where was she? I needed her to appear, to get rid of my aggression. I was ready. The longer she stayed away, the more determined I became. I knew she would turn up soon.

It was nine o'clock and I nipped to the bathroom, then

tucked myself into bed. I was wide awake, but ready to feign sleep.

*   *   *

I DON'T KNOW what time it was when Sonja finally came home. She moved around silently and left the light off, knowing I had to get up at 3.45am for my morning shift at the airport. She disappeared into the bathroom and only came back a long time later – after her seemingly everlasting routine. I faced the wall away from her, still wide awake and listening to her movements. When I heard nothing apart from soft breathing, I slowly turned over, my heart bashing against my ribcage. Sonja was lying on her back, her mouth slightly open.

I grabbed my phone from the floor next to my bed and pressed a key. The light of the screen came on. It was just enough to illuminate the two devils that were now sat on the windowsill. *Do it, do it, do it!*

I slid the phone back onto the carpet and sat up. With my hands clenching the edges of my pillow, I slipped out of my bed. I stared at Sonja's face. Her eyes shut, mouth still open. I took two slow steps towards her, pillow tight between my hands in front of me – ready to be pressed down. Another step closer, and I stood in the perfect position. No dizziness, no roller coaster. Nothing. I watched my arms stretch forward, the pillow calm like a tree's leaf before the storm, only a couple of inches away from Sonja's nose and mouth.

Cuckoo, cuckoo.

I jerked as if I'd suffered an electric shock, and pulled the pillow towards me as it trembled between my hands. *Jesus.* Frantically, I backed away from Sonja. She'd moved. The text message that had come in on my mobile prompted her to turn. I rushed back into my bed, pulled the duvet over me, and peeked through a tiny gap. Sonja had only changed her position, and was now lying on her front. Still asleep.

My arm sneaked out and snatched my phone back from the floor. Under the duvet, I pressed a key to see who the message was from: Mum. Weird, because in Germany it was one hour even further into the night.

I read Mum's text: *Hope you're having a good morning by the time you read this. I just thought I'd tell you that I don't think you should be too annoyed. Don't beat yourself up. It's all been down to the OCD. It's an illness! Mum.*

And so Mum was my angel this time. She was so understanding; and that was Sonja's good fortune. I glanced up to the windowsill. No more devils. They had vanished.

I held my phone in my hands for some minutes, then turned it off and dropped it back on the floor. If Sonja woke now, never mind. She'd stay alive anyway.

BACK TO DIRTY GERMANY

I HADN'T REALLY got any sleep. At 3.45am, when my alarm went off, I felt like a scrambled egg: totally beaten. After work at the airport, I was too weak to confront Sonja. I fell into bed. Lucky her, because with each hour that I didn't rant at her, my anger softened, Mum's understanding playing on my mind. I almost forgot Sonja had lied to me. Mum's words convinced me that calmness and support were the way to approach this. Sonja was *ill*, after all. Threating to leave her alone if she didn't undergo therapy was wrong. It hadn't worked back in 2002 after the clay pot scenario. The OCD didn't go away; it couldn't be switched off. We'd just come back to Munich with different-coloured corsets. Different meanings.

With lots of patience and encouragement, and the promise of parental support from her mum, Sonja agreed to get professional help. Therapy that wasn't self-prescribed, and not just to please other people; like I had wanted to please Sven, and she, possibly, her father once he'd offered to help make contact with Goran via his dad at the sports club. This time, she would go to stay at a clinic back in Germany.

* * *

AFTER A FEW weeks, Sonja and I left England for good. The airport shop I had worked at had closed down. When I first saw Mum and Dad, I was shocked. I hadn't seen them for five years. Dad's hair was all white; Mum's face wrinkly, her posture wearied. She would turn sixty in a couple of years.

For the next weeks, perhaps months, I would stay at Mum's and Dad's house in their guest room. Sonja stayed in her parents' guest room – her former bedroom. She registered with the doctor and enrolled at a clinic. Then she had to wait, for weeks, perhaps months. The waiting list for treatment was long.

Meanwhile, I went with Mum to Fessdorf's cemetery. Grandma was buried there, although she had lived in the centre of Gadburg. I stood by her grave, stared at her shiny headstone. It had no moss on it, and hardly any dirt. No surprise; it had only been there for about half a year. A couple of gravediggers were around. Mum had arranged for Grandad's urn to be put into the grave as well. It had been buried at a different cemetery, further away, for almost thirty years. Now my grandparents were going to be reunited.

"If you want, step a little closer. You'll see Grandma's urn," Mum said, pointing at the hole.

I stepped forward and looked at 'Grandma'. Then I backed away again, stood in the same spot, stared at the gravestone and listened to the short ceremony. Mum's Lord's Prayer. I clasped my hands like she and her two brothers did, and we all murmured along with her words.

In a blink of an eye it was over and Grandma was under the soil again. I had no time to think. Nothing was inside me; no feelings, not the tiniest tear in my eye, except for two loose words that dangled in my mind: *Bad timing*. Just some months before Sonja had prevented me from coming to Germany and going to Grandma's funeral. And just a few weeks before that, Grandma had expressed her last wish. Now, I'd only been able to have a second's glance at what was left of her – ashes in an urn.

Christmas Eve 2007

MUM ASKED ME to decorate the Christmas tree, and I did it with an awful lot of pleasure. I used almost all of her decorations. She had tons of them. The tree was close to being overloaded, but it looked absolutely fantastic. Dad confirmed it, and so I thought that this Christmas was going to be a good one. *Finally*.

I stood next to Dad at his desk and glanced over his shoulder as he designed a gift voucher on his computer for my brother. I helped with some Christmassy wording and watched the printing. Then Dad folded and slid the paper into an envelope. He was in such a good mood.

I couldn't stop thinking. I couldn't stop hoping. Surely, he would prepare something similar for me. Maybe he'd even done so already. I was almost as excited as when I was a little girl, full of hope that Dad had thrown away his principle of punishing me for my present-giving failure with Mum. Surely he was emotional enough about me being around for Christmas – I hadn't been for years. In fact, I hadn't been around *at all*.

I myself was quite emotional and had forgotten that I had stopped giving presents to my parents. It had been a joy strolling around Gadburg's city centre, searching for something for my daddy. I hoped for a smile when he unwrapped the tennis balls I'd decided to buy and read my Christmas letter I had tucked away under the bed I was sleeping in.

But Dad was, of course, Dad. And I was just naive. I was faced with pure cruelty when I sat around the Christmas tree that evening with my brother, his long-term girlfriend, Mum, and Dad. I watched as Dad handed my brother his envelope; how Dad smiled when he opened it, read the voucher and hugged him to say thank you. I also watched how Dad handed nothing to me, but told me he had almost gone to buy new tennis balls himself.

I tried to swallow the lump in my throat; however it just wouldn't go down. I couldn't stand it, but didn't want to cry in front of everybody, particularly as it would hurt Mum. I excused myself, went to the bathroom, opened a cupboard, stuck my head inside, and pressed my face down into a pile of towels. It worked like a silencer as I burst into tears.

The conclusion was so bitter. Dad wouldn't abandon his principles, or not for me at least.

* * *

WHILE SONJA WAS at the clinic for therapy, I gave her my utmost support. Every day I went to see her, for nine long weeks. She had to learn how to withstand her compulsions; not to execute them. Washing her hands for half a minute instead of nine was one of the tasks she was set. On paper, this is simple. In reality, though, it's a totally different story when anxiety arises, threatening to eat you whole if you don't comply.

In one of her group sessions, Sonja also heard how OCD covers up something deep inside – a trauma, maybe. A long-term problem. Something rooted in the family, established during childhood. The anxiety has a reason behind it!

Meanwhile, Dad got impatient with me. "You've got to do something, you've been here for a long time now!" He meant work, and settling down somehow, somewhere. Somewhere other than in his house.

Sonja had only left the clinic a few days ago and now the pressure was on. Problem: I didn't want to settle in or around Gadburg. Not even anywhere in Germany, really. I had loved being away, out in the world. But for the moment, I was okay with living in Fessdorf, in my parents' house, using their guest room. For two reasons: one, I didn't have a plan or idea of where to go (I was jobless), and two, my broken heart was struggling to heal after Nick's last text message to me: *I don't ever want to hear from you again.*

Yep, I would call it: *I was depressed.* Even more so since Sonja's OCD hadn't just been switched off, and we both knew there were people who were disappointed – not just us.

I had no clue what would come next in my life.

Mum had been happy about me being there. More than happy. I was sitting on the bed in the guest room when she came in. She tried to motivate me, rubbing my back in a motherly manner.

"You know, Dad is coming home soon. If he sees you here, not sending out more job applications, he'll get angry."

Dad was keen that I didn't do nothing. He wouldn't have accepted it. He pushed me to make sure I kept my chin up and didn't let myself down. And there was only one way he did this: applying pressure on me – the same technique that Sonja's father used on his daughter. Pressure, pressure, *fucking pressure.* No hugs. No love. Just fear. As a tough-minded non-princess, I didn't have the right to be devastated about Nick, nor to not have a plan for how to get on with life. At least not under Dad's roof.

I moaned to Mum. "But I'm feeling so low. I'm not motivated at all. I need some time, please, to think about what to do next. That's all."

Mum probably knew I would find a way to carry on. At some point. After some time. After a break. But Dad was against it. He didn't want to give me any time.

"If it was up to me, you could stay here forever. But I'm also scared of your dad," she said.

Her words were striking. It was what everybody had already known, but never said out loud. And yet I said nothing, just stayed slumped on the bed until Dad's car pulled in. He parked it in front of the garage.

I sent a couple of job applications out into the 'world' – or somewhere in Germany – for jobs I wasn't interested in, in cities I could never imagine living in. But it eased the pressure from Dad. At least for a day or two.

FROM MUM TO MOTHER

DAD KEPT ASKING what my future plans were and when I would move out. I hadn't let myself down, but had instead taken a couple of courses in computing. Maybe I wanted to get an office job one day. And still, Dad told me I had to find my own place, despite my pleas and explanations that I did not want to live in the area permanently. I did not like it. I couldn't imagine settling there again. But I was given no choice. Dad pushed for me to leave, and suddenly, Mum joined in.

It was beyond strange. I failed to recognise her; didn't know what had happened, who she had suddenly become. I didn't understand why she now used the same pressure on me. Had Dad made her? Forced her? Maybe blackmailed her? Was it some sort of deal?

Maybe she'd been infected by something. She must have been. A mutation of genes, perhaps, that had ruined her maternal instinct. Turned her into a bad mother, shrivelled up her *If it was up to me, you could stay here forever.*

Mum and I had definitely had some bonds between us from a long time ago. Now, with one shot, they were gone. A vacuum followed, sucking me in, eating, churning, whisking me up. Like a spewed-out blob, sick, I sat on the toilet and shat partly undigested food. My nerves were raw.

Mum ignored me. I was sat in tears on the sofa in the living room when she made sure she didn't turn her head towards me. It was unbelievable. Ungraspable. It just went against the universal law of motherhood. Why on earth? It frightened me. *Mum* frightened me!

It didn't matter to my parents that I didn't intend to have my own flat in Gadburg, or anywhere nearby. That I didn't want to stay in Germany forever. But as I couldn't come up with an alternative right away, I wasn't granted any more time to think while in their house. Whether or not I was still heartbroken about Nick wasn't considered. Only my brother, whose girlfriend had left him, got warm and loving support from Mum and Dad. Mum was really worried about his psyche and well-being.

My parents hadn't known Nick, but they knew my brother's girlfriend very well. They hadn't seen me together with a man, but they had seen my brother with his girlfriend. They'd welcomed her into the family, but they had never been involved with Florian, Sven or Nick.

My parents didn't know me. They didn't trust me – that I would leave their house when I was ready. They only wanted to support my brother in the right way. I don't think that, even if I'd cried about Nick in front of my parents, it would have made a difference. For them, I could just take anything.

"You will have to move out by the 31st October. If you haven't found a flat, you'll have to live in a hotel," Mum told me, and that was the moment she downgraded herself from Mum to only *my mother*.

When I did cry about this in front of my parents, Dad looked at me and said, "Do you really believe your tears still affect me?"

I didn't know if he meant my age with 'still'; or if I had cried too often in my life and he told me how he'd got used to that. But this was crystal clear: Dad was like Sonja's father – only *a father*. And, never mind the 31st October, it was now time for me to walk away.

* * *

IT WAS ONLY a few hundred metres from my parents' house to Sonja's, but they felt like miles. I couldn't get to her fast enough, so I ran. I needed to tell her that my father was an arsehole, and so was hers. That they were related – the family secret. I didn't care about my house money any more. I didn't care if I had to share it with Sonja. The truth had to come out. Her father and mine, the two half-brothers. It should cause a drama, a crisis. Her father truly was a son of a whore. He'd made his wife kneel down, made her beg him to talk to her again. And Grandad Ernst had cheated on Grandma Gerda – with Bertha.

I leaped onto the grassy path leading to Sonja's. I was still running when I saw her shoot from the door. She also ran towards me. Our bodies touched, our arms had flown open, and we wrapped them around each other like vines. I pressed my nose against Sonja's shoulder, smelled her. God damn it, was I glad to hold her, to have her close to me. She was the only faithful, reliable person I had to love me; my only ally now that Mum and Dad had abandoned me. Never would she have asked me to leave!

"My parents have given me an ultimatum. They're kicking me out!" I was actually panting into Sonja's ear.

"And mine have gone to court and made an application to get me a guardian. They've lost patience with me, maybe 'cause my clinic stay hasn't made the OCD go away," she said.

What? What had her parents done? They were getting someone else to be in charge of Sonja? What the fuck? How *sick*! I didn't understand the world any more. It felt like a conspiracy.

Sonja's parents seemed fed up with her mental problems, and keen for somebody else to take her over. It sounded very much like passing on their responsibility. So much for that promise of parental support from Sonja's mum... those enticing, hope-arousing words that had persuaded Sonja to finally agree to come back to Germany and be admitted to a clinic, after my second attempt on her life. My God, was I glad I had failed to kill her! My God, oh my God. I pushed back from our embrace, my hands grabbing Sonja's upper arms, eyes on hers.

"Come on, then, let's get the hell out of here. Forever." I shook her gently and totally forgot to tell her that her father and mine were half-brothers.

But I was still happy to share my house money with her. All of it. I pulled her by the hand, the German bank card for my account in my pocket, and we fled back to Switzerland. Yeah, we'd be staying in a hotel like my mother had threatened, but in a city that had been more of a home to me than anywhere else. I loved Zurich.

Auf Nimmer
Wiedersehen

Autumn 2010

OF COURSE, I also still loved Nick. But I didn't try to find
him in Zurich any more. I knew I had to move on. When
I once bumped into him on a tram, I pretended I had a
heart of steel and a pair of knees so strong they could have
supported the bridge we were crossing. When I got off, I
wobbled into a small gap between two buildings and secretly
cried over the three girls Nick had in tow, my father's words
Do you really believe your tears still affect me? swirling around
in my mind.

Sonja and I lived in a hotel first, then in a 'hole' behind
a hairdresser. I used my house money to pay for it. I bought
all the food for both of us. Morally, I was obliged. I also let
myself be all hers again, strapped on rules, restrictions and
corsets. Because I had no choice. I needed her and didn't
want to be completely alone. I wasn't able to.

My father had sent me an email, saying that it was his
last attempt to wake me up. *What from?* He told me that I
had to change, although I didn't think I was bad.

My father wasn't happy with me; he'd never really

accepted the way I was. In his email, he wrote how useless I was, noting all the things I hadn't managed to do. How I had failed: no job, not much money left, no house, no boyfriend, no husband and no child. *Yeah, I was a real damn shit-ass loser!*

I don't even know why I phoned and tried to defend myself. But I did.

"You are the problem of the family!" my father shouted at me.

And my mother listened via their second phone and said nothing. She didn't interfere, didn't deny my father's allegations, didn't speak up for me. She only breathed. Quietly. And when I started crying again, my father's words *Do you really believe your tears...* whipped, punched, tortured my mind.

I hung up and stood by the edge of the lake. It was dark and drizzling. It came at me from all angles; wind drove it everywhere. Streaks of my hair stuck to my cheeks. I didn't care. My sobs condensed in the air. The air smelled of autumn; decaying foliage. For a moment I thought I'd seen a reflection of my estranged mother scurry across the surface of the bleak, cold water. She'd confirmed there was no way I could come back to their house; not even in the most desperate situation.

"I would have a major problem with Dad if you came," she'd said, and I wished I could have slapped her for her use of that word; 'Dad'. I'd rather she'd used 'devil' – she had made a deal with him. I almost felt like I should wash my ears clean of the word – Dad – because a dad wouldn't give his wife a major problem for putting up her own child; wouldn't shut their door. Thank God, I had no desire to go back to my parents' anyway; I didn't want to email or even speak to them ever again. *Auf nimmer Wiedersehen.*

"Hey," I heard a voice next to me, "are you okay?"

I turned my head and saw a slim figure. She wore a long white skirt, almost touching the ground, which seemed rather inappropriate for the muddy weather. Her curly blonde hair cascaded around her neck, the tips resting on her white jacket. A small golden rucksack – her handbag, I supposed – hung low on her back. She reminded me of an angel. Her umbrella had kept her dry, and as she lifted it up she stood close to me, giving me shelter. Her left arm was tight around my shoulders.

I was still sobbing, but her company out of nowhere helped dry my tears. I didn't want to give up and jump into the freezing water of Lake Zurich. Some tiny hope for a better life was still flickering resiliently inside me. Not even the rain or the wind had put it out. I still hoped for something nice to happen to me, one day in my life.

"I could do with a fresh start. Somehow. Somewhere," I said.

"Well, once when I was desperate to forget and move on, I went far away as an au pair. Young children and their unconditional love helped heal my wounds." The Swiss accent of the woman holding me tickled my heart.

"Oh yes, maybe that is a good idea."

My house money was nearly used up. The job hunt had proved very difficult; I just didn't want to work as a lab technician any more and could only scrape together a bit of extra money working at a bar. Via the internet, I found a live-out au-pair position in Paris. A wealthy family invited both Sonja and me to come and stay in an accommodation building with lots of rooms to rent. In return for my work as an au pair, we would be allowed to live there for free. Neither of us was able to speak French, but it was the only reasonable au-pair position I'd been able to find. I asked Sonja if Paris was a clean enough spot, and because she knew we had no real other option, she said yes. Her parents hadn't been to Paris for a very long time at least and hopefully wouldn't be again. They knew she was in Zurich, so they might have sought her there. We underwent a transformation and left all our belongings behind to make a final clean break, as we were never going to return to our roots that had rejected us so harshly.

THE POINT OF NO RETURN?

2014

TWENTY-EIGHT YEARS — that's how long I've known Sonja.

Sonja. And where is she? In the schoolyard, hiding? Why isn't she here to meet me as she promised when she texted? Shall I text her, maybe? Not sure. Not sure if I want to give away that I've arrived, that I'm standing right here. She might think I'm still on my way.

I won't text. I won't phone. And I won't shout for her.

I can see straight through the passage and into the yard of this primary school. I tiptoe to the end of the passage. From there, I should be able to see one hundred per cent of the yard. I'm feeling brave. I put the pen and oven cloth into my bag, grab the knife and hold it in my right hand. The pointy blade is facing towards the yard. Zero distance to go, to run away. I'm standing at the edge of the yard, seeing it all, left and right. An ice-cold shower travels up and down my spine as I finally spot Sonja. But I cannot believe my eyes. The knife slips through my hand, plummets to the ground. Both my hands fly up to my face, one on each cheek. I scream out loud. I'm horrified. Blood! There is blood. Loads of it on a desk that Sonja is slumped over.

I race to her. Is she dead? She must be. Her head lies motionless in a purple pool. Her arms on either side, her right hand in a clenched fist. The left lies open and is the only body part on the desk not covered in blood. I've covered my mouth with my hands. Eyes wide open, I'm staring at her. *Oh. My. God!*

I rush around her, searching for a sign of life. She doesn't move, seems lifeless. Should I touch her?

The desk she's at is very low. Only half of it is bloody, the rest is clean. A small chair leans against it. Sonja is sitting in another chair. Both are so small that they must be meant for young children. Same for the desk: it's meant for two kids, sat next to each other at school. Sonja and me – her on the right-hand side, me on the left.

And there, on the ground, just under the desk, opposite Sonja, there is a paintbox. Twelve colours, arranged in the same way as those in my paintbox at primary school. All the colours are unused except for two. The blue and red are virtually washed out, like on the day we painted our pictures of Easter eggs and were unable to decide between violet and purple. Sonja was there; she'd only just entered my life.

I squat, checking out these two colours. My eyes held by the red, fascinated. Sonja's blood drips from the edge of the desk and hits the empty container, filling it up. *Plop, plop.*

I lift my head, look at Sonja. From this angle, I see she has a blue pen in her clenched fist. I'm sure it's a fountain pen; the one she used to have at primary school. Oh, and what's that her left hand is resting on? A folder. A brown one. Is it…? Well, no, this can't be true? But, yes, it is *the* one – the brown family meeting folder!

I stand up straight again. I still haven't touched her. Is

she really dead? Should I feel for her pulse? I'm scared. My middle and index fingers shake as they approach the left side of her neck. It is completely exposed, not a single hair covers it. Her head rests on her right cheek. My fingers close in on her neck. So shaky. I don't remember when I touched her last, but this seems like it might be the last time ever.

Fingers on her neck, I press down on her skin. Nothing. I feel nothing. I move them a few millimetres up, then press again. Nothing. Absolutely nothing. There is no pulse. Unless I'm incapable of sensing it, Sonja is dead. But still, I don't know where all this blood has come from. She looks so unharmed.

I sit down in the little chair to her left. No doubt, this is an invitation for me. It's the same way we used to sit at primary school, twenty-eight years ago. The day we met.

Suddenly I sigh. I'm sad. Although I wanted to kill her tonight, this is unexpected and makes me sad. I feel hollow. Am I lonely? Or just alone? Are they the same thing? I don't think so.

I look up at the sky. Dawn has broken. Birds are announcing the day. *Chirrup. Chirrup.*

What about the brown folder under Sonja's left hand? Carefully I pull it out and open it. The old reports are still in there. I turn straight to the back, where the most recent reports used to be filed. And there we go: the very last report is dated the 23rd July 2014 – today. The headline reads: *To my father.*

For being harsh and unloving with me, letting me down and denying any responsibility for screwing up my mind, which I believe led me to develop the obsessive-compulsive disorder that has wrecked my life, you'd deserve to be made to poo on your kitchen floor for the rest of your life. My friend – the only person who really cares about me – has suffered too, because I have coerced her. She has been unable to live the life she deserves and to work enough to receive a pension in the future. She is exhausted from taking care of me and has decided that one of us has to go. I wish for her to write a book about my life, sell it and make enough money for her pension!

FINCA

I close the brown family meeting folder and put it back on the little desk. Tears creep into my eyes, then stream through my fingers as I hold my face in my hands. I'm sobbing. Heavily. Very heavily. Inevitably.

I turn to Sonja.

"What a sad life you've had," I mutter, still crying, "and now you're here, dead, after I have known you for almost all my life."

I feel sorry for her and for myself.

I should call an ambulance, although I doubt they will be able to do much for Sonja. But I've got to do it; her body can't just stay here, can it?

I've never called an ambulance in France before. I need to think about the right number to dial. It might be three digits; something like 112. I get my phone out from my bag. It's switched on but still set to silent mode. No messages, no missed calls. Nobody has been thinking of me, it seems. But maybe I'm mistaken and Roger actually does think of me. He'd probably even offer his help right now, if I called him. Knowing this makes me a lot stronger. Emotional support is so important in life. Because it can be tough; unbearably so at times. I have learned that there are situations in which you must act on your own; that no one else can do it for you. And you can! I can. With help; emotional support!

I dial 112, still crying, but not as hard. Making this call isn't easy, but the main thing is that I'm doing it. The phone against my ear, I hear it ring. Then somebody answers. I stutter to begin with, then it gets easier. For about a minute I speak in French. Then I hang up. I don't exactly know what I've been saying but expect an ambulance to arrive shortly. So, I have my final few minutes with Sonja next to me.

I wipe away my tears and turn back to Sonja, to give her my full attention for the very last time. She is still slumped over this desk, the right side of her head in the purple pool, her fine, long blonde hair framing it prettily. Sonja used to tie her hair up in a bun or ponytail almost every day. Not tonight.

I still cannot recognise any injury, or where all the blood has come from. Instead, I realise how beautiful she is. Odd, really, because I have never truly seen it: she is *beautiful*. It's taken me all these years to realise that.

My hand reaches for her head, her cheek. Carefully, I stroke her face. Now I run my fingers through her hair. "Goodbye, Sonja. You've been such a close and faithful friend to me."

My fingers return to her cheek. Her skin feels very smooth, and suddenly warm. Glowing! Nothing like dead flesh. Bizarre. Utterly bizarre. Because, as I stroke her face, I feel something stroking my own.

I hear a noise in the distance. It sounds like a siren. The ambulance is approaching. I have a few seconds left with Sonja before they take her away.

I've stopped crying. My eyes are dry. No more sobbing. I'm able to breathe freely. My fingers are still on Sonja's face, and something is also still touching mine. Like a mirror.

The motions I make over her face, I feel exactly the same upon mine.

The siren is getting louder. They're coming closer. Really close. But I don't mind the noise at all. I like it. I *love* it. It sounds like music to me.

I move my hand back to Sonja's hair, and I feel a hand on mine. The siren's noise has become nothing more than music, and I'm enjoying it. I want this tune to be even louder, so I turn the volume of my headphones up. Back to Sonja's face, her skin so smooth and warm like my own. With my every stroke of her head, I feel it on mine. Because it *is* mine!

Sonja is me. And I am her. We are one and the same person. We've never been two different people. All she's been is the inner conflict that my OCD has brought to my life – the life that I have been forced to live. *I* have obsessive-compulsive disorder. Sonja does not physically exist. I am Finja.

I wipe my face and hair a few more times. Now I jump up from this chair, in this yard, turning the music in my ears up really loud. I sing along, throwing my arms towards the sky. Goosebumps run down my back. This time, it has happened! This time, it's really happened. I've made the right and most significant step to break free from my mental prison and start fighting my OCD.

I walk out of this courtyard. One last glance back at the chair I've just been sitting in. Two little shadows of an angel and a devil are in it now, both dangling their feet. Both winking and waving goodbye to me. I smile and wave back.

* * *

BACK IN THE road, I feel strong, positive and determined.

With music in my ears, I dance through the streets of Paris. I have no idea what the time is, but I don't care.

The sun has risen, shining warmly on me as I walk and dance. Through the roads of Paris, along the River Seine and past some *bouquinistes*. A couple of them are about to open, preparing for another busy day with plenty of tourists trying to catch a bit of the old Paris.

I reach the café, my favourite one. It is open. I go inside as I take off my headphones. A sweet smell mixed with coffee hits my nostrils. Mmmm, I love this. Most of the cute, round Parisian tables are unoccupied. Not many people are around yet, just a few. Most importantly: Roger in our usual spot by the bar, his coffee and *pain au chocolat* in front of him. He smiles when he sees me.

"*Bonjour, Finja. Qu'est-ce que tu désires aujourd'hui?*" the owner of the café asks.

"*Salut, ça va? Un café crème et un croissant, s'il te plaît,*" I reply.

I embrace Roger as I greet him, before taking a seat. I smile at him. But there is more to his happy face today. With one hand, he turns a tiny vase on the bar right in front of him. He's turning and turning it. The daisy inside it must be totally dizzy.

"And have you called your father?" Roger knows I have the desire to tell my father how I feel about him. And, of course, he also knows how scared I am of doing it.

"No, I haven't. I might call him one day. When I've written a book, and published it. So he can read about Sonja and the truth."

I've told Roger that I call my OCD 'Sonja'.

"The truth?" he asks.

"Yes. *My* truth. I believe *he* was the start of everything, the reason why I created Sonja. Why I was forced to live with her. Having OCD is *not* a choice!"

"Sounds reasonable." Roger smiles at me with pride in his eyes.

"I had to comfort myself. My father dumped his moods on the people around him, including me. *He* had the original problem, not me."

"Well, if ever you need my support when you're deciding what you'd like to tell him, I'd be there to hold your hand."

A goosebump shower.

My hands search my bag. I pull the golden envelope from it. "I've ripped it open, and I've slept without locking myself into my room. Four hours. Wasn't easy, but I did it. I'm able to move in with you now – no more locking in."

Roger's smile flashes up again. "I'm getting goosebumps all over my back."

"Me too."

He glances at the daisy in the vase. He's stopped turning it. Now he looks back at me, right into my eyes. "I love you!"

I want to answer him, but he doesn't let me. He has more to say, it seems.

"I love you regardless. With or without your OCD. I see the real you, not just the mental illness. And you are still special."

I've lost count of the goosebump showers now.

Roger pushes the vase over to me. "Here, now you have a daisy. Pluck it and you'll see it'll finish with *He loves me.*"

I stare at the daisy, hesitating. But not for long, as I push the vase back to him. "I don't need to pluck it. I know."

Roger's eyes flash at me. I'm reading them. He touches my hand, knowing I have such difficulty saying the words myself. But then, my courage rises. I get it; Roger really means them.

Enabling me: "And I love you, too."

AUTHOR'S MESSAGE

THANK YOU FOR having read my story. I feel truly honoured.

I'd like to emphasize my gratitude to other OCD-sufferers if you've made it to the end of my book, because I was worried I'd 'lose' you on the way due to the perspective from which I have told this story. It is very important to me that this hasn't been perceived as though there is little or no understanding for the OCD-sufferer and only for the sufferer with the OCD-sufferer. No, this is not the case because there is A LOT of understanding for the OCD-sufferer. To comfort you: I am one myself!

I wrote this story in this way as I believe that OCD is such a debilitating illness, such a beast, that it goes beyond the actual person who has it.

Please keep fighting and do *not* lose hope in your battle against OCD.

Unfortunately, nobody can lead this hard battle for you, but I strongly believe that it is easier if you've got somebody close – a good friend, a family member or an understanding lover – who is there to hold your hand. Remember: you are special – having a mental illness does not take this away from you.

ACKNOWLEDGEMENTS

I AM THANKFUL to those people who read passages of my manuscript or my entire work, enabling me to learn about writing in general.

Further, I must mention Literary Agent Janet Reid, even though I'm not represented by her, but I can truly say that I have learned from her blog and The Reef, and hopefully managed to get out of my writing-nappies. Also, thanks to Literary Agent Jessica Faust whose YouTube videos have been helpful.

Also, a genuine and heartfelt thank you to my Twitter friends of the #WritingCommunity – you guys are terrific! You've given me something I hadn't experienced before and so many of you have offered to help me with a certain issue. (I'm sure y'all know what I mean!)

Thank you to my editor. I was thrilled when I read your first comment about my work *This manuscript was presented to me in good condition with minimal intervention required*. However, I felt like a kid who thought they had brushed their teeth well and then chewed those plaque tablets afterwards… Once I opened my edited manuscript: *all red* ;).

I know… I *still* make English language mistakes, using word orders 'too German' at times or using the wrong preposition – things I should really have known until now…err *by* now.

Thank you to my cover/interior designers – you made my book look exactly how I wanted it.

And my biggest thank you just has to go to my fiancé, Neil, who has supported me on many levels while I wrote this book. He has continuously held my hand and made me stronger throughout my ongoing journey battling OCD!

Thank you SO much for reading my book!
If you can, please leave a review (good or bad) on Amazon or/AND Goodreads. Comments are so important for authors and their success.

Find me here:

Amazon:
https://www.katjagschulz.com/ , click on the grey 'BUY here'-button, click on my book, scroll down to 'Review this product'.
(You need an account with Amazon to do this.)

Goodreads:
https://www.katjagschulz.com/ , click on the black 'Goodreads reviews'-button, click on 'Rate this book' below the cover image & review.
(You need to sign up with Goodreads – it's easy!)

ABOUT THE AUTHOR

KATJA SCHULZ HAS lived with OCD for over thirty years. This debilitating mental illness has ruined far too much, but she has never lost hope and so managed to improve and fight her way back into life.

After leaving her native Germany, she lived in many different places, and is now settling for good with her future husband, Neil, in the UK. She wants to add a dog to the family.

Due to Katja's OCD, she has struggled with work, particularly full-time, but has found that her lately discovered love for writing suits both the needs related to her mental illness and a new possibility to work. She plans to publish her second book, LIVING LIES, one day in the future.

YOU CAN FIND her at www.katjagschulz.com and on Twitter @OneOfUsHasToGo